TAO II

Other Books in the Soul Power Series

Divine Transformation

Tao I

Divine Soul Mind Body Healing and Transmission System

Divine Soul Songs

The Power of Soul

Soul Communication

Soul Wisdom

TAO II

The Way of Healing,
Rejuvenation, Longevity,
and Immortality

Dr. & Master Zhi Gang Sha

ATRIA BOOKS
New York   London   Toronto   Sydney

Heaven's Library
Toronto

Heaven's Library

ATRIA BOOKS

A Division of Simon & Schuster, Inc.
1230 Avenue of the Americas
New York, NY 10020

Toronto, ON

The information contained in this book is intended to be educational and not for diagnosis,
prescription, or treatment of any health disorder whatsoever. This information should not replace
consultation with a competent health-care professional. The content of the book is intended to be
used as an adjunct to a rational and responsible health-care program prescribed by a health-care
practitioner. The author and publisher are in no way liable for any misuse of the material.

First Atria Books hardcover edition November 2010

ATRIA BOOKS and colophon are trademarks of Simon & Schuster, Inc.

Heaven's Library is a trademark of Heaven's Library Publication Corp.

For information about special discounts for bulk purchases, please contact
Simon & Schuster Special Sales at 1-866-506-1949 or business@simonandschuster.com.

The Simon & Schuster Speakers Bureau can bring authors to your live event.
For more information or to book an event, contact the Simon & Schuster Speakers Bureau
at 1-866-248-3049 or visit our website at www.simonspeakers.com.

Manufactured in the United States of America

10   9   8   7   6   5   4   3   2   1

Library of Congress Cataloging-in-Publication Data

Sha, Zhi Gang.
    Tao ii : the way of healing, rejuvenation, longevity, and immortality / Zhi Gang Sha.
        p.   cm.
    Includes bibliographical references and index.
    1. Taoism.   2. Taoist hygiene.   3. Spiritual healing.   4. Health.   5. Longevity.
I. Title.
BL1923.S473 2010
299.5'1431—dc22   2010038739

ISBN 978-1-4391-9865-0
ISBN 978-1-4391-9866-7 (ebook)

Contents

金丹大道修炼
Jin Dan Da Tao Xiu Lian

精 Jing

虚 Xu

道 Dao

精气神虚道合一 Jing Qi Shen Xu Dao He Yi

金丹 Jin Dan

治疗返老还童长寿永生之道
Zhi Liao Fan Lao Huan Tong Chang
Shou Yong Sheng Zhi Dao

Soul Power Series

THE PURPOSE OF life is to serve. I have committed my life to this purpose. Service is my life mission.

My total life mission is to transform the consciousness of humanity and all souls in all universes, and enlighten them, in order to create love, peace, and harmony for humanity, Mother Earth, and all universes. This mission includes three empowerments.

My first empowerment is to teach *universal service* to empower people to be unconditional universal servants. The message of universal service is:

> *I serve humanity and all universes unconditionally.*
> *You serve humanity and all universes unconditionally.*
> *Together we serve humanity and all souls in all universes unconditionally.*

My second empowerment is to teach *healing* to empower people to heal themselves and heal others. The message of healing is:

I have the power to heal myself.
You have the power to heal yourself.
Together we have the power to heal the world.

My third empowerment is to teach *the power of soul,* which includes soul secrets, wisdom, knowledge, and practical techniques, and to transmit Divine Soul Power to empower people to transform every aspect of their lives and enlighten their souls, hearts, minds, and bodies.

The message of Soul Power is:

I have the Soul Power to transform my consciousness and
every aspect of my life and enlighten my soul, heart, mind,
and body.
You have the Soul Power to transform your consciousness
and every aspect of your life and enlighten your soul,
heart, mind, and body.
Together we have the Soul Power to transform consciousness
and every aspect of all life and enlighten humanity and all
souls.

To teach the power of soul is my most important empowerment. It is the key for my total life mission. The power of soul is the key for transforming physical life and spiritual life. It is the key for transforming and enlightening humanity and every soul in all universes.

The beginning of the twenty-first century is the transition period into a new era for humanity, Mother Earth, and all universes. This era is named the Soul Light Era. The Soul Light Era began on August 8, 2003. It will last fifteen thousand years. Natural disasters—including tsunamis, hurricanes, cyclones, earthquakes, floods, tornados, hail, blizzards, fires, drought, extreme temperatures, famine, and disease—political, religious, and ethnic wars, terrorism, proliferation of nuclear weapons, economic challenges, pollution, vanishing plant and animal species, and other such upheavals are part of this transition. In addition, millions of people are suffering from depression, anxiety, fear, anger, and worry. They suffer from pain, chronic conditions, and life-threatening illnesses. Humanity needs help. The consciousness of humanity needs to be transformed. The suffering of humanity needs to be removed.

The books of the Soul Power Series are brought to you by Heaven's Library and Atria Books. They reveal soul secrets and teach soul wisdom, soul knowledge, and practical soul techniques for your daily life. The power of soul can heal, prevent illness, rejuvenate, prolong life, and transform consciousness and every aspect of life, including relationships and finances. The power of soul is vital to serving humanity and Mother Earth during this transition period. The power of soul will awaken and transform the consciousness of humanity and all souls.

In the twentieth century and for centuries before, *mind over matter* played a vital role in healing, rejuvenation, and life transformation. In the Soul Light Era, *soul over matter*—Soul Power—will play *the* vital role to heal, rejuvenate, and transform all life.

There are countless souls on Mother Earth—souls of human beings, souls of animals, souls of other living things, and souls of inanimate things. *Everyone and everything has a soul.*

Every soul has its own frequency and power. Jesus had miraculous healing power. We have heard many heart-touching stories of lives saved by Guan Yin's compassion.[1] Mother Mary's love has created many heart-moving stories. All of these great souls were given Divine Soul Power to serve humanity. In all of the world's great religions and spiritual traditions, including Buddhism, Taoism, Christianity, Judaism, Hinduism, Islam, and more, there are similar accounts of great spiritual healing and blessing power.

I honor every religion and every spiritual tradition. However, I am not teaching religion. I am teaching Soul Power, which includes soul secrets, soul wisdom, soul knowledge, and practical soul techniques. Your soul has the power to heal, rejuvenate, and transform life. An animal's soul has the power to heal, rejuvenate, and transform life. The souls of the sun, the moon, an ocean, a tree, and a mountain have the power to heal, rejuvenate, and transform life. The souls of healing angels, ascended masters, holy saints, Taoist saints, Hindu saints, buddhas, and other high-level spiritual beings have great Soul Power to heal, rejuvenate, and transform life.

Every soul has its own standing. Spiritual standing, or soul standing, has countless layers. Soul Power also has layers. Not every soul can perform miracles like Jesus, Guan Yin, and Mother Mary. Soul Power depends on the soul's spiritual standing in Heaven. The higher a soul stands in Heaven, the more Soul Power that soul is given by the Divine. Jesus, Guan Yin, and Mother Mary all have a very high spiritual standing.

Who determines a soul's spiritual standing? Who gives the appropriate Soul Power to a soul? Who decides the direction for humanity, Mother Earth, and all universes? The top leader of the spiritual world is the decision maker. This top leader is

---

1. Guan Yin is known as the Bodhisattva of Compassion and, in the West, as the Goddess of Mercy.

the Divine. The Divine is the creator and manifestor of all universes.

In the Soul Light Era, all souls will join as one and align their consciousnesses with divine consciousness. At this historic time, the Divine has decided to transmit divine soul treasures to humanity and all souls to help humanity and all souls go through Mother Earth's transition.

Let me share two personal stories with you to explain how I reached this understanding.

First, in April 2003, I held a Power Healing workshop for about one hundred people at Land of Medicine Buddha, a retreat center in Soquel, California. As I was teaching, the Divine appeared. I told the students, "The Divine is here. Could you give me a moment?" I knelt and bowed down to the floor to honor the Divine. (At age six, I was taught to bow down to my tai chi masters. At age ten, I bowed down to my qi gong masters. At age twelve, I bowed down to my kung fu masters. Being Chinese, I learned this courtesy throughout my childhood.) I explained to the students, "Please understand that this is the way I honor the Divine, my spiritual fathers, and my spiritual mothers. Now I will have a conversation with the Divine."

I began by saying silently, "Dear Divine, I am very honored you are here."

The Divine, who was in front of me above my head, replied, "Zhi Gang, I come today to pass a spiritual law to you."

I said, "I am honored to receive this spiritual law."

The Divine continued, "This spiritual law is named the Universal Law of Universal Service. It is one of the highest spiritual laws in the universe. It applies to the spiritual world and the physical world."

The Divine pointed to the Divine. "I am a universal servant."

The Divine pointed to me. "You are a universal servant." The Divine swept a hand in front of the Divine. "Everyone and everything is a universal servant. A universal servant offers universal service unconditionally. Universal service includes universal love, forgiveness, peace, healing, blessing, harmony, and enlightenment. *If one offers a little service, one receives a little blessing from the universe and from me. If one offers more service, one receives more blessing. If one offers unconditional service, one receives unlimited blessing.*"

The Divine paused for a moment before continuing. "There is another kind of service, which is unpleasant service. Unpleasant service includes killing, harming, taking advantage of others, cheating, stealing, complaining, and more. If one offers a little unpleasant service, one learns little lessons from the universe and from me. If one offers more unpleasant service, one learns more lessons. If one offers huge unpleasant service, one learns huge lessons."

I asked, "What kinds of lessons could one learn?"

The Divine replied, "The lessons include sickness, accidents, injuries, financial challenges, broken relationships, emotional imbalances, mental confusion, and any kind of disorder in one's life." The Divine emphasized, "This is how the universe operates. This is one of my most important spiritual laws for all souls in the universe to follow."

After the Divine delivered this universal law, I immediately made a silent vow to the Divine:

> *Dear Divine,*
>
> *I am extremely honored to receive your Law of Universal Service. I make a vow to you, to all humanity, and to all souls in all universes that I will be an unconditional universal servant. I will give my total GOLD* [gratitude, obedience, loyalty, devotion] *to you and to serving you.*

I am honored to be your servant and a servant of all humanity and all souls.

Hearing this, the Divine smiled and left.

My second story happened three months later, in July 2003, while I was holding a Soul Study workshop near Toronto. The Divine came again. I again explained to my students that the Divine had appeared, and asked them to wait a moment while I bowed down 108 times and listened to the Divine's message. On this occasion, the Divine told me, "Zhi Gang, I come today to choose you as my direct servant, vehicle, and channel."

I was deeply moved and said to the Divine, "I am honored. What does it mean to be your direct servant, vehicle, and channel?"

The Divine replied, "When you offer healing and blessing to others, call me. I will come instantly to offer my healing and blessing to them."

I was deeply touched and replied, "Thank you so much for choosing me as your direct servant."

The Divine continued, "I can offer my healing and blessing by transmitting my permanent healing and blessing treasures."

I asked, "How do you do this?"

The Divine answered, "Select a person and I will give you a demonstration."

I asked for a volunteer with serious health challenges. A man named Walter raised his hand. He stood up and explained that he had liver cancer, with a two-by-three-centimeter malignant tumor that had just been diagnosed from a biopsy.

Then I asked the Divine, "Please bless Walter. Please show

me how you transmit your permanent treasures." Immediately, I saw the Divine send a beam of light from the Divine's heart to Walter's liver. The beam shot into his liver, where it turned into a golden light ball that instantly started spinning. Walter's entire liver shone with beautiful golden light.

The Divine asked me, "Do you understand what software is?"

I was surprised by this question but replied, "I do not understand much about computers. I just know that software is a computer program. I have heard about accounting software, office software, and graphic design software."

"Yes," the Divine said. "Software is a program. Because you asked me to, I transmitted, or downloaded, my Soul Software for Liver to Walter. It is one of my permanent healing and blessing treasures. You asked me. I did the job. This is what it means for you to be my chosen direct servant, vehicle, and channel."

I was astonished. Excited, inspired, and humbled, I said to the Divine, "I am so honored to be your direct servant. How blessed I am to be chosen." Almost speechless, I asked the Divine, "Why did you choose me?"

"I chose you," said the Divine, "because you have served humanity for more than one thousand lifetimes. You have been very committed to serving my mission through all of your lifetimes. I am choosing you in this life to be my direct servant. You will transmit countless permanent healing and blessing treasures from me to humanity and all souls. This is the honor I give to you now."

I was moved to tears. I immediately bowed down 108 times again and made a silent vow:

> *Dear Divine,*
> *I cannot bow down to you enough for the honor you have given to me. No words can express my greatest gratitude.*

How blessed I am to be your direct servant to download your permanent healing and blessing treasures to humanity and all souls! Humanity and all souls will receive your huge blessings through my service as your direct servant. I give my total life to you and to humanity. I will accomplish your tasks. I will be a pure servant to humanity and all souls.

I bowed again. Then I asked the Divine, "How should Walter use his Soul Software?"

"Walter must spend time to practice with my Soul Software," said the Divine. "Tell him that simply to receive my Soul Software does not mean he will recover. He must practice with this treasure every day to restore his health, step by step."

I asked, "How should he practice?"

The Divine gave me this guidance: "Tell Walter to chant repeatedly: *Divine Liver Soul Software heals me. Divine Liver Soul Software heals me. Divine Liver Soul Software heals me. Divine Liver Soul Software heals me.*"

I asked, "For how long should Walter chant?"

The Divine answered, "At least two hours a day. The longer he practices, the better. If Walter does this, he could recover in three to six months."

I shared this information with Walter, who was excited and deeply moved. Walter said, "I will practice two hours or more each day."

Finally I asked the Divine, "How does the Soul Software work?"

The Divine replied, "My Soul Software is a golden healing

ball that rotates and clears energy and spiritual blockages in Walter's liver."

I again bowed to the Divine 108 times. Then I stood up and offered three Soul Softwares to every participant in the workshop as divine gifts. Upon seeing this, the Divine smiled and left.

Walter immediately began to practice as directed for at least two hours every day. Two and a half months later, a CT scan and MRI showed that his liver cancer had completely disappeared. At the end of 2006 I met Walter again at a signing in Toronto for my book *Soul Mind Body Medicine.*[2] In May 2008 Walter attended one of my events at the Unity Church of Truth in Toronto. On both occasions Walter told me that there was still no sign of cancer in his liver. For nearly five years his Divine Soul Download healed his liver cancer. He was very grateful to the Divine.

This major event of being chosen as a direct divine servant happened in July 2003. As I mentioned, a new era for Mother Earth and all universes, the Soul Light Era, began on August 8, 2003. The timing may look like a coincidence but I believe there could be an underlying spiritual reason. Since July 2003 I have offered divine transmissions to humanity almost every day. I have offered more than ten divine transmissions to all souls in all universes.

I share this story with you to introduce the power of divine transmissions or Divine Soul Downloads. Now let me share the commitment that I made in *Soul Wisdom,*[3] the first book of my Soul Power Series, and that I have renewed in every one of my books since:

---

2. *Soul Mind Body Medicine: A Complete Soul Healing System for Optimum Health and Vitality* (Novato, California: New World Library, 2006).

3. *Soul Wisdom: Practical Soul Treasures to Transform Your Life* (Toronto/New York: Heaven's Library/Atria Books, 2008).

From now on, I will offer Divine Soul Downloads in every book I write.

Divine Soul Downloads are permanent divine healing and blessing treasures for transforming your life. There is an ancient saying: *If you want to know if a pear is sweet, taste it.* If you want to know the power of Divine Soul Downloads, experience it.

Divine Soul Downloads carry divine frequency with divine love, forgiveness, compassion, and light. Divine frequency transforms the frequency of all life. Divine love melts all blockages, including soul, mind, and body blockages, and transforms all life. Divine forgiveness brings inner peace and inner joy. Divine compassion boosts energy, stamina, vitality, and immunity. Divine light heals, prevents sickness, rejuvenates, and prolongs life.

A Divine Soul Download is a new soul created from the heart of the Divine. The Divine Soul Download transmitted to Walter was a Soul Software. Since then, I have transmitted several other types of Divine Soul Downloads, including Divine Soul Herbs, Divine Soul Acupuncture, Divine Soul Massage, Divine Soul Operation, and Divine Soul Mind Body Transplants.

A Divine Soul Transplant is a new divine soul of an organ, a part of the body, a bodily system, cells, DNA, RNA, the tiny matter in cells, or the spaces between cells. When it is transmitted, it replaces the recipient's original soul of the organ, part of the body, system, cells, cell units, DNA, RNA, tiny matter in cells, or spaces between cells. A new divine soul can also replace the soul of a home or a business. A new divine soul can be transmitted to a pet, a mountain, a city, or a country to replace their original souls. A new divine soul can even replace the soul of Mother Earth.

A Divine Mind Transplant is also a light being created by the Divine. It carries divine consciousness to replace the original consciousness of the recipient's system, organ, part of the body, cells, cell units, DNA, RNA, tiny matter, or spaces.

A Divine Body Transplant is another light being created by the Divine. This light being carries divine energy and divine tiny matter to replace the original energy and tiny matter of the recipient's system, organ, part of the body, cells, cell units, DNA, RNA, tiny matter, or spaces.

Everyone and everything has a soul. The Divine can download any soul you can conceive of. These Divine Soul Downloads are permanent divine healing, blessing, and life transformation treasures. They can transform the lives of anyone and anything. Because the Divine created these divine soul treasures, they carry Divine Soul Power, which is the greatest Soul Power among all souls. All souls in the highest layers of Heaven will support and assist Divine Soul Downloads. Divine Soul Downloads are the crown jewel of Soul Power.

Divine Soul Downloads are divine presence. The more Divine Soul Downloads you receive, the faster your soul, heart, mind, and body will be transformed. The more Divine Soul Downloads your home or business receives and the more Divine Soul Downloads a city or country receives, the faster their souls, hearts, minds, and bodies will be transformed.

In the Soul Light Era, the evolution of humanity will be created by Divine Soul Power. Soul Power will transform humanity. Soul Power will transform animals. Soul Power will transform nature and the environment. Soul Power will assume the leading role in every field of human endeavor. Humanity will deeply understand that *the soul is the boss.*

Soul Power, including soul secrets, soul wisdom, soul knowledge, and practical soul techniques, will transform every aspect of human life. Soul Power will transform every aspect of organizations and societies. Soul Power will transform cities, countries, Mother Earth, all planets, stars, galaxies, and all universes. Divine Soul Power, including Divine Soul Downloads, will lead this transformation.

I am honored to have been chosen as a divine servant to offer Divine Soul Downloads to humanity, to relationships, to homes, to businesses, to pets, to cities, to countries, and more. In the last few years I have already transmitted countless divine souls to humanity and to all universes. I repeat to you now: *I will offer Divine Soul Downloads within each and every book of the Soul Power Series.* Clear instructions on how to receive these Divine Soul Downloads will be provided in the next section, "How to Receive the Divine Soul Downloads Offered in the Books of the Soul Power Series," as well as on the appropriate pages of each book.

I am a servant of humanity. I am a servant of the universe. I am a servant of the Divine. I am extremely honored to be a servant of all souls. I commit my total life and being as an unconditional universal servant.

I will continue to offer Divine Soul Downloads for my entire life. I will offer more and more Divine Soul Downloads to every soul. I will offer Divine Soul Downloads for every aspect of life for every soul.

I am honored to be a servant of Divine Soul Downloads.

Human beings, organizations, cities, and countries will receive more and more Divine Soul Downloads, which can transform every aspect of their lives and enlighten their souls, hearts, minds, and bodies. The Soul Light Era will shine Soul Power. The books in the Soul Power Series will spread Divine Soul Downloads, together with Soul Power—soul secrets, soul wisdom, soul knowledge, and practical soul techniques—to serve humanity, Mother Earth, and all universes. The Soul Power Series is a pure servant for humanity and all souls. The Soul Power Series is honored to be a Total GOLD[4] servant of the Divine, humanity, and all souls.

The final goal of the Soul Light Era is to join every soul as one in love, peace, and harmony. This means that the consciousness of every soul will be totally aligned with divine consciousness. There will be difficulties and challenges on the path to this final goal. Together we will overcome them. We call all souls of humanity and all souls in all universes to offer unconditional universal service, including universal love, forgiveness, peace, healing, blessing, harmony, and enlightenment. The more we offer unconditional universal service, the faster we will achieve this goal.

The Divine gives his heart to us. The Divine gives his love to us. The Divine gives Divine Soul Downloads to us. Our hearts meld with the Divine's heart. Our souls meld with the Divine's soul. Our consciousnesses align with the Divine's consciousness. We will join hearts and souls together to create love, peace, and harmony for humanity, Mother Earth, and all universes.

> *I love my heart and soul*
> *I love all humanity*
> *Join hearts and souls together*
> *Love, peace and harmony*
> *Love, peace and harmony*

Love all humanity. Love all souls.
Thank all humanity. Thank all souls.
Thank you. Thank you. Thank you.

Zhi Gang Sha

---

4. Total GOLD means total gratitude, total obedience, total loyalty, and total devotion to the Divine.

How to Receive the Divine Soul Downloads Offered in the Books of the Soul Power Series

THE BOOKS OF the Soul Power Series are unique. For the first time in history, the Divine is downloading the Divine's soul treasures to readers as they read these books. Every book in the Soul Power Series will include Divine Soul Downloads that have been preprogrammed. When you read the appropriate paragraphs and pause for a minute, divine gifts will be transmitted to your soul.

In April 2005 the Divine told me to "leave Divine Soul Downloads to history." I thought, "A human being's life is limited. Even if I live a long, long life, I will go back to Heaven one day. How can I leave Divine Soul Downloads to history?"

In the beginning of 2008, as I was editing the paperback edition of *Soul Wisdom,* the Divine suddenly told me: "Zhi Gang, offer my downloads within this book." The Divine said, "I will preprogram my downloads in the book. Any reader can receive them as he or she reads the special pages." At the moment the Divine gave me this direction, I understood how I could leave Divine Soul Downloads to history.

Preprogrammed Divine Soul Downloads are permanently stored within this book and every book in the Soul Power Series. If people read this book thousands of years from now, they will still receive the Divine Soul Downloads. As long as this book exists and is read, readers will receive the Divine Soul Downloads.

Allow me to explain further. The Divine has placed a permanent blessing within certain paragraphs in these books. These blessings allow you to receive Divine Soul Downloads as permanent gifts to your soul. Because these divine treasures reside with your soul, you can access them twenty-four hours a day—as often as you like, wherever you are—for healing, blessing, and life transformation.

It is very easy to receive the Divine Soul Downloads in these books. After you read the special paragraphs where they are preprogrammed, close your eyes. Receive the special download. It is also easy to apply these divine treasures. After you receive a Divine Soul Download, I will immediately show you how to apply it for healing, blessing, and life transformation.

You have free will. If you are not ready to receive a Divine Soul Download, simply say *I am not ready to receive this gift.* You can then continue to read the special download paragraphs, but you will not receive the gifts they contain. The Divine does not offer Divine Soul Downloads to those who are not ready or not willing to receive the Divine's treasures. However, the moment you are ready, you can simply go back to the relevant paragraphs and tell the Divine *I am ready.* You will then receive the stored special download when you reread the paragraphs.

The Divine has agreed to offer specific Divine Soul Downloads in these books to all readers who are willing to receive them. The Divine has unlimited treasures. However, you can receive only the ones designated in these pages. Please do not ask for different or additional gifts. It will not work.

After receiving and practicing with the Divine Soul Downloads in these books, you could experience remarkable healing results in your spiritual, mental, emotional, and physical bodies. You could receive incredible blessings for your love relationships and other relationships. You could receive financial blessings and all kinds of other blessings.

Divine Soul Downloads are unlimited. There can be a Divine Soul Download for anything that exists in the physical world. The reason for this is very simple. *Everything has a soul.* A house has a soul. The Divine can download a soul to your house that can transform its energy. The Divine can download a soul to your business that can transform your business. If you are wearing a ring, that ring has a soul. If the Divine downloads a new divine soul to your ring, you can ask the divine soul in your ring to offer divine healing and blessing.

I am honored to have been chosen as a servant of humanity and the Divine to offer Divine Soul Downloads. For the rest of my life, I will continue to offer Divine Soul Downloads. I will offer more and more of them. I will offer Divine Soul Downloads for every aspect of every life.

I am honored to be a servant of Divine Soul Downloads.

What to Expect After You Receive Divine Soul Downloads

Divine Soul Downloads are new souls created from the heart of the Divine. When these souls are transmitted, you may feel a strong vibration. For example, you could feel warm or excited. Your body could shake a little. If you are not sensitive, you may not feel anything. Advanced spiritual beings with an open Third Eye can actually see a huge golden, rainbow, purple, or crystal light soul enter your body.

These divine souls are your yin companions[1] for life. They will stay with your soul forever. Even after your physical life ends, these divine treasures will continue to accompany your soul into your next life and all of your future lives. In these books, I will teach you how to invoke these divine souls anytime, anywhere to give you divine healing or blessing in this life. You also can invoke these souls to radiate out to offer divine healing or blessing to others. These divine souls have extraordinary abilities to heal, bless, and transform. If you develop advanced spiritual abilities in your next life, you will discover that you have these divine souls with you. Then you will be able to invoke these divine souls in the same way in your future lifetimes to heal, bless, and transform every aspect of your life.

It is a great honor to have a divine soul downloaded to your own soul. The divine soul is a pure soul without bad karma. The divine soul carries divine healing and blessing abilities. The download does not have any side effects. You are given love and light with divine frequency. You are given divine abilities to serve yourself and others. Therefore, humanity is extremely honored

---

1. A yang companion is a physical being, such as a family member, friend, or pet. A yin companion is a soul companion without a physical form, such as your spiritual fathers and mothers in Heaven.

that the Divine is offering Divine Soul Downloads. I am extremely honored to be a servant of the Divine, of you, of all humanity, and of all souls to offer Divine Soul Downloads. I cannot thank the Divine enough. I cannot thank you, all humanity, and all souls enough for the opportunity to serve.

⁎

Thank you. Thank you. Thank you.

Foreword to the Soul Power Series

I HAVE ADMIRED DR. Zhi Gang Sha's work for some years now. In fact, I clearly remember the first time I heard him describe his soul healing system, Soul Mind Body Medicine. I knew immediately that I wanted to support this gifted healer and his mission, so I introduced him to my spiritual community at Agape. Ever since, it has been my joy to witness how those who apply his teachings and techniques experience increased energy, joy, harmony, and peace in their lives.

Dr. Sha's techniques awaken the healing power already present in all of us, empowering us to put our overall well-being in our own hands. His explanation of energy and message, and how they link consciousness, mind, body, and spirit, forms a dynamic information network in language that is easy to understand and, more important, to apply.

Dr. Sha's time-tested results have proven to thousands of students and readers that healing energies and messages exist within specific sounds, movements, and affirmative perceptions. Weaving in his own personal experiences, Dr. Sha's theories and practices of working directly with the life-force energy and spirit are practical, holistic, and profound. His recognition that Soul Power is most important for every aspect of life is vital to meeting the challenges of twenty-first-century living.

The worldwide representative of his renowned teacher, Dr. Zhi Chen Guo, one of the greatest qi gong masters and healers in the world, Dr. Sha is himself a master of ancient disciplines such as tai chi, qi gong, kung fu, the *I Ching,* and feng shui. He has blended the soul of his culture's natural healing methods with his training as a Western physician, and generously offers his wisdom to us through the books in his Soul Power Series. His contribution to those in the healing professions is undeniable, and the way in which he empowers his readers to understand themselves, their feelings, and the connection between their bodies, minds, and spirits is his gift to the world.

Through his Soul Power Series, Dr. Sha guides the reader into a consciousness of healing not only of body, mind, and spirit, but also of the heart. I consider his healing path to be a universal spiritual practice, a journey into genuine transformation. His professional integrity and compassionate heart are at the root of his being a servant of humankind, and my heartfelt wish for his readers is that they accept his invitation to awaken the power of the soul and realize the natural beauty of their existence.

Dr. Michael Bernard Beckwith
Founder, Agape International Spiritual Center

How to Read This Book

*I*N EVERY BOOK of my Soul Power Series, I reveal soul secrets and teach soul wisdom, soul knowledge, and practical soul techniques. Secret and sacred wisdom and knowledge are important. *Practice is even more important.* Since ancient times, serious Buddhist, Taoist, qi gong, and kung fu practitioners have spent hours and hours a day in practice. Their dedication empowers them to develop and transform their frequency, their consciousness, and their purification further and further. In the modern world, successful professionals in every field similarly spend hours a day for months and years in practice. Their commitment empowers them to develop and transform their power and abilities further and further.

Every book in my Soul Power Series offers new approaches to healing, rejuvenation, and life transformation. Along with the teachings of sacred wisdom and knowledge, I also offer Divine Soul Downloads and Tao Soul Downloads as a servant, vehicle, and channel of the Divine and Tao. I am honored to serve you through these books. However, *the most important service offered*

in these books is the practices. In this book I lead you in many practices. If you spend four or five minutes to do each practice, I fully
understand that it will take you some time to finish all of them.
Do a few practices today. Tomorrow do another few practices. Do
a few more the day after tomorrow. The practices are vital. The
practices in this book will help you clear your bad karma. They
will help you heal, rejuvenate, and prolong your life. They can
lead you to reach Tao and meld with Tao.

If you do not do the practices, how can you experience their
power and benefits? If you do not experience their power and
benefits, how can you fully understand and absorb the teaching?
In fact, the teaching is the practice; the practice is the teaching.

For this particular book, *Tao II: The Way of Healing, Rejuvenation, Longevity, and Immortality,* the practices are absolutely vital.
They are lifelong practices for self-clearing bad karma, healing,
prevention of sickness, purification, rejuvenation, and longevity.
For beginning and serious Tao practitioners, they are an essential
part of my ten-year Tao training program. For every spiritual being, the practices in this book also give you some of the fastest
and most powerful ways to offer universal service and advance on
your spiritual journey. They can lead you to reach and meld with
Tao. They can lead you toward immortality to be a better servant
for humanity, Mother Earth, and all universes.

If you do not do the practices, this book will be only a theo-
retical exercise for you. You may find it interesting, even fascinat-
ing, but you will not receive the tremendous potential benefits for
every aspect of your life.

The CD or audio download included with this book is to
teach you and support you in singing or chanting the sacred texts
that carry the highest Tao secrets, wisdom, knowledge, and practical techniques available at this time and offered to you in this

book. For the serious Tao student and practitioner, the audio version of this book (available in a boxed set of CDs or via a digital download) is also an essential complement and supplement to this print version that you have in your hands.

As you read this book, my message to you is make sure you do not miss the practices. Use the included CD or audio download, as well as the audio version of this book, as essential practice guides and aids that could significantly boost and accelerate the results you obtain. I deliberately guide you in this book and lead you in the audio version of this book to do the highest Tao practices for healing, rejuvenation, prolonging life, and more. Reading this book and, even more, practicing with the audio version of this book, are like being at a workshop with me. When you go to a workshop and the teacher leads you in a meditation or practice, you do not run off to do something else, do you?

Do not rush through this book. Do every practice that I ask you to do. You will receive ten, fifty, a hundred times the benefit that you would receive if you simply read through the book quickly. Also, to receive Divine and Tao Soul Downloads does not mean you automatically receive their benefits. You must invoke them and practice to receive and experience divine healing and blessing. Remember also that going through this book just once is not enough. My advanced students go through my books many times. Every time they read and do the practices, they reach more and more "aha!" moments. They receive more and more remarkable healing, purification, and life transformation results.

These are important messages for you to remember as you read this book. I wish each of you will receive great rejuvenation, purification, and life transformation by doing the practices in this book. Receive the benefits of *soul over matter*, which is the power of soul. Receive the benefits of Divine Soul Power and Tao Soul Power.

Practice. Practice. Practice.

Experience. Experience. Experience.

Benefit. Benefit. Benefit.

Hao! Hao! Hao!

Thank you. Thank you. Thank you.

Editor's Note on Pinyin (Chinese Romanization) and Chinese Pronunciation

The Chinese romanization used in this book generally follows pinyin, which has for decades been the standard romanization system used in the People's Republic of China itself, as well as now around the world. Some divine flexibility has been applied, however. Most notably, Dao and Tao are both used as romanizations of the same word—the word that represents the main subject and source of this book. I also chose to capitalize certain words and phrases but not others that could be expected to be capitalized for similar reasons. Again, the only "rule" is that of divine flexibility.

Pronunciation of Chinese is difficult to transliterate using the English alphabet. Here, I was also somewhat systematic but again not rigidly so. Because Chinese is a tonal language, and for other reasons, understand that the pronunciations given can only be rough approximations.

List of Divine Soul Downloads

List of Figures

Tao I and Tao II Teaching Is Extremely Simple, Profound, and Powerful: Realizations of a Serious Tao Practitioner

As a serious student and practitioner of Taoism and Tao (or Dao) for more than forty years, I am very honored to share my insights on the divine and Tao teachings and practices in Master Sha's books *Tao I* and *Tao II*.

In the last three decades, there has been a notable surge of interest in the West in ancient Chinese wisdom and arts. I have witnessed numerous translated and original books on acupuncture, traditional Chinese medicine, tai chi, qi gong, and feng shui. Even more striking is that translations of various parts of Dao Zang, the massive ancient collection of canonical Tao texts, have also appeared in the West. In recent decades, many teachers of qi gong and tai chi chuan have also emerged to teach westerners. Some of them present themselves as having knowledge of Tao. However, studying Tao in this way can usually produce only limited results. There are several reasons for this.

First, there are immense gaps in culture and time between the twenty-first-century West and ancient China. Take something as seemingly simple as the words "square" and "round." If you do not know what these words really signify in the ancient Taoist texts of the Han Dynasty, you can never understand the true meaning of these texts, even if you were fortunate enough to have a good translation—which is an entire issue in itself!

Let me give you an example. The *I Ching*, the ancient Chinese oracle book, gives the advice to "be square" in the text hexagram 2 (Kun). I spent many years wondering what this could mean. When I went to China in 2005 with Master Sha and one hundred of his students to study with Master and Dr. Zhi Chen Guo, Master Sha's beloved spiritual father, one of the Master Guo's daughters taught us not to "square" our heads. What she meant was to have a broad perspective, and not limited thinking. At that moment, it clicked in me—to be square means to apply limits!

In addition, ancient Taoist texts would often refer to historical events or persons to explain particular points. If you don't understand the reference, you cannot get the teaching. For example, someone who upset the emperor could be punished by having a foot chopped off. That was a huge public disgrace that had to be carried to the end of life. Anyone who saw such a person knew right away that this one was in public disgrace and must not be associated with. Throughout Chinese history, many excellent persons become Taoists after being exposed to jealousy and intrigue from corrupt officials. Such a person would fall unfairly into disfavor, be punished by an angry emperor, and would have to leave court in disgrace (but fortunate and grateful just to be alive). Ostracized by society, the person would often go into seclusion in caves or on mountains to do inner work and reach Tao. Therefore, some Taoists refer to having a foot chopped off (meaning to be disgraced and humiliated) as a very beneficial thing to happen, because it serves as a wake-up call to let go of desires for fame, wealth, and power, and turn to spiritual development.

The second difficulty is that ancient texts outline only a part of the necessary knowledge. The bottom 25 percent, the simplest knowledge, was considered not necessary to write about, because it was presumed that everyone knew this as part of common Chinese culture. Even today, most Chinese, even if they do not study Tao, know what yin, yang, and the five elements are.

We are fortunate that an enormous amount of spiritual knowledge was written down to preserve it for future generations. However, to protect the sacred wisdom, the highest teachings are written in codes and metaphors that require a knowledgeable master to explain their meaning. These codes were very secret and without a proper master to decode the texts, they can appear to be just a garble of incomprehensible words, even if well translated. For example, how is one to practice the teaching that husband and wife should "join in the heart?" How is one to "let the tiger and dragon fight in the crucible?" The differences introduced by various lineages have made things even more obscure.

Moreover, about 15 percent of the top knowledge, the highest secrets, was never committed to paper, but memorized and transmitted only orally from masters to selected disciples. Therefore, even with a superb and complete translation of the original texts, one could never figure out all of the necessary wisdom.

The third major difficulty for westerners is that few are fluent in Chinese and very, very few can read ancient Chinese. Ancient Chinese characters often have multiple meanings. From one phrase consisting of four characters, one can get several totally different sentences.

In the West, the first translations of Taoist texts were done by academic linguists who had no direct personal knowledge of Taoism. In many cases, these professors set precedents for the understanding of certain characters and phrases that were followed by succeeding generations of translators. However, to a real Taoist, many of their works sound totally confusing.

The fourth problem is that even good translations were never able to capture the true beauty, flavor, and power of the original texts. For example, Lao Zi's *Dao De Jing* is written as poetry and so its sentences evoke a very special feeling in the heart, as all good poetry does. Poetry works on our deepest emotions and feelings. This essence can be very difficult to capture in translation. Therefore, in almost all western translations, this special effect of the Taoist texts on our hearts and psyche is lost.

The fifth and most difficult obstacle to overcome in studying Tao is experience. Relying only on books is not enough. It is absolutely essential to study directly from a teacher. This, however, can be the most difficult obstacle in the journey to Tao.

Centuries ago, Lu Tung-Pin (Lü Dongbin), a famous Taoist wizard master, lamented that there were only very few real masters, but thousands of impostors. That is as true now as it was then. Most of the available teachers in our time have only some superficial knowledge of Taoist principles, mostly as they relate to the practice of acupuncture or martial arts, yet they unscrupulously present themselves to hungry audiences as genuine experts. They mislead sincere students and to study with them is a waste.

I myself have spent my whole life searching for and practicing Tao. My first experiences were at the age of ten, when I was enrolled in a judo class. Judo in fact means "gentle Tao." My master at that time constantly reminded me not to use my muscles against an opponent, but to let Tao do it for me. If I had only understood that profound wisdom then, and applied it throughout my adult life, things would have been so much different!

I spent forty years of endless searching, studying, trying this and that, until I finally realized, now in my fifties, that really, the best thing I can do is to surrender myself totally to God, to Tao. But I had to go through the long way, as anybody else, of self-discovery and pursuit of all sorts of things, because it is exactly as Lao Zi said: "True Tao is a simple and straightforward road, but people like convoluted sidewalks."

So, for many years, I studied all sorts of Taoist esoteric arts. I studied and mastered the Taoist system of food, acupuncture, divination, martial arts, energy exercises, and sexual practices. For several years before I met Master Sha, I was heavily involved in the waterwheel energy practice (rotation of energy in the microcosmic circle, the small Tao energy circle known as *xiao zhou tian* that starts in the genital area, goes up the spinal cord to the top of the head, and then flows down the front side of the body), and in mind exercises by Ssu-ma Cheng-chen (Sima Qian) from his work *Zuo Wang Lun,* which means "sitting in oblivion." In the late 1990s, I was steadily progressing in the secret art of creating an immortal baby, as a way of achieving immortality.

However, my practices had one serious drawback.

For all those years, I had studied without a physical teacher, relying on the *I Ching* oracle system to guide me. I had no choice because I was born in a communist country in the middle of Europe, where there were no Taoists. Nevertheless, I had inside me, all my life, an insatiable thirst to reach Tao, undoubtedly because I had been a Taoist in previous lives.

My interest was totally outside the cultural context in which

I grew up so, to fulfill my dream, I had to overcome obstacles that many have no idea of. There was simply no one to talk to about these things in my country. Therefore, my journey was long and difficult, relying mostly on trial and error, following my intuition or, as I now know, my soul guidance and, of course, frequent consultation with *I Ching*.

Of course, I did not get everything right. That would have simply been impossible. To achieve Tao is the most complex human endeavor. How can you possibly hope to start from complete scratch, proceed alone, and succeed?

I translated many books into my native language, including about fifty books from Dao Zang. During the Ming Dynasty, one of the emperors who was very fond of Taoist practices had ordered the compilation of all available Taoist books into this one large collection. About fifteen hundred books were collected and reprinted into one single collection, Dao Zang, under this order. Eventually, by the end of the Qin Dynasty and the transition from the ancient Chinese imperial order to a republic, only two copies survived. One was held in the imperial archives in the Forbidden City, the other in the White Cloud Taoist Monastery.

In the 1920s, a French scholar by the name of Maspero found this treasure in the monastery. With the great support of monks, he had blueprint copies made of all of the books. This task took more than two years but then Maspero took the blueprints to Taiwan where the entire canon was printed on a commercial press. This saved the collection. Although there is only one known original copy in China, now the whole Dao Zang is available in many libraries both in China and in many universities around the world.

After I arrived in Canada, I spent many hours, as well as many consecutive days studying the texts most relevant to me. These books contain many diagrams and charts that helped me understand how energy functions in the human body. I compared what I learned with the results of my practices and, of course, continued to check with *I Ching*.

That I was able to succeed even partially with this approach amazes me. Now, after studying with Master Sha for ten years, I see that without a proper teacher, spiritual progress is almost impossible. Even though there were some failures in my progress, there were significant victories also. I want to mention two of my "achievements" from those early days.

One day in April 1994, as I was meditating in front of my altar, I heard a clear voice say, "Now I will show you something very special." Within seconds, energy rushed up my spine, over my head, down my face, and through my chest into my Lower Dan Tian. I was greatly surprised and very happy that my small circle, my *xiao zhou tian,* spontaneously opened!

There is a hint of Tao practice in the first chapter of the Huang Di Nei Jing Su Wen, *The Yellow Emperor's Internal Classic,* that I read in my twenties. In this chapter, called "Universal Truth of the Ancient Time," there is a discussion between Huang Di (the Yellow Emperor) and his teacher, Chi Po.

Chi Po explained to the Yellow Emperor that the secret of reaching Tao, the secret of immortality, and the secret of living a long life and being a high saint lie in the circle in the body. Second, she explained how the highest ancient saints were uniting with Tao and with Heaven and Earth. Her description was very poetic, but there was no mention about any possible practices that could help explain things.

It took many years for me to finally come to the works of

Chang Po Tuan, a great teacher of Taoism in China, who described the circle and how to practice it. Yet, the practice was based on the power of the mind only and was not combined with chanting mantras. There was also no mention of creating saliva in this practice nor in any book I have read and I can assure you that I have read just about anything that could have been read about Taoism.

From that moment, I practiced this energy circle exercise often. That was, however, not a very wise thing to do. The rotations of energy in this circle made my qi very hot. I remember occasions where I felt very hot energy coming down from my palate to my tongue and down to Chong Mai, the central meridian.

After doing this practice for several years, my mouth become quite dry and I knew that this was not right. I become quite tired too, but I had no one to consult. It was not until 2004, when I met professor De Hua Liu, who showed me an exercise to combat this issue, that I was able to try something different. I did not have much success with that exercise either.

In 2007, Master Zhi Chen Guo showed me his version of the small circle and that indeed made things much different. Finally, I was able to produce some saliva in my mouth.

I was therefore extremely grateful when Master Sha introduced the divine teaching of Tian Yi Zhen Shui, which is Heaven's unique sacred liquid. Right from the beginning of applying this teaching, I was able to produce saliva and, over time, my mouth became moist and quite watery.

When I practice this exercise with mantras and Divine Downloads, within a few short minutes I have a mouth filled with sweet saliva. Once this is swallowed and directed to the Lower Dan Tian, the whole body is filled with a very comfortable feeling. I have been practicing this for about ten months now, and perhaps this is the reason that my body feels very comfortable. This exercise is really working for me.

The second practice I wish to mention is the creation of an immortal baby, which is named *xiao zhen ren.* "Xiao" means *small.* "Zhen ren" means *true being.* Xiao zhen ren is a soul baby. This was a main goal of my Taoist practices. It is a very advanced Taoist secret path, during which we can create a new soul within our own body.

This new soul is made of our essence—from our jing (essence of matter), qi (our energy), and shen (Yuan Shen). When the father's sperm and the mother's egg join together to form an embryo, Tao gives Yuan Shen to this embryo.

The process of creating *xiao zhen ren* starts with building a huge supply of jing that we can further transform to higher frequencies. Then, we have to develop a lot of pure qi (energy) and finally jing, qi, and Yuan Shen join as one. Ancient Taoists have developed very complex techniques to do this, but they are very difficult to learn and practice.

To succeed, you need to work very hard for many years to collect a lot of jing, then transform jing into qi, and then change qi into shen. You continue to gather *jing qi shen,* purify them, and then you bring *jing qi shen* together to the top of your head, where they blend together. Afterward, you bring this one unified essence down into the Lower Dan Tian. This is the way that I practiced. In this book, *Tao II,* Master Sha has a new teaching. Please follow Master Sha's teaching. It is simpler. I went through a much more complicated way and spent more than twenty years to achieve this *xiao zhen ren.*

In the ancient way, you slowly grow the unified jing qi shen until the soul baby is formed. The soul baby will ascend to the top of the head, to *Tian Men,* "Heaven's Gate." Finally, you practice the technique called "nine years of facing the wall." You sit and meditate to empty your mind, doing nothing else for nine years in order to finish the maturation of *xiao zhen ren*.

These are the ancient ways to create an immortal baby to reach immortality. They take about twenty to thirty years of dedicated hard work.

I did not have all the techniques, as I did this without the guidance of a teacher. I did not know how to produce enough jing and consequently, my body weakened quite a lot. But I persevered and finally, at the beginning of 2001, the baby was conceived. I owe this in part to my first meeting with Master Sha in October 2000. Although Master Sha did not teach Tao at that time, he taught me how to harness enormous quantities of light. In addition, he taught me how to communicate with the Divine so that I could bring a lot of light to my Lower Dan Tian.

Around March 2001, jing qi shen had combined on the top of my head and a purple ball descended into my Lower Dan Tian. The baby was conceived. I spent a lot of time doing more practices with the baby until 2006, when the baby finally emerged from my Bai Hui, an acupuncture point on the top of my head.

This achievement was the result of several decades of extensive search, practice, and many sacrifices. It was not easy at all. Professor De Hua Liu, who recognized my *xiao zhen ren* in 2003, told me to be very happy to have produced a *xiao zhen ren*. He said very few people in history have succeeded in this quest.

However, the Divine Xiao Zhen Ren that Master Sha transmits from the Divine, is a different story. The immortal baby that I created according to original Taoist teachings, although it was a considerable feat, was created from my own bodily energies. It cannot be compared to a baby created by God, which has divine energies. How can our own energies match the purity of divine energies? The Divine has the purest and most exquisite energy in the whole universe. Xiao Zhen Ren is an incredible divine treasure that the Divine has decided to offer to humanity at this time.

I feel so happy for all the students of Master Sha who can have an immortal baby transmitted from the Divine within minutes at his retreats. So much time and effort saved and so much virtue and power gifted by divine generosity!

There was one additional secret Taoist practice that I knew of, but did not venture to try. This was the teaching of creating a Golden Pill, the elixir of immortality. During the entire history of China, emperors across many dynasties were literally wild to get ahold of this profound secret. Of course, emperors in ancient China had the whole country at their disposal, with enormous wealth, many wives, and the most comfortable lives. Is it any wonder that all the emperors wanted was to be able to enjoy their lives and its offerings as long as possible? Therefore, many emperors were pursuing the quest of immortality.

The recipes to concoct the elixir of immortality were known as Wai Dan. "Wai" means *external.* "Dan" means *medicine that can make one immortal.* Dan is also in a round shape like a ball, so "Wai Dan" means *a specially cooked medicine ball for longevity and immortality.*

Many Taoist masters have cooked Wai Dan. They were all cooking minerals, mainly lead and quicksilver. Needless to say, the product was highly poisonous. Throughout history, many emperors were carried to the grave after ingesting this type of Wai Dan. I am sure nobody would blame me not to have given Wai Dan a try, but I tried everything else and boy, did I get burned!

After many emperors and many others died after drinking Wai Dan, Taoist masters started to realize that true power comes from inside. It does not come from outside materials. The Tao masters then started to search and practice in order to form the internal Dan, which is the Jin Dan ("Golden Dan").

Jin Dan practice has been experienced and developed by many great masters. There is only one way to form a Jin Dan. This secret has been kept by masters only for their lineage holders. It has not been delivered to the public. Through history, people have heard about Jin Dan practices, but very few have accomplished the Jin Dan practice. When you read a Tao book, it clearly states that to receive the true secret of Jin Dan, it has to be delivered orally. Jin Dan has been kept secret in history.

These days we are extremely fortunate, because Master Sha has been authorized by the Divine to transmit a Divine Jin Dan to us. Divine Jin Dan is not a concoction from poisonous minerals. To the contrary, it is a divine soul of highest purity that carries the frequencies of an elixir of immortality.

To receive a Divine Jin Dan takes literally seconds. There is no need for complex and time consuming preparation as in the old days. However, that is not the main difference here. The elixir of immortality, at least the one for which we have written information, is made from minerals, while the Divine Jin Dan is created by the Divine. It is a divine soul that constantly radiates high frequencies of very pure divine love and light. For more than six months, I have been practicing with the Divine Jin Dan that I have received and the results have been heart-touching. I use my Divine Jin Dan in all of my meditations.

To summarize from my experiences of the traditional Taoist practices that were available to me, and those that I learned from Master Sha, I see three main differences.

The original Taoist teachings are passed to us in ancient language that not many understand, and the top secrets are written in secret codes. This leads to the possibility of misunderstandings and misapplication of techniques.

The Tao that Master Sha teaches is not Taoism, although some names and concepts are similar. The wisdom that Master Sha shares with us is divine revelation, new concepts of Tao that Master Sha received directly from the Divine and Tao. The techniques are unique and unprecedented.

The teachings of Master Sha's books, *Tao I: The Way of All Life* and *Tao II: The Way of Healing, Rejuvenation, Longevity, and Immortality,* are extremely simple and practical with clear explanations that everyone can understand and put into practice. There are no secret codes so one can grasp the meaning of concepts easily. But you do need to read these books more than once and seriously practice. Then you can understand his teaching much more deeply and receive many more "aha!" moments.

Second, there is one thing that is even more remarkable: Master Sha treats everyone equally. You may study with him for ten years or you may have just attended his Tao Retreat for the first time. It does not matter; you will receive the same teaching and you will receive the same opportunities to receive the spiritual transmissions. There are no hidden secrets, no preferences. This is his true Tao teaching.

Finally, as we experienced in the past, the combination of simple and effective techniques Master Sha teaches together with Divine and Tao Downloads can help students achieve high states even during home practices.

It was my great joy when I found Master Sha in 2000 and soon discovered that he does teach some Taoist principles. Our very first meditation together was a meditation on the Lower Dan Tian. Dan Tian is a Taoist term and that was in principle a Taoist meditation. Ever since, we have practiced some qi gong exercises, some of which were Taoist and some of which were Master Guo's meditations with visualization, and practices with energy circles that use Taoist principles.

Over the years, we have progressed in our spiritual practices from working on energy centers, to promoting energy flow in the main energy circle inside the body, to forming the Jin Dan, and up to creating *xiao zhen ren*. Master Sha has received the divine authority to offer transmissions of Divine Xiao Zhen Ren. Words are not enough to explain this greatest honor for the true spiritual Tao seeker or practitioner.

But, Master Sha has not stopped there. Master Sha teaches by offering direct experience. When he writes compassion, you can feel compassion. When he writes love, you can feel love. In the same way, when he writes Tao, you can feel Tao.

Master Sha defines Tao as emptiness, oneness, without shape or form, unlimitedly big and small, beyond space and time. This is obviously not possible to describe, but can only be experienced.

In the divine way of Tao, or One, just by chanting mantras together with Master Sha and his special energy field, one can go directly into states of Tao that are just hinted at in Taoist books. To get there, we do not need secret complex Taoist techniques that were in Taoist tradition transmitted only to very few and that take many years to master. But by direct experience through chanting sacred phrases of Tao mantras, we can receive the meaning of Tao teaching that goes well beyond the intellect.

To be in Master Sha's special force field and to be able to link through the connection that Master Sha has with Tao, we can, using the very simple techniques that Master Sha teaches, enter very special states in a relatively short time. Each book includes a CD or audio download with Master Sha chanting that can help you create this special field. Moreover, there are permanent transmissions of power included in the text of both *Tao I* and *Tao II*. You really receive incredible tools for your spiritual quest.

The direct experience of Tao and the energies emanating from every line of new divine and Tao wisdom that Master Sha has received gives us, the readers, the opportunity to be attuned to different aspects of the Divine and Tao. Every line of the Tao mantras has tremendous power for healing and blessing. All of this gives you and every reader an incredible opportunity to progress on your spiritual journey very fast and to go very high.

According to Master Sha, the final goal of one's spiritual journey is to meld with Tao, to become Tao. Tao is the source and creator of all things. It is The Way. Tao is both emptiness and nothingness. Tao creates One. Tao is Oneness, unity. There are countless planets, stars, galaxies, and universes, but they are all one.

Up to 2009, Master Sha has revealed and emphasized practices to develop one's soul. We, his students, were given techniques to purify, develop, and enlighten the soul and were guided towards unconditional service in order to reach the highest levels of soul standing.

In his second, more recent phase of teachings, Master Sha offers the divine way of practicing Tao. He shares the essence of the traditional Taoist wisdom and practice, but he emphasizes divine and Tao practice. The divine way to practice Tao and to meld with Tao is clearly presented in the *Tao I* and *Tao II* books.

Now Master Sha is teaching us how to discover in ourselves the seed of Tao. This seed is our Yuan Shen. Once we discover it, we nurture it, then develop it, and finally, meld our body soul with it. That is the final achievement. That is the union with Tao.

Another way to achieve union with Tao is to achieve emptiness, for every time we reach emptiness, in that moment, we are melding with Tao.

Finally, there is a practice of Jin Dan in Kun Gong, the Kun Temple, as Jin Dan is a gateway to Tao.

Master Sha emphasizes that as a prerequisite to any success, we must achieve purity inside and outside. We do not think, say, or do any impure things. We do not even allow any impurity to be heard, seen, or experienced. As we progress on the journey to Tao, we have to be kind by developing unconditional love, forgiveness, compassion, generosity, integrity, sincerity, and honesty. We must remove any type of evil, greed, and ignorance by purifying our hearts. Then we can embark on the divine path to achieving Tao, the practice of Jin Dan Da Tao Xiu Lian.

While in his previous book, *Tao I*, Master Sha teaches how to develop the Jin Dan, in this book, *Tao II*, he goes further to explain how to use the Jin Dan practice to achieve union with Tao.

Jin Dan is the highest treasure in Xiu Lian. Jin Dan Da Tao Xiu Lian is the root foundation of Xiu Lian and we practice this highest treasure for *fan lao huan tong* (transforming old age to the health and purity of the baby state), longevity, and immortality.

Jin Dan Da Tao Xiu Lian is the absolute truth. It is the highest philosophy.

Jin Dan Da Tao Xiu Lian has four steps:

The first step of Jin Dan Da Tao Xiu Lian is recovery of health by removing all sickness. The second step is to reach fan lao huan tong. The third step is to develop long life. The fourth and final step of Jin Dan Da Tao Xiu Lian is to meld with Tao, to become Tao.

In the first step, we have to remove all our sickness, which is caused by the imbalance of yin and yang. Sickness exhausts jing (the matter in every cell and the entire body), qi (the energy and life force of the body), and shen (soul, or message, that directs the transformation between matter and energy), the vital forces of our being. During this practice, we gather jing qi shen xu Tao and transform them further.

In the second step, we practice rejuvenation, specifically fan lao huan tong, which means "return from old age to become like a baby." It is achieving such a level of health and transformation of the body that the practitioner becomes younger. The main emphasis at this stage is to align the soul, mind, and body (in Tao terms, shen, qi, and jing). We achieve fan lao huan tong by practicing Jin Dan Da Tao Xiu Lian.

In the third step of Jin Dan Da Tao Xiu Lian, we achieve longevity. To do so we have to reach *ming xin jian xing* (enlighten the heart to see your true self, which is your Yuan Shen) by quietness and stillness. Then we develop intelligence of the mind, of our heart, of our soul, and finally, Yuan Shen intelligence. At this level, our Yuan Shen can start to guide our body to practice the most advanced Xiu Lian. Yuan Shen will guide our Shi Shen (body soul) to transform every aspect of our life.

At the final stage, we reach high levels of enlightenment and our Shi Shen (body soul) will completely meld with Yuan Shen.

The last and final stage is to arrive at union with Tao. During this time, Yuan Shen will continue to guide our body soul or Shi Shen, until Shi Shen completely melds with Yuan Shen. When this happens, you are melded with Tao, because Yuan Shen is Tao. Moreover, our physical body also has to meld with the Tao. Once we meld our physical body with the Tao, we have reached immortality. This means to stop reincarnation.

This is my understanding of Master Sha's divine Tao teachings. In all the books I have read, I have never seen anything so simple and effective. It is easy to understand and easy to practice—simply wonderful.

I have great respect for all Taoist teachers and I feel great gratitude for all the wisdom that they passed to us. I always think how extremely difficult it must have been to practice in hunger, cold, and poverty in isolated mountains. They had such dedication and such generosity. They recorded for our convenience all the experiences they had and literally gave us their hearts.

Many great Tao masters have practiced seriously for many lifetimes to find the truth to heal, to reach *fan lao huan tong* and longevity, and to move to immortality. The top secrets are kept without delivery to the public.

How fortunate we are that Master Sha has revealed this absolute truth to reach *fan lao huan tong*, longevity, and immortality. How generous Master Sha is! How grateful and appreciative we are to Master Sha! We cannot thank the Divine and Tao enough that they have chosen Master Sha as a messenger and a servant to deliver this sacred teaching to humanity.

Let me use myself as an example. I have been on the Tao practice journey for more than forty years. Master Sha's divine and Tao teaching has accelerated my Tao practice beyond comprehension. I am extremely grateful to my beloved spiritual father and teacher for his compassionate heart and unconditional service to me, humanity, and all souls.

From my own experience, Master Sha's Tao teaching is an absolute treasure for anyone who is searching to reach Tao and accelerate his or her own spiritual journey.

In my opinion, Master Sha's divine and Tao teaching will guide millions and millions of spiritual seekers in the future on their spiritual journeys and help transform every aspect of their lives.

I strongly recommend that you read this book from the bottom of your heart. Do not rush to read fast. Read slowly. Digest well. Absorb well. To read one time is not enough. To read three times is not enough. The more you read this book, the more "aha!" moments you will receive.

Every time you read this book in this way, you will continue to receive "aha!" moments. These "aha!" moments will speed your journey to meld with Tao.

Now, we can sit in a comfortable room, have plenty of food and support beside us, and just read books we order online. The difference between what was available to the ancients then and what is available to us now is just incredible.

But, as with everything in the universe, the teachings have to undergo a change. The universe is in a constant flux, ever changing, and our practices have to change also.

Therefore, we must have great reverence for the old teachings and at the same time we have to be flexible enough to accept new teachings that reflect a new era in the universe.

Master Sha is offering divine Tao teaching. It is new, breathing with beautiful light and freshness, and although it is quite a deep topic, Master Sha has offered the theory and explained the techniques quite clearly, without any secret codes. Anyone who is willing to learn, can.

I am honored to have read *Tao II: The Way of Healing, Rejuvenation, Longevity, and Immortality* before it was published. I am humbled to have this opportunity to share my personal experiences and my realizations of Master Sha's Tao teachings.

I thank my spiritual father and teacher, Master Zhi Gang Sha.

I thank the Divine.

I thank Tao.

I thank all of my spiritual fathers and mothers in all of my lifetimes.

I thank each of you.

In summary, the Tao teaching in Master Sha's books is extremely simple, profound, and powerful. Words are not enough to express my greatest gratitude for this new divine Tao teaching. I wish you and each reader will read the Tao books and all the books of the Soul Power Series seriously and practice diligently. It will save a spiritual seeker twenty to thirty years, even one's entire life or lifetimes, of trying to find the true teachings.

The sacred teaching is released in Master Sha's Tao books. They are absolute treasures.

Practice more. The more you practice, you may have the same realization that I have had about Master Sha's Tao teachings, or even more.

The benefits could be beyond your comprehension.

I wish for you to have great success in your Tao journey.

Peter Hudoba

Introduction

$\mathcal{T}$HERE ARE NEARLY seven billion human beings on Mother Earth. Every day, hundreds of millions of them suffer from different sicknesses. Everyone can understand the feeling of sickness. Everyone has experienced sickness. How does someone feel when he or she suffers from pain, from inflammation, from a fever, from diabetes, from arthritis, from emotional blockages, such as depression, anxiety, or fear, from suicidal thoughts, or from mental confusion? How would you feel if your loved one had a mental disorder or was paralyzed from a stroke? For all of these sicknesses and more, what are the feelings of these unhealthy people?

There are thousands and thousands of healing modalities to help people when they become sick, including conventional modern medicine, traditional Chinese medicine, ayurvedic medicine, and many other kinds of medicine.

Why does a person get sick? What is the root cause of the sickness? How can we remove the root cause of the sickness? Is there a way that a person can help him or herself by removing the root cause of all sickness and by self-healing all sickness? This book could have the answers to these questions for you.

Countless people since creation have been searching for rejuvenation. People put great effort into rejuvenating their bodies in order to become younger and more beautiful. People spend thousands of dollars for plastic surgery to make themselves look younger. Do you want to learn the sacred way to truly make yourself younger inside as well as outside? This book could give you the way.

People have tried countless herbs, fruits, all kinds of natural nutrients, supplements, and other material remedies, such as oils and lotions, for rejuvenation. There are all kinds of physical exercises and spiritual practices to help people become younger. How can a person really become younger? Is there a special way that anyone can use to become younger? This book could give you the answers.

Fan lao huan tong (pronounced *fahn lao hwahn tawng*) is a special historical term in traditional Tao practice. "Fan" means *return*. "Lao" means *old age*. "Huan" means *return to*. "Tong" means *baby*. "Fan lao huan tong" means *transform old age to the health and purity of the baby state*. Imagine an old person who can transform his or her old age to the state of a baby. This may be very hard to believe. Is it possible to reach fan lao huan tong? This book could give you the answer.

The normal process of a human being's life is birth, infancy, childhood, adolescence, adulthood, senior citizenship, sickness or infirmity, and death. Millions of people are searching for anti-aging secrets. Millions of people wish to have a long life. Many seniors would like to live longer. Think about your family and friends. Think about yourself. Would you like to have true anti-aging secrets? This book could give them to you.

In ancient times, a serious spiritual seeker, including Tao masters, would hide in a cave in the mountains for thirty years, fifty years, and even for his or her whole life searching for the secrets for a long, long life. There are sacred teachings from many religions and other spiritual groups about longevity.

Have you found the true way to prolong your life? If you really want to prolong your life, what kinds of practices do you need to do? How can you actually achieve longevity? This book could give you the answers.

Millions of people throughout history have dreamed of reaching immortality. Very few people have actually reached immortality. People find it very difficult to believe that immortality is even possible. They use their logical minds to think: *If immortality is possible, why haven't I ever seen an immortal being?*

Lao Zi is the author of the revered classic text, *Dao De Jing.* I was honored to be chosen as a lineage holder of Lao Zi's teacher, Peng Zu, the renowned Chinese "long life star" who is a major Taoist saint. Peng Zu lived to the age of 880. I have visited the tomb of the founder of tai chi, Master Zhang San Feng. The plaque on his tomb lists the years of his birth and death. He lived for about 450 years. Nobody knows how long Lao Zi lived.

Is immortality possible? The answer could be found in the Jin Dan Da Tao Xiu Lian and the Tao of Healing, Rejuvenation, Longevity, and Immortality that I share in this book in chapters 2 and 3, respectively.

"Jin Dan" (pronounced *jeen dahn*) means *golden light ball.* In Tao practice, this special golden light ball is formed by gathering souls, energy, and matter from Heaven, Mother Earth, and humanity, and from countless planets, stars, galaxies, and universes. Tao is The Way. "Da Tao" (pronounced *dah dow*) means *The Big Way.* "Xiu" means *purification.* "Lian" means *practice.* "Xiu Lian" (pronounced *sheo lyen*) or *purification practice* represents *the totality of one's spiritual journey*. Jin Dan Da Tao Xiu Lian means *The Big Tao Golden Light Ball Xiu Lian*.

How can you believe in immortality? Gain this belief little by little by reading this book and through your own Xiu Lian practice.

If you practice Jin Dan Da Tao Xiu Lian and the Tao of Healing, Rejuvenation, Longevity, and Immortality, your sicknesses could be healed. If you are healed, you could believe the teachings, sacred wisdom, and practices shared in this book more.

If you practice Jin Dan Da Tao Xiu Lian and the Tao of Healing, Rejuvenation, Longevity, and Immortality, you could clearly see and feel that you are becoming younger. You could have more energy, stamina, vitality, and immunity. Although you may have gray or white hair, your skin could be getting smoother and smoother. In other words, you could have the condition that is described as "white hair, baby face." This is an important physical signal. Your vitality, energy, flexibility, and memory could be like a child's. When you clearly feel and experience that you are becoming younger and younger, you could believe the teachings, sacred wisdom, and practices shared in this book more.

You could live to the age of one hundred, which relatively few people can do at this time. When you do Jin Dan Da Tao Xiu Lian and you reach the age of one hundred, everything in your body could have the health, vitality, and purity of a young child. This indicates that you have reached the fan lao huan tong condition. You have transformed your old age to the health and purity of the baby state. If you reach this condition, you could believe the teachings, sacred wisdom, and practices shared in this book even more.

Five thousand years ago, *The Yellow Emperor's Internal Clas-*

sic, the authority book of traditional Chinese medicine, and many other books shared that many people in that time lived to be one hundred to one hundred fifty years old. They followed nature's way. They ate proper food regularly and in moderation. They rested properly by following nature's way, sleeping at sunset and waking upon sunrise. (Very few people today follow this simple and natural rule.) They balanced their emotions. They purified their hearts. They did spiritual practices and physical exercises. They left many profound and valuable teachings for humanity.

When you practice Jin Dan Da Tao Xiu Lian and the Tao of Healing, Rejuvenation, Longevity, and Immortality, you could live to the age of one hundred fifty. If you can do this, then you could believe the teachings, sacred wisdom, and practices shared in this book much more.

There is no rush to believe in immortality. Gain your belief little by little. A short while ago, I thought that if I could live to the age of one hundred, then I could write a book on longevity and immortality. The Divine and Tao told me that I do not need to wait until I am a hundred years old to write such a book. This book is in front of you now.

The reason for the Divine's and Tao's direction is simple. Millions of people are seniors. The teachings, sacred wisdom, and especially the practical techniques for rejuvenation, longevity, and immortality shared in this book can directly benefit so many people who are searching for answers to the questions I asked above.

In the sixth book of my Soul Power Series, *Tao I: The Way of All Life*,[1] I shared two phrases from *Dao De Jing*: Tao ke Tao (pronounced *dow kuh dow*), fei chang Tao (pronounced *fay chahng dow*). These phrases can be translated as: *Tao that can be*

---

1. *Tao I: The Way of All Life* (Toronto/New York: Heaven's Library/Atria Books, 2010).

*explained by words or comprehended by thoughts is not the eternal
Tao or true Tao.*

Tao is The Way of all life. Tao is the source of all things. I also
shared in *Tao I* the normal creation of Tao and the reverse creation of Tao. Tao normal creation is a process: Tao creates One.
One creates Two. Two creates Three. Three creates all things. Tao
reverse creation is the reverse process: All things return to Three.
Three returns to Two. Two returns to One. One returns to Tao.

The normal path of a human being's life progresses from baby
to child, teenager, adult, senior, sickness or infirmity, and death.
This follows Tao normal creation.

A human being has many bodily systems. Each system consists of many organs. Every organ has millions and billions of
cells. This is Tao sheng yi (Tao creates One), yi sheng er (One creates Two), er sheng san (Two creates Three), san sheng wan wu
(Three creates all things).[2] This process moves from macrocosm
to microcosm.

Generally speaking, a human being is formed when a sperm
and an egg join as one to become an embryo. The embryo grows
and develops to become a fetus and then further to become a baby
who has many systems, organs, and cells. This is the normal creation of Tao, from the simplest embryo to a being with trillions
of cells. This process is from macrocosm to microcosm. A microcosm has limited life. Therefore, a human being's life is limited.

To prolong life, one must follow Tao reverse creation. Reverse
creation is to join the soul, mind, and body of billions and trillions of cells as one. This process moves from microcosm to macrocosm. A macrocosm has unlimited life. Tao is the source. Tao

---

2. The phrases in Chinese are pronounced *dow shung yee, yee shung ur, ur shung sahn, sahn
shung wahn woo.*

is the creator. Tao is the macrocosm. Tao has unlimited life. If a person can reach Tao, immortality is possible.

When you practice Tao reverse creation (I will show you how in this book), Yuan Shen (pronounced *ywen shun*) is in charge. "Yuan Shen" means *original soul* or *source soul*. At the moment the father's sperm and the mother's egg join as one, Tao gives Yuan Shen to the embryo. Yuan Shen *is* Tao. Yuan Shen is the true self of a human being. Yuan Shen will be with a person for his or her whole life. However, Yuan Shen remains hidden for normal human beings.

For a normal human being, one's Shi Shen (pronounced *shr shun*) is in charge. Shi Shen is one's "body soul." It is the soul who reincarnates. Shi Shen is not the real true self of a human being. After Tao Xiu Lian practice, one can reach ming xin jian xing. "Ming xin" means *enlighten the heart*. "Jian xing" means *see Yuan Shen hidden in the heart*. Ming xin jian xing (pronounced *ming sheen jyen shing*) means *enlighten your heart to see your true self, your Yuan Shen*.

When you reach ming xin jian xing, your Yuan Shen takes charge over your Shi Shen. Yuan Shen is Tao. Yuan Shen will guide Shi Shen to gather the soul, mind, and body of every system, every organ, every cell, every cell unit, every cell DNA and RNA, every space between the cells, and every tiny matter inside the cells to join as one. To completely join the soul, mind, and body of all systems, organs, and cells as one is to return to Tao. To return to Tao is to have unlimited life. This is Tao reverse creation. Yuan Shen leads one's Xiu Lian to make it happen.

I am not talking about Taoism. Tao is One. Tao is emptiness and nothingness. Tao is the source and creator of all things. Tao is unlimited. If you reach Tao, you could have unlimited life.

Tao is profound and mysterious. Since ancient times, millions of people have studied Tao and wanted to reach Tao. People do not know how to do it. In fact, **Tao is inside everyone's heart.** Yuan Shen is inside everyone's heart. Your nationality, the color of your skin, or your belief system do not matter. Tao gives Yuan Shen to you and every human being equally. If you can really understand how to see your Yuan Shen, and then have your Yuan Shen guide your Xiu Lian, then the following will happen:

All sickness will be healed.
All kinds of suffering will be removed.
True happiness and joy will accompany you.
Rejuvenation will happen.
Longevity will occur.
Immortality will be on the way.
Humanity will evolve in a new direction.
World love, peace, and harmony will manifest.
Wan ling rong he will be accomplished.

"Wan" means *ten thousand,* which in Chinese represents *all* or *every.* "Ling" means *soul.* "Rong he" means *join as one.* "Wan ling rong he" (pronounced *wahn ling rawng huh*) means *all souls join as one.*

Tao or Yuan Shen in everyone's heart can make this happen for us.

In *Dao De Jing,* Lao Zi shared clearly with humanity the sacred code for developing Yuan Shen and reaching Tao. But because Lao Zi's words are difficult to understand, very few people have really realized the absolute truth that he presented in *Dao De Jing* thousands of years ago. Even in China, not many people at all have really understood and realized the true sacred code to reach Tao.

How can you find this true sacred code? I am honored to release this sacred code for you and humanity now. This sacred code can be summarized in one sentence:

Jin Dan Da Tao Xiu Lian is the sacred code to reach Tao.

It can be summarized further in two words:

Lian Dan

"Lian Dan" (pronounced *lyen dahn*) means *form the Jin Dan*. It can be summarized even further in one word:

Yi

"Yi" (pronounced *yee*) means *one*. One is Jin Dan. One is Yuan Shen. One is Tao.

This is the root of Xiu Lian.

This is the foundation to meld with Tao.

This is the absolute truth.

This is the only way to meld with Tao.

Every Tao practitioner must go through three special periods of practice and achievement:

- Bai Ri Zhu Ji (pronounced *bye rr joo jee*). Practice one hundred days of Jin Dan Da Tao Xiu Lian to build a foundation for your body.
- Qian Ri Xiao Cheng (pronounced *chyen rr shee-yow chung*). Practice one thousand days of Jin Dan Da Tao Xiu Lian to reach a "small achievement," which is to form the Jin Dan and to reach ming xin jian xing.

- Shi Nian Da Cheng (pronounced *shr nyen dah chung*). Do Jin Dan Da Tao Xiu Lian for ten years to reach a "big achievement." The big achievement is to meld with Tao.

These three periods of time will take a total of ten years doing Jin Dan Da Tao Xiu Lian.

In ancient times, serious Tao masters spent ten years of their lives just doing Tao Xiu Lian and nothing else. Many of them lived to the age of one hundred, one hundred fifty, or even longer because of their Xiu Lian practice.

A human's average life expectancy is about eighty years. If you do ten years of practice for the Jin Dan, you could add seventy years to your life. If you practice Jin Dan Da Tao seriously and reach *yu Dao he zhen* (pronounced *yü dow huh jun*), which means *meld with Tao*, longevity and immortality are waiting for you.

A human being has a family life and work life. It is very difficult to devote ten years just to Tao practice without doing anything else. But by following the sacred Tao teachings, wisdom, and especially the practical techniques in chapter 2, "Jin Dan Da Tao Xiu Lian," and chapter 3, "The Tao of Healing, Rejuvenation, Longevity, and Immortality," you can take more than ten years to meld with Tao, but you can do it. In this book, I will share the highest secrets for reaching fan lao huan tong, longevity, and immortality as quickly as possible.

Chapter 2, "Jin Dan Da Tao Xiu Lian," is the absolute truth to remember. It is also the highest practical technique. It is the secret code to reach fan lao huan tong, longevity, and immortality.

As I am flowing this book, the Divine, Tao, the highest Tao

saints, buddhas, and other spiritual fathers and mothers are above my head to guide me. I am extremely humbled and honored. I am a servant for you, humanity, and all souls. I am the vehicle to share the Tao of Healing, Rejuvenation, Longevity, and Immortality.

I am your servant forever.

I am a servant for humanity and all souls forever.

This book will help anyone who is ready and willing to study Tao and to reach Tao.

This book shares the absolute truth to reach fan lao huan tong and immortality. "Absolute truth" means it is the only way to reach immortality. I said earlier that you need to gain this belief little by little. To do Jin Dan Da Tao Xiu Lian is to yu Dao he zhen (meld with Tao).

Chapter 2 is the absolute truth and the highest practice to meld with Tao. In chapter 3, I will explain the four stages to meld with Tao.

Study well.

Practice hard.

Form your Jin Dan.

Heal all sickness.

Prevent all sickness.

Reach ming xin jian xing (enlighten your heart to see your true self, which is your Yuan Shen).

Reach fan lao huan tong (transform old age to the health and purity of the baby state).

Prolong your life.

Move to immortality.

I am honored to share these special teachings and share the sacred wisdom, knowledge, and practical techniques that millions of people are waiting for.

I love my heart and soul
I love all humanity
Join hearts and souls together
Love, peace and harmony
Love, peace and harmony

Essence of Tao I

$\mathcal{I}$ SHARED MUCH SACRED wisdom, knowledge, and practical techniques in *Tao I: The Way of All Life*. I will summarize them in this chapter because they are an essential foundation for the new sacred Tao wisdom, knowledge, and practical techniques in this book.

What Is Tao?

Tao is The Way. Tao is the source and creator of all things. Tao is emptiness and nothingness. Tao is the universal principles and laws. Tao cannot be explained in words or comprehended by thought.

What Is the Normal Creation of Tao?

The normal creation of Tao is:

TAO → One → Two → Three → all things
   creates

Tao creates One. One creates Two. Two creates Three. Three creates all things. The greatest significance of Tao normal creation is that it describes how Heaven, Mother Earth, humanity, and countless planets, stars, galaxies, and universes are created.

What Is the Reverse Creation of Tao?

The reverse creation of Tao is:

all things → Three → Two → One → Tao
        return to

All things return to Three. Three returns to Two. Two returns to One. One returns to Tao. The greatest significance of Tao reverse creation is that it describes how to reach fan lao huan tong (transform old age to the health and purity of the baby state), longevity, and immortality.

Significance of Studying and Practicing Tao

Studying and practicing Tao has unlimited benefits, which include:

- learning and realizing that Tao is The Way of all life
- applying Tao to transform all life
- learning and realizing that Tao is the source of all universes
- applying Tao to transform all universes
- learning and realizing that Tao is the universal principles and laws that everyone and everything must follow

- learning and realizing the universal principles and laws in order to truly understand: "Follow the Tao, flourish. Go against the Tao, finish."
- applying Tao to flourish in every aspect of life
- learning and realizing Tao normal creation and Tao reverse creation
- applying Tao normal creation and Tao reverse creation to guide and transform every aspect of your life
- learning and applying Tao for healing
- learning and applying Tao for prevention of illness
- learning and applying Tao for rejuvenation (fan lao huan tong)
- learning and applying Tao for prolonging life
- learning and applying Tao for immortality
- learning and applying Tao for transforming relationships
- learning and applying Tao for transforming finances
- learning and applying Tao for enlightening the soul
- learning and applying Tao for enlightening the heart
- learning and applying Tao for enlightening the mind
- learning and applying Tao for enlightening the body
- learning and applying Tao for the evolution of humanity
- learning and applying Tao for developing the potential powers of the soul, including soul wisdom, intelligence, and abilities to transform all life
- learning and applying Tao for developing the potential powers of the mind, including mind wisdom, intelligence, and abilities to transform all life

- learning and applying Tao for developing the potential powers of the body, including body wisdom, intelligence, and abilities to transform all life
- learning and applying Tao for developing extraordinary saints' abilities
- learning and applying Tao to become a Total GOLD unconditional universal servant and a Tao servant

What Is the Tao Jing?

In December 2008 the Divine and Tao gave me the Tao Jing, consisting of seventy-five sacred phrases. "Tao Jing" means *Tao Classic*. Each phrase is extremely sacred and powerful. As I write this, *Tao I* was published less than three months ago. Already, thousands of students worldwide chant Tao Jing regularly.

The complete Tao Jing follows. A CD with me singing the Tao Jing accompanied by divine Tao music flowed by Divine Music Composer Chun-Yen Chiang is available.

道可道	**Tao Ke Tao**	*dow kuh dow*
	Tao that can be explained by words or comprehended by thoughts	
非常道	**Fei Chang Tao**	*fay chahng dow*
	Is not the eternal Tao or true Tao	
大无外	**Da Wu Wai**	*dah woo wye*
	Bigger than Biggest	
小无内	**Xiao Wu Nei**	*shee-yow woo nay*
	Smaller than Smallest	

无方圆	**Wu Fang Yuan**	*woo fahng ywen*
	No Square, No Circle	
无形象	**Wu Xing Xiang**	*woo shing shyahng*
	No Shape, No Image	
无时空	**Wu Shi Kong**	*woo shr kawng*
	No Time, No Space	
顺道昌	**Shun Tao Chang**	*shwun dow chahng*
	Follow Tao, Flourish	
逆道亡	**Ni Tao Wang**	*nee dow wahng*
	Go against Tao, Finish	
道生一	**Tao Sheng Yi**	*dow shung yee*
	Tao creates One	
天一真水	**Tian Yi Zhen Shui**	*tyen yee jun shway*
	Heaven's unique sacred liquid	
金津玉液	**Jin Jin Yu Ye**	*jeen jeen yü yuh*
	Gold Liquid, Jade Liquid (Mother Earth's sacred liquid)	
咽入丹田	**Yan Ru Dan Tian**	*yahn roo dahn tyen*
	Swallow into the Lower Dan Tian	
一生二	**Yi Sheng Er**	*yee shung ur*
	One creates Two	
道丹道神	**Tao Dan Tao Shen**	*dow dahn dow shun*
	Tao Light Ball, Tao Heart Soul	
服务人类	**Fu Wu Ren Lei**	*foo woo wren lay*
	Serve all humanity	
服务万灵	**Fu Wu Wan Ling**	*foo woo wahn ling*
	Serve all souls	

服务地球	**Fu Wu Di Qiu**	*foo woo dee cheo*
	Serve Mother Earth	
服务宇宙	**Fu Wu Yu Zhou**	*foo woo yü joe*
	Serve all universes	
治愈百病	**Zhi Yu Bai Bing**	*zhr yü bye bing*
	Heal all sickness	
预防百病	**Yu Fang Bai Bing**	*yü fahng bye bing*
	Prevent all sickness	
返老还童	**Fan Lao Huan Tong**	*fahn lao hwahn tawng*
	Return old age to the health and purity of a baby	
长寿永生	**Chang Shou Yong Sheng**	*chahng sho yawng shung*
	Longevity and immortality	
和谐人类	**He Xie Ren Lei**	*huh shyeh wren lay*
	Harmonize all humanity	
道业昌盛	**Tao Ye Chang Sheng**	*dow yuh chahng shung*
	Tao career flourishes	
功德圆满	**Gong De Yuan Man**	*gawng duh ywen mahn*
	Serve unconditionally and gain complete virtue to reach enlightenment	
万灵融合	**Wan Ling Rong He**	*wahn ling rawng huh*
	All souls join as one	
丹神养肾	**Dan Shen Yang Shen**	*dahn shun yahng shun*
	Tao Dan, Tao Shen nourish kidneys	
二生三	**Er Sheng San**	*ur shung sahn*
	Two creates Three	

三万物	**San Wan Wu** Three creates all things	*sahn wahn woo*
天地人	**Tian Di Ren** Heaven, Earth, Human Being	*tyen dee wren*
神气精	**Shen Qi Jing** Soul Energy Matter	*shun chee jing*
肾生精	**Shen Sheng Jing** Kidneys create Jing	*shun shung jing*
精生髓	**Jing Sheng Sui** Jing creates marrow	*jing shung sway*
髓充脑	**Sui Chong Nao** Spinal cord fills brain	*sway chawng now*
脑神明	**Nao Shen Ming** Mind reaches enlightenment	*now shun ming*
炼精化气	**Lian Jing Hua Qi** Transform Jing to Qi	*lyen jing hwah chee*
炼气化神	**Lian Qi Hua Shen** Transform Qi to Shen	*lyen chee hwah shun*
炼神还虚	**Lian Shen Huan Xu** Return Shen to Xu	*lyen shun hwahn shü*
炼虚还道	**Lian Xu Huan Tao** Return Xu to Tao	*lyen shü hwahn dow*
合道中	**He Tao Zhong** Meld with Tao	*huh dow jawng*
无穷尽	**Wu Qiong Jin** The benefits for your life are endless	*woo chyawng jeen*

道灵宫	**Tao Ling Gong** Tao Soul Temple	*dow ling gawng*
信息雪山	**Xin Xi Xue Shan** Message Center, Snow Mountain	*sheen shee shoo-eh* *shahn*
灵语言	**Ling Yu Yan** Soul Language	*ling yü yahn*
灵信通	**Ling Xin Tong** Soul Communication	*ling sheen tawng*
灵歌舞	**Ling Ge Wu** Soul Song, Soul Dance	*ling guh woo*
灵敲打	**Ling Qiao Da** Soul Tapping	*ling chee-yow dah*
灵草药	**Ling Cao Yao** Soul Herbs	*ling tsow yow*
灵针灸	**Ling Zhen Jiu** Soul Acupuncture	*ling jun jeo*
灵按摩	**Ling An Mo** Soul Massage	*ling ahn maw*
灵治疗	**Ling Zhi Liao** Soul Healing	*ling jr lee-yow*
灵预防	**Ling Yu Fang** Soul Prevention of Illness	*ling yü fahng*
灵转化	**Ling Zhuan Hua** Soul Transformation	*ling jwahn hwah*
灵圆满	**Ling Yuan Man** Soul Enlightenment	*ling ywen mahn*
灵智慧	**Ling Zhi Hui** Soul Intelligence	*ling jr hway*
灵潜能	**Ling Qian Neng** Soul Potential	*ling chyen nung*

换灵脑身	**Huan Ling Nao Shen** Soul Mind Body Transplant	*hwahn ling now shun*
服务三界	**Fu Wu San Jie** Serve Heaven, Earth, and Human Being	*foo woo sahn jyeh*
灵光普照	**Ling Guang Pu Zhao** Shining Soul Light	*ling gwahng poo jow*
万物更新	**Wan Wu Geng Xin** Everything is renewed	*wahn woo gung sheen*
誓为公仆	**Shi Wei Gong Pu** Vow to be a servant	*shr way gawng poo*
世代服务	**Shi Dai Fu Wu** Serve in all lifetimes	*shr dye foo woo*
灵光圣世	**Ling Guang Sheng Shi** Soul Light Era	*ling gwahng shung shr*
创新纪元	**Chuang Xin Ji Yuan** Create a new era	*chwahng sheen jee ywen*
道道道	**Tao Tao Tao** Tao Tao Tao	*dow dow dow*
道定得	**Tao Ding De** Tao stillness	*dow ding duh*
道慧明	**Tao Hui Ming** Tao intelligence, Tao realization	*dow hway ming*
道喜在	**Tao Xi Zai** Tao happiness and joy	*dow shee dzye*
道体生	**Tao Ti Sheng** Tao body is produced	*dow tee shung*
道圆满	**Tao Yuan Man** Tao enlightenment	*dow ywen mahn*

道合真	**Tao He Zhen**	*dow huh jun*
	Meld with Tao and become a true being	
道果成	**Tao Guo Cheng**	*dow gwaw chung*
	Tao harvest	
道神通	**Tao Shen Tong**	*dow shun tawng*
	Complete Tao saint abilities	
道法自然	**Tao Fa Zi Ran**	*dow fah dz rahn*
	Follow Nature's Way	

What Is the Jin Dan?

Jin Dan is a golden light ball located in one's lower abdomen, just below the navel and in the center of the body. No one is born with a Jin Dan. Special Tao practice is required to create a Jin Dan.

The Power and Significance of the Jin Dan

Jin Dan has the following powers and abilities:

- Jin Dan is the source of message, energy, and matter.
- Jin Dan has the highest power for healing your spiritual, mental, emotional, and physical bodies.
- Jin Dan is the key to preventing sickness in your spiritual, mental, emotional, and physical bodies.
- Jin Dan is the highest treasure for purifying your soul, heart, mind, and body.
- Jin Dan has the highest abilities for rejuvenating your soul, heart, mind, and body.

- Jin Dan has the highest strength for transforming all of your relationships.
- Jin Dan has the highest potential for transforming your business.
- Jin Dan has the highest honor for enlightening your soul, heart, mind, and body.
- Jin Dan has the highest power and abilities for healing, blessing, and transforming others.
- Jin Dan has the highest power and abilities for offering service to humanity, Mother Earth, and all universes.

How to Build a Jin Dan

We will apply the Four Power Techniques, which are Body Power, Soul Power, Mind Power, and Sound Power. Let me summarize the key wisdom of the Four Power Techniques:

Body Power is special body positions and hand positions for healing and rejuvenation.

Soul Power is to say *hello* to the inner souls of your body, including the souls of your systems, organs, cells, cell units, DNA and RNA, as well as to outer souls, including saints, healing angels, archangels, ascended masters, lamas, gurus, all kinds of spiritual fathers and mothers, the Divine, and Tao, to invoke their power for healing, rejuvenation, and life transformation.

Mind Power is creative visualization. The most important wisdom is to visualize golden or rainbow light to transform your health, relationships, finances, and more.

Sound Power is to chant or sing ancient healing mantras, Divine Soul Songs, and Tao songs for healing, rejuvenation, and transformation of relationships, finances, and every aspect of life.

Here is one basic practice that I shared in *Tao I*. A detailed explanation follows the practice itself. Later in this book, I will introduce new sacred practices to build a Jin Dan.

Use the Four Power Techniques with a secret and sacred mantra:

Body Power. Sit up straight. Put the tip of your tongue as close as you can to the roof of your mouth without touching. Put both palms on your lower abdomen below the navel.

Soul Power. Say *hello:*

> *Dear soul mind body of Tao,*
> *Dear soul mind body of the Divine,*
> *Dear soul mind body of all universes, galaxies, stars, and*
>   *planets,*
> *Dear soul mind body of Heaven,*
> *Dear soul mind body of Mother Earth,*
> *Dear soul mind body of all my spiritual fathers and mothers*
>   *in all layers of Heaven,*
> *Dear soul mind body of all my systems, organs, cells, cell*
>   *units, DNA, RNA, tiny matter in the cells, and spaces*
>   *between the cells,*
> *I love you all, honor you all, and appreciate you all.*
> *You have the power to create and form my Jin Dan.*
> *I am extremely blessed.*
> *I cannot honor you enough.*
> *Thank you.*

Mind Power. Visualize a beautiful, bright, and powerful golden light ball forming in your lower abdomen, just below your navel.

Sound Power. Sing or chant in Chinese:

Tao Sheng Yi	*dow shung yee*	Tao creates One
Tian Yi Zhen Shui	*tyen yee jun shway*	Heaven's unique sacred liquid
Jin Jin Yu Ye	*jeen jeen yü yuh*	Gold liquid, jade liquid
Yan Ru Dan Tian	*yahn roo dahn tyen*	Swallow into the Lower Dan Tian
Shen Qi Jing He Yi	*shun chee jing huh yee*	Soul energy matter join as one
Tian Di Ren He Yi	*tyen dee wren huh yee*	Heaven, Mother Earth, human being join as one
Jin Dan Lian Cheng	*jeen dahn lyen chung*	Jin Dan is formed

Tao Sheng Yi	*dow shung yee*
Tian Yi Zhen Shui	*tyen yee jun shway*
Jin Jin Yu Ye	*jeen jeen yü yuh*
Yan Ru Dan Tian	*yahn roo dahn tyen*
Shen Qi Jing He Yi	*shun chee jing huh yee*
Tian Di Ren He Yi	*tyen dee wren huh yee*
Jin Dan Lian Cheng	*jeen dahn lyen chung*

Tao Sheng Yi　　　　　　*dow shung yee*
Tian Yi Zhen Shui　　　　*tyen yee jun shway*
Jin Jin Yu Ye　　　　　　*jeen jeen yü yuh*
Yan Ru Dan Tian　　　　　*yahn roo dahn tyen*
Shen Qi Jing He Yi　　　　*shun chee jing huh yee*
Tian Di Ren He Yi　　　　　*tyen dee wren huh yee*
Jin Dan Lian Cheng　　　　*jeen dahn lyen chung*

Tao Sheng Yi　　　　　　*dow shung yee*
Tian Yi Zhen Shui　　　　*tyen yee jun shway*
Jin Jin Yu Ye　　　　　　*jeen jeen yü yuh*
Yan Ru Dan Tian　　　　　*yahn roo dahn tyen*
Shen Qi Jing He Yi　　　　*shun chee jing huh yee*
Tian Di Ren He Yi　　　　　*tyen dee wren huh yee*
Jin Dan Lian Cheng　　　　*jeen dahn lyen chung*

Tao Sheng Yi　　　　　　*dow shung yee*
Tian Yi Zhen Shui　　　　*tyen yee jun shway*
Jin Jin Yu Ye　　　　　　*jeen jeen yü yuh*
Yan Ru Dan Tian　　　　　*yahn roo dahn tyen*
Shen Qi Jing He Yi　　　　*shun chee jing huh yee*
Tian Di Ren He Yi　　　　　*tyen dee wren huh yee*
Jin Dan Lian Cheng　　　　*jeen dahn lyen chung*

Tao Sheng Yi　　　　　　*dow shung yee*
Tian Yi Zhen Shui　　　　*tyen yee jun shway*
Jin Jin Yu Ye　　　　　　*jeen jeen yü yuh*
Yan Ru Dan Tian　　　　　*yahn roo dahn tyen*
Shen Qi Jing He Yi　　　　*shun chee jing huh yee*
Tian Di Ren He Yi　　　　　*tyen dee wren huh yee*
Jin Dan Lian Cheng　　　　*jeen dahn lyen chung*

Tao Sheng Yi	*dow shung yee*
Tian Yi Zhen Shui	*tyen yee jun shway*
Jin Jin Yu Ye	*jeen jeen yü yuh*
Yan Ru Dan Tian	*yahn roo dahn tyen*
Shen Qi Jing He Yi	*shun chee jing huh yee*
Tian Di Ren He Yi	*tyen dee wren huh yee*
Jin Dan Lian Cheng . . .	*jeen dahn lyen chung . . .*

Chant or sing for at least fifteen minutes. It is best to chant or sing for thirty minutes to one hour. Building a Jin Dan takes time and effort. The more you chant or sing, the more quickly you will build your Jin Dan.

Let me explain each line of the seven-line mantra used as the Sound Power in this practice to build a Jin Dan.

TAO SHENG YI

Tao is The Way, the source of all universes. Tao is the creator. "Sheng" means *creates*. "Yi" means *one*. "Tao sheng yi" means *Tao creates One*.

TIAN YI ZHEN SHUI

"Tian" means *Heaven*. "Yi" means *one* or *unique*. "Zhen" means *true* or *sacred*. "Shui" means *liquid* or *water*. "Tian yi zhen shui" means *Heaven's unique sacred liquid*. Heaven's sacred liquid gathers the message, energy, and matter of Heaven. *Tian yi zhen shui* falls down from Heaven through the crown chakra (just above the top of the head), and then goes through the brain and the palate into the mouth.

JIN JIN YU YE

The first "Jin" means *gold*. The second "jin" means *liquid*. "Yu" means *jade*. "Ye" means *liquid*. "Jin jin yu ye" means *gold liquid, jade liquid*. Gold and jade express the preciousness of this liquid. Jin Jin and Yu Ye are also the names of two acupuncture points that are located under the tongue. Jin jin yu ye is Mother Earth's sacred liquid. It gathers the message, energy, and matter of Mother Earth. Jin jin yu ye comes in through the Yong Quan (Kidney 1) acupuncture points, which are located on the soles of the feet between the second and third metatarsal bones, one-third of the distance from the webs of the toes to the heel. It then goes up through the center of the legs to the Hui Yin acupuncture point in the perineum (between the genitals and the anus), and then up through the first five soul houses (the seven soul houses correspond closely to the seven chakras) in the center of the body. From the fifth soul house in the throat, it moves to the Jin Jin and Yu Ye acupuncture points under the tongue, from which it then flows out into the mouth.

YAN RU DAN TIAN

"Yan" means *swallow*. "Ru" means *into*. "Dan" means *light ball*. "Tian" means *field*. This Dan Tian refers to the Lower Dan Tian, which is one of the most important energy centers in the body. Jin Dan is located slightly above the Lower Dan Tian.

SHEN QI JING HE YI

"Shen" means *all of one's souls, including one's body soul, system souls, organ souls, cell souls, cell unit souls, DNA and RNA souls, tiny matter souls, and space souls*. "Qi" means *all of one's energies, including the energies of the body, systems, organs, cells, cell units, DNA and RNA, tiny matter, and spaces.* "Jing" means *all matter in one's body.* "He" means *join as.* "Yi" means *one.* "Shen qi jing he yi" means *all souls, energies, and matter join as one.* They all join as one in the Jin Dan.

TIAN DI REN HE YI

"Tian" means *Heaven.* "Di" means *Earth.* "Ren" means *human being.* "He" means *join as.* "Yi" means *one.* "Tian di ren he yi" means *Heaven, Mother Earth, and human being join as one.* They all join as one in the Jin Dan.

JIN DAN LIAN CHENG

"Jin" means *gold.* "Dan" means *light ball.* "Lian" means *cook.* "Cheng" means *done.* "Jin dan lian cheng" means *golden light ball is formed.*

Let me summarize the essence of the meaning and significance of each line in this sacred mantra:

Tao Sheng Yi. Tao creates One. One includes all universes, galaxies, stars, and planets. Chanting *Tao sheng yi* gathers message, energy, and matter from Tao and from all universes.

Tian Yi Zhen Shui. Chanting this line gathers Heaven's unique sacred liquid, which gathers the message, energy, and matter of Heaven.

Jin Jin Yu Ye. Chanting this line gathers Mother Earth's sacred liquid, which gathers the message, energy, and matter of Mother Earth.

Yan Ru Dan Tian. The message, energy, and matter from Tao and from all universes, are gathered in the mouth with Heaven's unique sacred liquid and Mother Earth's sacred liquid, and then swallowed into the Lower Dan Tian to form the Jin Dan. From the Lower Dan Tian, it is formed and moves up a little to the location of the Jin Dan.

Shen Qi Jing He Yi. All the souls, energies, and matter of the whole body join as one in the Jin Dan.

Tian Di Ren He Yi. All the essence of Heaven, Mother Earth, and human beings join as one in the Jin Dan.

Jin Dan Lian Cheng. From *Tao sheng yi, tian yi zhen shui, jin jin yu ye, yan ru dan tian, shen qi jing he yi*, and *tian di ren he yi*, the Jin Dan is formed.

This is the simplest way to form a Jin Dan: by gathering message, energy, and matter from Tao, the Divine, all universes, all galaxies, all stars, all planets, all layers of Heaven, Mother Earth, the human realm, and from your own soul, mind, and body.

For a new but dedicated practitioner who practices for one hour each day, it generally takes about four hundred hours to build a Jin Dan. It would take such a practitioner more than one year to build a Jin Dan through dedicated daily hour-long practice. Someone who practices two hours per day could form a Jin Dan in about two hundred days.

The Divine and Tao are guiding me at this moment that this sacred divine and Tao teaching could help you build your Jin Dan eight to ten times faster than traditional ways. The traditional ways and practices could even take decades.

Developing a Jin Dan is a "must" step for a Tao practitioner. In one sentence:

Jin Dan can bring you to Tao.

Jin Dan Da Tao Xiu Lian
The Big Tao Golden
Light Ball Xiu Lian

Xiu Lian (pronounced *sheo lyen*), a term from ancient and traditional Tao practice, is the totality of one's spiritual journey. "Xiu" means *purification of soul, heart, mind, and body*. "Lian" means *practice*.

There are many ways to do Xiu Lian in traditional Tao. Since creation, all spiritual groups and beings worldwide have created countless Xiu Lian techniques. What is the best way to do Xiu Lian?

In this chapter, I will share the divine and Tao soul secrets, wisdom, knowledge, and practical techniques of Jin Dan Da Tao Xiu Lian, which can be translated as "The Big Tao Golden Light Ball Xiu Lian." Jin Dan Da Tao Xiu Lian is the best way to do Xiu Lian. Jin Dan Da Tao practice is the fastest way to reach Tao and meld with Tao. "Jin" (pronounced *jeen*) means *golden*. "Dan" (pronounced *dahn*) means *light ball*. Jin Dan is a special golden light ball located in one's lower abdomen, just below the navel in the center of the body. As you have learned and done in the practice that concludes chapter 1, the Tao practitioner must form and develop the Jin Dan.

Chapter 3 of my book *Tao I: The Way of All Life* is about the Jin Dan. There, I explain what the Jin Dan is, the significance and power of the Jin Dan, and how to form the Jin Dan. To study the Tao of fan lao huan tong (transforming old age to the health and purity of the baby state), longevity, and immortality, you must understand the third chapter of *Tao I*. For your convenience, I gave you the essence of that teaching in chapter 1 of this book.

In this book, I will share much new wisdom, secrets, knowledge, and practical techniques of the Jin Dan. I will teach you a different way to form the Jin Dan. You will definitely understand the importance of the Jin Dan much further. You will pay attention to Jin Dan practice for your entire spiritual journey.

Tao practitioners have always searched for sacred wisdom and practices for good health and, especially, to live a long, long life. Why does a person have to go through the process of birth, growth, maturing through childhood and adolescence, adulthood, old age, sickness and infirmity, and then death? People have realized that this process is the natural law of humanity.

In ancient times, the saints observed Heaven and Earth. They wondered, "Why is Mother Earth not getting older? Why is Heaven not getting older?" Human beings are born, grow, mature, become sick, and then die. But the sun, the moon, the Big Dipper, Heaven, and Mother Earth have a constant existence. Why do they not get old? Why do they not die?

These saints wondered further, "Can a human being's life be

as long as the life of the sun, the moon, the Big Dipper, Heaven, and Mother Earth? What sacred and mysterious power controls Heaven and Mother Earth to allow them to have unlimited life?" The saints realized that Heaven and Mother Earth are actually very close to human life. For example, food grows on Mother Earth. The sun and the rain, even the moon and the snow, are important for food to grow. As another example, natural disasters from Heaven and Mother Earth greatly affect people's lives.

Recognizing this vital connection, people started to honor Heaven and Mother Earth. They held special ceremonies on special days during the year to honor the sacred and mysterious power in Heaven and to request good fortune, balance among the rain, the snow, and other natural elements, peace for Mother Earth, avoidance of natural disasters, and more.

With greater connection and harmony with Mother Earth, people began to discover that eating or even just touching some plants and herbs brought healing results. There is a famous ancient statement: *Shen Nong chang bai cao* (pronounced *shun nawng chahng bye tsow*). "Chang" means *taste* or *eat*. "Bai" means *one hundred*; it represents "all" or "every" in Chinese. "Cao" means *herbs*. Shen Nong ("saint farmer") is the father of Chinese agriculture. Five thousand years ago, he tasted hundreds of herbs to evaluate their healing characteristics. He wrote an encyclopedia of his findings, which includes not only herbs, plants, and flowers, but also all kinds of minerals and animal parts. As a high-level being, he was not harmed by poisonous herbs and minerals. To this day, Shen Nong has been revered as the founder of the Chinese herbs system.

People around the world have realized more and more that herbs can heal and nourish the body in order to prolong life. Some intelligent people started to think about creating an herb formula that could prolong life. They tried cooking some special herbs in order to help people have a long, long life. To preserve herbs for longer use, they cooked them in a ball with honey. They named these herbs "longevity herbs." They also called them Dan Wan (pronounced *dahn wahn*), which means *round herbs ball*. In this context, "dan" carries the further meaning of *saint's herbs for longevity*. "Wan" refers to the *herbs ball mixed with honey*. Therefore, "Dan Wan" means *herbs ball that carries saint's power to prolong life*.

This Dan Wan helped some people heal sickness, but they did not succeed in bringing long life. Some experiments involved cooking metallic ore in an urn. These preparations actually harmed many people because of poisonous content that could include mercury, arsenic, or lead, for example. There are several renowned stories in Chinese history, including stories about emperors who wanted to live long, long lives. They ate this kind of cooked metallic ore ball that was called Xian Dan (pronounced *shyen dahn*), which means *saint's ball*. They wanted a long, long life, but instead they were poisoned and died earlier.

Although these were unpleasant experiences, this kind of alchemy could be considered to be the historical beginning of chemistry. The ancient masters used such intense fire that they burned the urn itself to cook the material placed within the urn. Cooking the Xian Dan was a totally secret way to prolong life. The ancient Tao masters did this when they were hidden in forests and mountains.

As these masters cooked the Xian Dan, they meditated and chanted. They discovered that through this meditation and chanting, their sicknesses were healed. They then naturally started to think about prolonging life. These Tao practitioners felt they needed to create an internal power and force to rejuvenate the body with energy, vitality, and immunity.

Through their meditation and internal study of the whole body, they discovered the energy centers in the body and determined how these energy centers were interrelated. These energy centers are vital for healing, rejuvenation, and longevity.

I have shared some of this fundamental wisdom and practice of Tao in my earlier books, such as *Power Healing: The Four Keys to Energizing Your Body, Mind & Spirit*.[1] In particular, the five most important energy centers in the body are:

- Lower Dan Tian
- Snow Mountain Area
- Message Center
- Zu Qiao
- Third Eye

See pp. 162–183 of *Power Healing* or pp. 304–322 of my book *Soul Mind Body Medicine: A Complete Soul Healing System for Optimum Health and Vitality* for teachings about these five energy centers.

For thousands of years, every generation of Tao saints has experienced all kinds of Xiu Lian methods, including meditation, chanting, tai chi, qi gong, and other practices. Some of these high-level practitioners have realized that the Jin Dan is the most important internal power for healing, rejuvenation, and longevity, but the Jin Dan wisdom and practice have not been spread enough to humanity. The deep wisdom and power of the Jin Dan have not been revealed at all to humanity.

How powerful is the Jin Dan? What can the Jin Dan really do

---

1. *Power Healing: The Four Keys to Energizing Your Body, Mind & Spirit* (San Francisco: HarperSanFrancisco, 2002).

for one's life? The Jin Dan has layers. To form a complete Jin Dan is not easy at all. Heaven has countless layers. Can you absorb the essence of, and nutrients from, all layers of Heaven? It is not easy.

Where does the ultimate power of the Jin Dan come from? Tao is the source of the ultimate power of the Jin Dan.

Lao Zi's *Dao De Jing* shared with humanity the normal creation of Tao:

Tao sheng yi
Yi sheng er
Er sheng san
San sheng wan wu

Tao creates One.
One creates Two.
Two creates Three.
Three creates all things.

Tao ➔ One ➔ Two ➔ Three ➔ all things
       creates

Heaven and Mother Earth are Two. They are created by Tao. Tao is the source of all universes. Let me remind you of and emphasize the first few sacred phrases of the Tao Jing (Tao Classic) that I received in December 2008 and shared in *Tao I: The Way of All Life*:

道可道   **Tao Ke Tao**   *dow kuh dow*
           Tao that can be explained
           by words or comprehended
           by thoughts

非常道	**Fei Chang Tao**	*fay chahng dow*
	Is not the eternal Tao or true Tao	
大无外	**Da Wu Wai**	*dah woo wye*
	Bigger than Biggest	
小无内	**Xiao Wu Nei**	*shee-yow woo nay*
	Smaller than Smallest	
无方圆	**Wu Fang Yuan**	*woo fahng ywen*
	No Square, No Circle	
无形象	**Wu Xing Xiang**	*woo shing shyahng*
	No Shape, No Image	
无时空	**Wu Shi Kong**	*woo shr kawng*
	No Time, No Space	
顺道昌	**Shun Tao Chang**	*shwun dow chahng*
	Follow Tao, Flourish	
逆道亡	**Ni Tao Wang**	*nee dow wahng*
	Go against Tao, Finish	

These sacred phrases explain the nature of Tao. Tao cannot be explained and cannot be comprehended. Tao is bigger than biggest and smaller than smallest. Tao has no square, no circle, no shape, no image, no time, no space.

Tao is *wu* (pronounced *woo*), which means *emptiness* or *nothingness*. Heaven, Mother Earth, countless planets, countless stars, countless galaxies, and countless universes are *you* (pronounced *yoe*), which means *existence*.

"Wu sheng you" means *wu creates you*. Nothingness creates existence. This is so simple, but it is the biggest Tao. To truly realize this simplicity is the deepest wisdom. Many people on Mother Earth are always searching for complicated solutions. This can be seen in every aspect of life. Da Tao zhi jian (pronounced *dah dow jr jyen*), *The Big Way is extremely simple.*

Lao Zi shared two statements in *Dao De Jing*:

为学日增
Wei Xue Ri Zeng

"Wei" means *for.* "Xue" means *study* (of all kinds, including wisdom and knowledge from one's parents, all formal education, and more). "Ri" means *daily.* "Zeng" means *increase.* "Wei xue ri zeng" (pronounced *way shoo-eh rr dzung*) means *to study daily increases wisdom and knowledge.*

为道日损
Wei Dao Ri Sun

"Dao" or Tao is The Way, *the truth of all life.* "Sun" means *correct and transform.* "Wei Dao ri sun" (pronounced *way dow rr swun*) means *to study and practice Tao daily corrects your mistakes and transforms your incorrect thoughts and actions.*

Jin Dan is absolutely Da Tao zhi jian. To practice Jin Dan is to practice Tao.

Jin Dan is the unity of the jing, qi, and shen (matter, energy, and soul) of one's body. One must gather the essence of and all kinds of nutrients from Heaven, Mother Earth, and all universes to form the Jin Dan.

"Jing" means *matter.* "Qi" (pronounced *chee*) means *energy.* "Shen" (pronounced *shun*) means *soul.* For centuries, Tao masters have done special meditations and special chants to form the Jin Dan. They used three kinds of secrets:

- **Shen Mi** (pronounced *shun mee*). "Shen" means *body*. "Mi" means *secret*. "Shen mi," or *body secrets*, are special hand and body positions to form the Jin Dan and to support other spiritual practices for healing, rejuvenation, and longevity.
- **Kou Mi** (pronounced *koe mee*). "Kou" means *mouth*. "Kou mi," or *mouth secrets*, are to chant special mantras to form the Jin Dan and to support other spiritual practices for healing, rejuvenation, and longevity.
- **Yi Mi** (pronounced *yee mee*). "Yi" means *thinking*. "Yi mi," or *thinking secrets*, are to use mind power, including creative visualization, to form the Jin Dan and to support other spiritual practices for healing, rejuvenation, and longevity.

Millions of people in history have practiced Tao. Millions of people today are searching for the secrets of longevity. Millions of people are dreaming for immortality. There are so many Xiu Lian methods to accomplish all of this and more.

What is the highest sacred and most profound Xiu Lian method for healing, for rejuvenation in order to reach fan lao huan tong (transforming old age to the health and purity of the baby state), for longevity, and, finally, for moving to immortality? I want to emphasize again and clearly present to you and humanity that the answer is Jin Dan Da Tao Xiu Lian, the Big Tao Golden Light Ball Xiu Lian.

Grab this top sacred treasure.

Jump into practice.

Form your complete Jin Dan.

Heal all of your sicknesses.

Prevent all sicknesses.

Purify your soul, heart, mind, and body.

Rejuvenate your soul, heart, mind, and body.

Reach fan lao huan tong—transform old age to the health and purity of the baby state.

Prolong life.

Move in the direction of immortality.

Jin Dan Da Tao Xiu Lian is the key for your spiritual journey.

Jin Dan Da Tao Xiu Lian is the answer for healing, rejuvenation, and longevity.

Jin Dan Da Tao Xiu Lian is the path to immortality.

Enjoy it.

Benefit from it.

This is a long journey.

Wish you great success.

Text of Jin Dan Da Tao Xiu Lian

On July 9, 2010, as I flew from Sydney, Australia to China, I received a direct teaching from Tao. I was extremely moved and touched. I have no words to express my gratitude and honor enough. Jin Dan Da Tao Xiu Lian is the new Tao teaching to form the Jin Dan.

金丹大道修炼

Jin Dan Da Tao Xiu Lian

The Big Tao Golden Light Ball Xiu Lian

精
Jing

Matter

天之精	**Tian Zhi Jing**	*tyen jr jing*
	Heaven's jing	
地之精	**Di Zhi Jing**	*dee jr jing*
	Mother Earth's jing	
人之精	**Ren Zhi Jing**	*wren jr jing*
	Humanity's jing	
天地人之精	**Tian Di Ren Zhi Jing**	*tyen dee wren jr jing*
	Heaven's, Mother Earth's, humanity's jing	
万物之精	**Wan Wu Zhi Jing**	*wahn woo jr jing*
	Jing of countless planets, stars, and galaxies	
全宇宙之精	**Quan Yu Zhou Zhi Jing**	*chwen yü joe jr jing*
	Jing of countless universes	
皆是道之精	**Jie Shi Dao Zhi Jing**	*jyeh shr dow jr jing*
	All are Tao's jing	

气
Qi

Energy

天之气	**Tian Zhi Qi**	*tyen jr chee*
	Heaven's qi	
地之气	**Di Zhi Qi**	*dee jr chee*
	Mother Earth's qi	
人之气	**Ren Zhi Qi**	*wren jr chee*
	Humanity's qi	

天地人之气   **Tian Di Ren Zhi Qi**   *tyen dee wren jr chee*
              Heaven's, Mother Earth's,
              humanity's qi

万物之气   **Wan Wu Zhi Qi**   *wahn woo jr chee*
              Qi of countless planets,
              stars, and galaxies

全宇宙之气   **Quan Yu Zhou Zhi Qi**   *chwen yü joe jr chee*
              Qi of countless universes

皆是道之气   **Jie Shi Dao Zhi Qi**   *jyeh shr dow jr chee*
              All are Tao's qi

神

Shen

Soul

天之神   **Tian Zhi Shen**   *tyen jr shun*
             Heaven's soul

地之神   **Di Zhi Shen**   *dee jr shun*
             Mother Earth's soul

人之神   **Ren Zhi Shen**   *wren jr shun*
             Humanity's soul

天地人之神   **Tian Di Ren Zhi Shen**   *tyen dee wren jr shun*
             Heaven's, Mother Earth's,
             humanity's souls

万物之神   **Wan Wu Zhi Shen**   *wahn woo jr shun*
             Souls of countless planets,
             stars, and galaxies

全宇宙之神   **Quan Yu Zhou Zhi Shen**   *chwen yü joe jr shun*
             Souls of countless universes

皆是道之神   **Jie Shi Dao Zhi Shen**   *jyeh shr dow jr shun*
             All are Tao's soul

虚
Xu

Emptiness

天之虚	**Tian Zhi Xu**	*tyen jr shü*
	Heaven's emptiness	
地之虚	**Di Zhi Xu**	*dee jr shü*
	Mother Earth's emptiness	
人之虚	**Ren Zhi Xu**	*wren jr shü*
	Humanity's emptiness	
天地人之虚	**Tian Di Ren Zhi Xu**	*tyen dee wren jr shü*
	Heaven's, Mother Earth's, humanity's emptiness	
万物之虚	**Wan Wu Zhi Xu**	*wahn woo jr shü*
	Emptiness of countless planets, stars, and galaxies	
全宇宙之虚	**Quan Yu Zhou Zhi Xu**	*chwen yü joe jr shü*
	Emptiness of countless universes	
皆是道之虚	**Jie Shi Dao Zhi Xu**	*jyeh shr dow jr shü*
	All are Tao's emptiness	

道
Dao

Complete Emptiness

天之道	**Tian Zhi Dao**	*tyen jr dow*
	Heaven's Tao	
地之道	**Di Zhi Dao**	*dee jr dow*
	Mother Earth's Tao	

人之道 **Ren Zhi Dao** *wren jr dow*
Humanity's Tao

天地人之道 **Tian Di Ren Zhi Dao** *tyen dee wren jr dow*
Heaven's, Mother Earth's,
humanity's Tao

万物之道 **Wan Wu Zhi Dao** *wahn woo jr dow*
Tao of countless planets,
stars, and galaxies

全宇宙之道 **Quan Yu Zhou Zhi Dao** *chwen yü joe jr dow*
Tao of countless universes

皆是大道 **Jie Shi Da Dao** *jyeh shr dah dow*
All are Big Tao

精气神虚道合一
Jing Qi Shen Xu Dao He Yi

Matter Energy Soul Emptiness Tao Join as One

天精气神虚 **Tian Jing Qi Shen Xu** *tyen jing chee shun*
道合一 **Dao He Yi** *shü dow huh yee*
Heaven's matter energy
soul emptiness Tao join
as one

地精气神虚 **Di Jing Qi Shen Xu** *dee jing chee shun shü*
道合一 **Dao He Yi** *dow huh yee*
Mother Earth's matter
energy soul emptiness
Tao join as one

人精气神虚 **Ren Jing Qi Shen Xu** *wren jing chee shun*
道合一 **Dao He Yi** *shü dow huh yee*
Humanity's matter energy
soul emptiness Tao join as one

天地人精气 **Tian Di Ren Jing Qi** *tyen dee wren jing*
神虚道合一 **Shen Xu Dao He Yi** *chee shun shü dow*
Heaven's, Mother Earth's, *huh yee*
humanity's matter energy
soul emptiness Tao join
as one

万物精气神 **Wan Wu Jing Qi Shen** *wahn woo jing chee*
虚道合一 **Xu Dao He Yi** *shun shü dow huh yee*
Matter energy soul
emptiness Tao of
countless planets, stars,
and galaxies join
as one

全宇宙精气 **Quan Yu Zhou Jing Qi** *chwen yü joe jing chee*
神虚道合一 **Shen Xu Dao He Yi** *shun shü dow huh yee*
Matter energy soul
emptiness Tao of
countless universes
join as one

皆是与道 **Jie Shi Yu Dao** *jyeh shr yü dow huh*
合一 **He Yi** *yee*
All are joining as one
with Tao

金丹
Jin Dan

Golden Light Ball

天金丹 **Tian Jin Dan** *tyen jeen dahn*
Heaven's Jin Dan

地金丹　　　**Di Jin Dan**　　　*dee jeen dahn*
Mother Earth's Jin Dan

人金丹　　　**Ren Jin Dan**　　　*wren jeen dahn*
Humanity's Jin Dan

天地人金丹　**Tian Di Ren Jin Dan**　*tyen dee wren jeen dahn*
Heaven's, Mother Earth's, humanity's Jin Dan

万物金丹　　**Wan Wu Jin Dan**　　*wahn woo jeen dahn*
Jin Dan of countless planets, stars, and galaxies

全宇宙金丹　**Quan Yu Zhou Jin Dan**　*chwen yü joe jeen dahn*
Jin Dan of countless universes

皆是道金丹　**Jie Shi Dao Jin Dan**　*jyeh shr dow jeen dahn*
All are Tao's Jin Dan

与道合真
Yu Dao He Zhen

Meld with Tao

天与道合真　**Tian Yu Dao He Zhen**　*tyen yü dow huh jun*
Heaven melds with Tao

地与道合真　**Di Yu Dao He Zhen**　*dee yü dow huh jun*
Mother Earth melds with Tao

人与道合真　**Ren Yu Dao He Zhen**　*wren yü dow huh jun*
Humanity melds with Tao

天地人与道合真　**Tian Di Ren Yu Dao He Zhen**　*tyen dee wren yü dow huh jun*
Heaven, Mother Earth, humanity meld with Tao

万物与道	**Wan Wu Yu Dao**	*wahn woo yü dow*
合真	**He Zhen**	*huh jun*
	Countless planets, stars, and galaxies meld with Tao	
全宇宙与道	**Quan Yu Zhou Yu Dao**	*chwen yü joe yü dow*
合真	**He Zhen**	*huh jun*
	Countless universes meld with Tao	
皆是与道	**Jie Shi Yu Dao**	*jyeh shr yü dow*
合真	**He Zhen**	*huh jun*
	All meld with Tao	

You can listen to me sing the Jin Dan Da Tao Xiu Lian text on the CD or audio download that accompanies this book. Receive the Tao frequency and vibration, with Tao love, forgiveness, compassion, and light. Practice with me to build your complete Jin Dan. I am honored to include this recording as an additional major blessing of this book.

What Is Jin Dan Da Tao Xiu Lian?

Now let me explain Jin Dan Da Tao Xiu Lian. You will understand its power and significance more. You will appreciate the importance of singing or chanting it yourself. You will be prepared to receive the greatest benefits that this book offers.

Tao is The Way. Tao can be divided into Da Tao (Big Tao) and Xiao Tao (Small Tao). Da Tao is the Tao of all universes, galaxies, stars, and planets, including Heaven, Mother Earth, and humanity. Xiao Tao is the Tao of every aspect of life, including eating, sleeping, working, relationships, and finances.

Jin Dan Da Tao Xiu Lian is the highest Tao Xiu Lian. Practicing Jin Dan Da Tao is the simplest and most powerful way to practice Tao in order to reach Tao. Practicing Jin Dan Da Tao is the *direct* way to reach Tao.

Jin Dan Da Tao practice is the highest divine Tao practice I have received up to now. I am honored to share it with you, humanity, and all universes. This practice gathers the *jing qi shen xu dao* of Heaven, Mother Earth, humanity, and countless planets, stars, galaxies, and universes to form Tao Dan (Tao Light Ball), which is the complete Jin Dan. This practice is *zhi zhi Da Tao* (pronounced *jr jr dah dow*). "Zhi zhi" means *direct point*. Da Tao is The Big Way. "Zhi zhi Da Tao" means *directly come to Tao*.

In *Tao I: The Way of All Life,* I shared Jin Dan secrets with humanity. I would like to emphasize three paragraphs from pages 389–390 of that book:

Jin Dan is one of the highest treasures of Tao teaching. Jin Dan is one of the highest treasures from the Divine and Tao. **To reach Tao, Jin Dan is the key.**

THE POWER AND SIGNIFICANCE OF JIN DAN

Jin Dan has the following powers and abilities:

- Jin Dan is the source of message, energy, and matter.
- Jin Dan has the highest power for healing your spiritual, mental, emotional, and physical bodies.
- Jin Dan is the key to preventing sickness in your spiritual, mental, emotional, and physical bodies.
- Jin Dan is the highest treasure for purifying your soul, heart, mind, and body.
- Jin Dan has the highest abilities for rejuvenating your soul, heart, mind, and body.

- Jin Dan has the highest strength for transforming all of your relationships.
- Jin Dan has the highest potential for transforming your business.
- Jin Dan has the highest honor for enlightening your soul, heart, mind, and body.
- Jin Dan has the highest power and abilities for healing, blessing, and transforming others.
- Jin Dan has the highest power and abilities for offering service to humanity, Mother Earth, and all universes.

In one sentence:

Jin Dan is the greatest treasure for all life.

The Power and Significance of Jin Dan Da Tao Xiu Lian

The Jin Dan that I shared in my book, *Tao I,* and whose essence I just reviewed above, is a *human* Jin Dan. All of the practices in *Tao I* are to develop a human Jin Dan. The Jin Dan Da Tao Xiu Lian in this book is a practice to form the Jin Dan of Heaven, the Jin Dan of Mother Earth, the Jin Dan of all humanity, the Jin Dan of *wan wu* (all things), including countless planets, stars, and galaxies, and the Jin Dan of all universes. Finally, it is a practice to form Tao Dan.

Heaven can form Heaven's Jin Dan. Mother Earth can form Mother Earth's Jin Dan. Humanity can form humanity's Jin Dan. Countless planets, stars, and galaxies can form their Jin Dans. Countless universes can form their Jin Dans. Tao has Tao Jin Dan.

One must follow certain steps to form any Jin Dan. There is no way that anyone can form a complete Jin Dan right away. The process to form the Jin Dan has three major steps:

1. Purify your soul, heart, mind, and body

During the Jin Dan Da Tao practice, you will gather the *jing qi shen xu dao* (pronounced *jing chee shun shü dow*) of Heaven, Mother Earth, humanity, wan wu (including countless planets, stars, and galaxies), and countless universes. Suddenly, you could reach emptiness. That moment could be very short, a few seconds or even less. However, that moment is very important. Every time you reach the emptiness condition, even for a moment, purification happens. Soul mind body blockages in every aspect of life will be reduced in that moment.

One must reach emptiness many times for purification to be deeper and deeper. Soul mind body blockages in life will be reduced further and further.

2. Transform your jing qi shen xu dao

During the Jin Dan Da Tao practice, the *jing qi shen xu dao* of Heaven, Mother Earth, humanity, wan wu (including countless planets, stars, and galaxies), and countless universes will transform the frequency of your *jing qi shen* to the *jing qi shen* of Heaven, Mother Earth, and humanity, and meld with all of them in order to reach Tao.

To practice *jing qi shen xu dao* is to practice the five steps of practicing Tao: *jing, qi, shen, xu,* and *dao.* These five steps are not separate. When you practice *jing,* the *qi, shen, xu,* and *dao* will also transform. When you practice *qi,* the *shen, xu, dao,* and *jing* will also transform, and similarly when you practice *shen* or *xu* or *dao.*

Every time you reach the emptiness condition, in that moment you are melding with Tao, even if that moment is very limited. Every time you reach such an emptiness moment, you are receiving purification and transformation of your soul, heart, mind, and body and of your *jing qi shen xu dao.*

The more you practice and the more you reach emptiness, the deeper the purification and transformation you receive. To meld with Tao takes a long, long time. It takes absolute persistence and constancy to practice again and again and again.

3. Meld with Tao

To meld with Tao means to completely meld with Tao in every aspect of your life. It is very difficult to do, but it is possible. What you do in every activity, what you say in every word you speak, and what you think in every thought you have will meld with Tao. Complete purity, honesty, and sincerity, complete humbleness and selflessness, and complete love, forgiveness, compassion, and light will appear when you completely meld with Tao.

Since creation, only a very limited number of human beings have melded with Tao. Now, Mother Earth *is* in a transition period. Mother Earth is facing incredible challenges in every aspect of her life, including all kinds of natural disasters, human disasters (for example, the Bhopal disaster in 1984, the Chernobyl disaster in 1986, and the Deepwater Horizon oil spill in 2010), wars, economic challenges, sicknesses, and more. In this historic period, humanity, Mother Earth, Heaven, and countless planets, stars, galaxies, and universes need purification and transformation in order to meld with Tao. It is most important. It is absolutely urgent.

I am not teaching Taoism. In *Tao I,* I explained very clearly that the Tao teaching that I am offering is The Way of all life and comes directly from Tao and the Divine. The Jin Dan Da Tao practice serves all life, including healing, prevention of sickness, rejuvenation, prolonging life, transformation of relationships, finances, and every aspect of life, and purification and enlightenment of soul, heart, mind, and body. The Jin Dan Da Tao practice serves all life in ways beyond any words, comprehension, and imagination.

You can meld with Tao by following the Jin Dan Da Tao practice.

All humanity can meld with Tao by following the Jin Dan Da Tao practice.

Heaven, Mother Earth, and countless planets, stars, galaxies, and universes can meld with Tao by following the Jin Dan Da Tao practice.

Wan ling (all souls) can meld with Tao by following the Jin Dan Da Tao practice.

Melding with Tao takes a long, long time.

A single human being could take thousands or millions of lifetimes or even longer to meld with Tao.

It could take all humanity and all of Heaven, Mother Earth, and countless planets, stars, galaxies, and universes a much longer time than a single highly developed spiritual being to meld with Tao.

But it *is* possible.

HOW TO DO JIN DAN DA TAO XIU LIAN

I am formally introducing Jin Dan Da Tao Xiu Lian in this book. Jin Dan Da Tao Xiu Lian practice begins near the end of 2010. This practice will serve humanity in a special way.

Every human being needs good health, prevention of sickness, rejuvenation, and long life. Every human being needs transformation of relationships and finances. Every soul needs soul enlightenment to uplift its soul standing in Heaven. Humanity and Mother Earth need love, peace, and harmony now more than at any other time. Jin Dan Da Tao Xiu Lian can serve all of these.

I am extremely honored that Tao has delivered this Jin Dan Da Tao Xiu Lian teaching to me. I am introducing the Jin Dan Da Tao teaching and practice now. We will apply the Four Power Techniques, which are Body Power, Soul Power, Mind Power, and Sound Power. Let me repeat the key wisdom of the Four Power Techniques:

Body Power is special body positions and hand positions for healing and rejuvenation.

Soul Power is to say *hello* to the inner souls of your body, including the souls of your systems, organs, cells, cell units, DNA, RNA, spaces between cells, and tiny matter in the cells, as well as to outer souls, including saints, healing angels, archangels, ascended masters, lamas, gurus, all kinds of spiritual fathers and mothers, the Divine, and Tao, to invoke their power for healing, rejuvenation, and life transformation.

Mind Power is creative visualization. The most important wisdom is to visualize golden or rainbow light to transform your health, relationships, finances, and more.

Sound Power is to chant or sing ancient healing mantras,

Divine Soul Songs, and Tao songs for healing, rejuvenation, and transformation of relationships, finances, and every aspect of life.

Let us practice Jin Dan Da Tao Xiu Lian now. Apply the Four Power Techniques:

Body Power. Sit up straight. Put the tip of your tongue as close as you can to the roof of your mouth without touching. Make a circle with your hands and fingers. Your thumbs will be at the top of the circle, pointing at each other without touching. Rest the fingers of one hand (it does not matter which hand) over the fingers of the other hand. Your fingers will be at the bottom of the circle. Place the tips of your thumbs in front of your navel, so that someone looking directly at you will see the circle made by your hands and fingers. This is called the Jin Dan Da Tao Xiu Lian Hand Position. See figure 1.

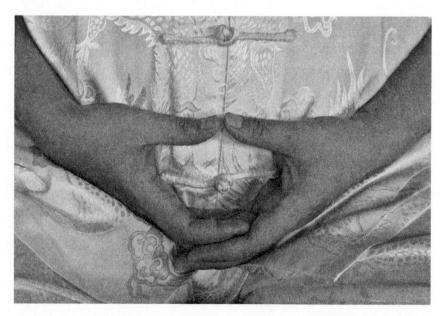

Figure 1. Jin Dan Da Tao Xiu Lian Hand Position

Soul Power. Say *hello:*

> *Dear Tao,*
> *Dear Divine,*
> *Dear soul mind body of countless universes,*
> *Dear soul mind body of countless galaxies, stars, and planets,*
> *Dear soul mind body of Mother Earth,*
> *Dear soul mind body of all humanity,*
> *Dear soul mind body of all animals,*
> *Dear soul mind body of everything in countless planets, stars,*
> *   galaxies, and universes,*
> *Dear soul mind body of all spiritual fathers and mothers in*
> *   all layers of Heaven and on Mother Earth,*
> *I love you, honor you, and appreciate you.*
> *Please come to my Jin Dan area to form my Jin Dan,*
> *   Heaven's Jin Dan, Mother Earth's Jin Dan, humanity's*
> *   Jin Dan, countless planets', stars', and galaxies' Jin Dan,*
> *   and countless universes' Jin Dan.*
> *Finally, form Tao Dan.*
> *I am extremely honored and blessed to do this practice to*
> *   form all kinds of Jin Dan as an unconditional universal*
> *   servant.*
> *Thank you. Thank you. Thank you.*

Mind Power. Focus on your Jin Dan area to observe the countless souls you have invoked. This Tao secret is beyond any words.

Sound Power. Chant in Chinese, silently or aloud:

天之精   **Tian Zhi Jing**   *tyen jr jing*
              Heaven's jing

地之精	**Di Zhi Jing** Mother Earth's jing	*dee jr jing*
人之精	**Ren Zhi Jing** Humanity's jing	*wren jr jing*
天地人之精	**Tian Di Ren Zhi Jing** Heaven's, Mother Earth's, humanity's jing	*tyen dee wren jr jing*
万物之精	**Wan Wu Zhi Jing** Jing of countless planets, stars, and galaxies	*wahn woo jr jing*
全宇宙之精	**Quan Yu Zhou Zhi Jing** Jing of countless universes	*chwen yü joe jr jing*
皆是道之精	**Jie Shi Dao Zhi Jing** All are Tao's jing	*jyeh shr dow jr jing*
天之气	**Tian Zhi Qi** Heaven's qi	*tyen jr chee*
地之气	**Di Zhi Qi** Mother Earth's qi	*dee jr chee*
人之气	**Ren Zhi Qi** Humanity's qi	*wren jr chee*
天地人之气	**Tian Di Ren Zhi Qi** Heaven's, Mother Earth's, humanity's qi	*tyen dee wren jr chee*
万物之气	**Wan Wu Zhi Qi** Qi of countless planets, stars, and galaxies	*wahn woo jr chee*
全宇宙之气	**Quan Yu Zhou Zhi Qi** Qi of countless universes	*chwen yü joe jr chee*
皆是道之气	**Jie Shi Dao Zhi Qi** All are Tao's qi	*jyeh shr dow jr chee*

天之神	**Tian Zhi Shen**	*tyen jr shun*
	Heaven's soul	
地之神	**Di Zhi Shen**	*dee jr shun*
	Mother Earth's soul	
人之神	**Ren Zhi Shen**	*wren jr shun*
	Humanity's soul	
天地人之神	**Tian Di Ren Zhi Shen**	*tyen dee wren jr shun*
	Heaven's, Mother Earth's, humanity's souls	
万物之神	**Wan Wu Zhi Shen**	*wahn woo jr shun*
	Souls of countless planets, stars, and galaxies	
全宇宙之神	**Quan Yu Zhou Zhi Shen**	*chwen yü joe jr shun*
	Souls of countless universes	
皆是道之神	**Jie Shi Dao Zhi Shen**	*jyeh shr dow jr shun*
	All are Tao's soul	
天之虚	**Tian Zhi Xu**	*tyen jr shü*
	Heaven's emptiness	
地之虚	**Di Zhi Xu**	*dee jr shü*
	Mother Earth's emptiness	
人之虚	**Ren Zhi Xu**	*wren jr shü*
	Humanity's emptiness	
天地人之虚	**Tian Di Ren Zhi Xu**	*tyen dee wren jr shü*
	Heaven's, Mother Earth's, humanity's emptiness	
万物之虚	**Wan Wu Zhi Xu**	*wahn woo jr shü*
	Emptiness of countless planets, stars, and galaxies	
全宇宙之虚	**Quan Yu Zhou Zhi Xu**	*chwen yü joe jr shü*
	Emptiness of countless universes	

皆是道之虚 **Jie Shi Dao Zhi Xu**   *jyeh shr dow jr shü*
All are Tao's emptiness

天之道 **Tian Zhi Dao**   *tyen jr dow*
Heaven's Tao

地之道 **Di Zhi Dao**   *dee jr dow*
Mother Earth's Tao

人之道 **Ren Zhi Dao**   *wren jr dow*
Humanity's Tao

天地人之道 **Tian Di Ren Zhi Dao**   *tyen dee wren jr dow*
Heaven's, Mother Earth's,
humanity's Tao

万物之道 **Wan Wu Zhi Dao**   *wahn woo jr dow*
Tao of countless planets,
stars, and galaxies

全宇宙之道 **Quan Yu Zhou Zhi Dao**   *chwen yü joe jr dow*
Tao of countless universes

皆是大道 **Jie Shi Da Dao**   *jyeh shr dah dow*
All are Big Tao

天精气神虚 **Tian Jing Qi Shen Xu**   *tyen jing chee shun*
道合一 **Dao He Yi**   *shü dow huh yee*
Heaven's matter energy soul
emptiness Tao join as one

地精气神虚 **Di Jing Qi Shen Xu**   *dee jing chee shun*
道合一 **Dao He Yi**   *shü dow huh yee*
Mother Earth's matter energy
soul emptiness Tao join as one

人精气神 **Ren Jing Qi Shen**   *wren jing chee shun*
虚道合一 **Xu Dao He Yi**   *shü dow huh yee*
Humanity's matter energy
soul emptiness Tao join as one

天地人精气
神虚道合一
Tian Di Ren Jing Qi Shen Xu Dao He Yi
Heaven's, Mother Earth's, humanity's matter energy soul emptiness Tao join as one
tyen dee wren jing chee shun shü dow huh yee

万物精气神
虚道合一
Wan Wu Jing Qi Shen Xu Dao He Yi
Matter energy soul emptiness Tao of countless planets, stars, and galaxies join as one
wahn woo jing chee shun shü dow huh yee

全宇宙精气
神虚道合一
Quan Yu Zhou Jing Qi Shen Xu Dao He Yi
Matter energy soul emptiness Tao of countless universes join as one
chwen yü joe jing chee shun shü dow huh yee

皆是与道合一
Jie Shi Yu Dao He Yi
All are joining as one with Tao
jyeh shr yü dow huh yee

天金丹
Tian Jin Dan
Heaven's Jin Dan
tyen jeen dahn

地金丹
Di Jin Dan
Mother Earth's Jin Dan
dee jeen dahn

人金丹
Ren Jin Dan
Humanity's Jin Dan
wren jeen dahn

天地人金丹
Tian Di Ren Jin Dan
Heaven's, Mother Earth's, humanity's Jin Dan
tyen dee wren jeen dahn

万物金丹	**Wan Wu Jin Dan** Jin Dan of countless planets, stars, and galaxies	*wahn woo jeen dahn*
全宇宙金丹	**Quan Yu Zhou Jin Dan** Jin Dan of countless universes	*chwen yü joe jeen dahn*
皆是道金丹	**Jie Shi Dao Jin Dan** All are Tao's Jin Dan	*jyeh shr dow jeen dahn*
天与道合真	**Tian Yu Dao He Zhen** Heaven melds with Tao	*tyen yü dow huh jun*
地与道合真	**Di Yu Dao He Zhen** Mother Earth melds with Tao	*dee yü dow huh jun*
人与道合真	**Ren Yu Dao He Zhen** Humanity melds with Tao	*wren yü dow huh jun*
天地人与道 合真	**Tian Di Ren Yu Dao He Zhen** Heaven, Mother Earth, humanity meld with Tao	*tyen dee wren yü dow huh jun*
万物与道 合真	**Wan Wu Yu Dao He Zhen** Countless planets, stars, and galaxies meld with Tao	*wahn woo yü dow huh jun*
全宇宙与 道合真	**Quan Yu Zhou Yu Dao He Zhen** Countless universes meld with Tao	*chwen yü joe yü dow huh jun*
皆是与道 合真	**Jie Shi Yu Dao He Zhen** All meld with Tao	*jyeh shr yü dow huh jun*

It could take you about five minutes to finish chanting this Jin Dan Da Tao Xiu Lian text one time. To chant it one time is wonderful and will benefit you. To chant it more times could benefit you much, much more. You can chant for healing. For healing chronic and life-threatening conditions, chant a total of two hours or more per day. In fact, there is no time limit. The more you chant, the better.

You can chant for prevention of sickness. You can chant to purify your soul, heart, mind, and body. You can chant to transform your relationships and finances. You can chant to enlighten your soul, heart, mind, and body.

When you chant, you are forming your Jin Dan, as well as Heaven's Jin Dan, Mother Earth's Jin Dan, humanity's Jin Dan, countless planets', stars' and galaxies' Jin Dan, countless universes' Jin Dan, and Tao Dan. You are self-clearing karma. You are transforming life for yourself, humanity, Mother Earth, and countless planets, stars, galaxies, and universes. The power of this Jin Dan Da Tao Xiu Lian practice cannot be explained by any words or comprehended by any thoughts.

Jin Dan is the highest treasure for healing, prevention of sickness, complete rejuvenation to *fan lao huan tong,* longevity, and, finally, for moving in the direction of immortality.

Practice Practice Practice
Heal Heal Heal
Prevent sickness Prevent sickness Prevent sickness
Purify Purify Purify
Self-clear karma Self-clear karma Self-clear karma
Transform Transform Transform
Enlighten Enlighten Enlighten
Jing Jing Jing
Qi Qi Qi

Shen Shen Shen
Xu Xu Xu
Dao Dao Dao
Jing Qi Shen Xu Dao He Yi
Jing Qi Shen Xu Dao He Yi
Jing Qi Shen Xu Dao He Yi
Jin Dan Jin Dan Jin Dan
Yu Dao He Zhen
Yu Dao He Zhen
Yu Dao He Zhen

More on Mind Power

Mind Power is "mind over matter." In ancient times, it was named *yi mi*. "Yi" means *thinking*. "Mi" means *secret,* so "yi mi" means *thinking secrets.*

Mind Power is meditation. Mind Power can be summarized in one sentence:

Mind Power is creative visualization.

If your Third Eye is open, you can directly see spiritual images. If your Third Eye is not open, visualize the images. The secret is in *how* you visualize. To visualize something is to communicate with the soul, mind, and body of that thing. For example, if you visualize Heaven's temple, you are invoking the soul, mind, and body of Heaven's temple. You will receive nourishment from Heaven's temple.

If you visualize the Divine, you are invoking the Divine. You are connecting with the Divine. The moment that you think about the Divine, the Divine knows right away. The Divine will give you love, forgiveness, compassion, and light. The Divine will give you nourishment.

Creative visualization is very important. There is no limitation to what you can visualize. This means that you can connect and communicate with anyone and anything you wish to connect with. The important wisdom is to communicate only with the Light Side.

Some people on Mother Earth communicate with the Dark Side. If you communicate with the Dark Side, you will receive the Dark Side's influence. This is a very important teaching. Some people purposely connect with the Dark Side to receive the Dark Side's support.

I cannot emphasize this wisdom enough. Remember to connect only with the Light Side. Do not invoke or call the Dark Side. The Dark Side can be very powerful.

I am going to give you some examples of what you could visualize when you chant Jin Dan Da Tao Xiu Lian. Remember the one-sentence secret: *Mind Power is creative visualization*. Meditation is creative visualization. Meditation is unlimited. You have the freedom to visualize anything you wish. Just remember to communicate only with the Light Side.

When you are chanting, focus your mind on your Jin Dan area to observe the souls, minds, and bodies of everyone and everything that you invoke, connect, and communicate with. Remember that in the following Mind Power applications, I am simply sharing some principles and examples. You absolutely can create your own way to meditate with creative visualization. Divine creation, divine manifestation, and divine flexibility should be the guidance for your meditation.

I taught Universal Meditation in chapter 5 of *Soul Mind Body Medicine,* which is one of my major books on healing. Find some time to study that chapter. It could help you understand meditation much better.

Now I am going to give you examples of how you can meditate when you do Jin Dan Da Tao Xiu Lian practice. Visualize at the same time you are chanting. Applying Mind Power and Sound Power simultaneously is the best way to use the Four Power Techniques. The visualizations are very flexible. I give you the following examples to share and guide you to learn Universal Meditation.

Universal Meditation is Tao meditation. The purpose of all of the meditations that you do is to reach Tao. Tao meditation is sacred and profound. Tao meditation is beyond words, comprehension, and imagination.

Enjoy it.

Benefit from it.

Transform every aspect of your life.

Finally, meld with Tao.

This is the Tao secret that is beyond any words.

Jin Dan Da Tao Jing Xiu Lian Meditation

Let me explain further. The following teaching is a Tao guided meditation. Every section of Jin Dan Da Tao Xiu Lian can be practiced as a separate meditation or they can be practiced together. This meditation is being created as I am flowing this chapter. Tao, the Divine, and all of the major spiritual fathers and mothers are above my head. They are giving this meditation to me on the spot. I am extremely grateful to be a vehicle and servant for you, humanity, and *wan ling* (all souls).

精

Jing

Matter

天之精	**Tian Zhi Jing**	*tyen jr jing*
	Heaven's jing	
地之精	**Di Zhi Jing**	*dee jr jing*
	Mother Earth's jing	
人之精	**Ren Zhi Jing**	*wren jr jing*
	Humanity's jing	
天地人之精	**Tian Di Ren Zhi Jing**	*tyen dee wren jr jing*
	Heaven's, Mother Earth's, humanity's jing	
万物之精	**Wan Wu Zhi Jing**	*wahn woo jr jing*
	Jing of countless planets, stars, and galaxies	
全宇宙之精	**Quan Yu Zhou Zhi Jing**	*chwen yü joe jr jing*
	Jing of countless universes	
皆是道之精	**Jie Shi Dao Zhi Jing**	*jyeh shr dow jr jing*
	All are Tao's jing	

金丹大道
JIN DAN DA TAO

THE BIG WAY GOLDEN LIGHT BALL

精修炼冥想
JING XIU LIAN MING XIANG

JING XIU LIAN MEDITATION

Apply the Four Power Techniques:

Body Power. Sit up straight on the floor or on a cushion with legs crossed in the full-lotus position, half-lotus position, or naturally. You may also sit in a chair. Keep your back straight. Put the tip of your tongue as close as you can to the roof of your mouth without touching. Put one palm on your lower abdomen. Put your other palm over this hand.

Soul Power. Say *hello:*

> *Dear Tian Zhi Jing, Heaven's jing,*
> *Dear Di Zhi Jing, Mother Earth's jing,*
> *Dear Ren Zhi Jing, humanity's jing,*
> *Dear Tian Di Ren Zhi Jing, Heaven's, Mother Earth's, and*
>   *humanity's jing,*
> *Dear Wan Wu Zhi Jing, jing of countless planets, stars, and*
>   *galaxies,*
> *Dear Quan Yu Zhou Zhi Jing, jing of countless universes,*
> *Dear Tao Zhi Jing, Tao's jing,*
> *Dear all spiritual fathers and mothers in all layers of Heaven*
>   *and on Mother Earth,*
> *Dear Divine,*
> *Dear Tao,*
> *I love you all, honor you all, and appreciate you all.*
> *Please come to my lower abdomen to form my Jin Dan.*
> *I am extremely honored.*
> *I cannot thank you enough.*

Mind Power. Visualize Heaven's temple inside your lower ab-domen. This Heaven's temple is filled with all kinds of divine light: golden light, rainbow light, purple light, crystal light, and all kinds of light of mixed colors. All kinds of light shine in your body from head to toe, skin to bone. All divine light comes into your lower abdomen to form your Jin Dan.

Sound Power. Chant repeatedly, silently or aloud:[2]

> *Heaven's liquid comes into my abdomen to form my Jin Dan. Thank you.*
> *Heaven's nectar comes into my abdomen to form my Jin Dan. Thank you.*
> *Heaven's fruit juice comes into my abdomen to form my Jin Dan. Thank you.*
> *Heaven's herbs come into my abdomen to form my Jin Dan. Thank you.*
> *Heaven's vitamins, minerals, amino acids, proteins, and all essential nutrients come into my abdomen to form my Jin Dan. Thank you.*
> *Mother Earth's oceans come into my abdomen to form my Jin Dan. Thank you.*
> *Mother Earth's rivers come into my abdomen to form my Jin Dan. Thank you.*
> *The Himalayas come into my abdomen to form my Jin Dan. Thank you.*
> *The Great Wall of China comes into my abdomen to form my Jin Dan. Thank you.*
> *The pyramids of Egypt come into my abdomen to form my Jin Dan. Thank you.*

---

2. Chanting silently is yin chanting. It stimulates the small cells and spaces in the body. Chanting aloud is yang chanting. It stimulates the large cells and spaces.

The Amazon rain forest comes into my abdomen to form my
Jin Dan. Thank you.
All of my spiritual fathers and mothers come into my
abdomen to form my Jin Dan. Thank you.
Humanity comes into my abdomen to form my Jin Dan.
Thank you.
Mother Earth comes into my abdomen to form my Jin Dan.
Thank you.
Countless planets, stars, and galaxies come into my abdomen
to form my Jin Dan. Thank you.
Countless universes come into my abdomen to form my Jin
Dan. Thank you.
The Divine comes into my abdomen to form my Jin Dan.
Thank you.
Tao comes into my abdomen to form my Jin Dan.
Thank you.

Hao! You are extremely blessed.

There is no time limit for this meditation and chanting. The more you repeat it, the more benefits you will receive and the faster you will build your Jin Dan.

Jin Dan Da Tao Qi Xiu Lian Meditation

气

Qi

Energy

天之气   **Tian Zhi Qi**   *tyen jr chee*
        Heaven's qi

地之气	**Di Zhi Qi**	*dee jr chee*
	Mother Earth's qi	
人之气	**Ren Zhi Qi**	*wren jr chee*
	Humanity's qi	
天地人之气	**Tian Di Ren Zhi Qi**	*tyen dee wren jr chee*
	Heaven's, Mother Earth's, humanity's qi	
万物之气	**Wan Wu Zhi Qi**	*wahn woo jr chee*
	Qi of countless planets, stars, and galaxies	
全宇宙之气	**Quan Yu Zhou Zhi Qi**	*chwen yü joe jr chee*
	Qi of countless universes	
皆是道之气	**Jie Shi Dao Zhi Qi**	*jyeh shr dow jr chee*
	All are Tao's qi	

金丹大道

JIN DAN DA TAO

THE BIG WAY GOLDEN LIGHT BALL

气修炼冥想

QI XIU LIAN MING XIANG

QI XIU LIAN MEDITATION

Apply the Four Power Techniques:

Body Power. Sit up straight on the floor or on a cushion with legs crossed in the full-lotus position, half-lotus position, or naturally. You may also sit in a chair. Keep your back straight. Put the tip of your tongue as close as you can to the roof of your mouth without touching. Put one palm on your lower abdomen. Put your other palm over this hand.

Soul Power. Say *hello:*

> *Dear Tian Zhi Qi, Heaven's qi,*
> *Dear Di Zhi Qi, Mother Earth's qi,*
> *Dear Ren Zhi Qi, humanity's qi,*
> *Dear Tian Di Ren Zhi Qi, Heaven's, Mother Earth's, and*
>   *humanity's qi,*
> *Dear Wan Wu Zhi Qi, qi of countless planets, stars, and*
>   *galaxies,*
> *Dear Quan Yu Zhou Zhi Qi, qi of countless universes,*
> *Dear Tao Zhi Qi, Tao's qi,*
> *Dear all spiritual fathers and mothers in all layers of Heaven*
>   *and on Mother Earth,*
> *Dear Divine,*
> *Dear Tao,*
> *I love you all, honor you all, and appreciate you all.*
> *Please come to my lower abdomen to form my Jin Dan.*
> *I am extremely honored.*
> *I cannot thank you enough.*

Mind Power. Visualize as follows inside your abdomen:

You are sitting in front of a beautiful mountain with countless pine trees all around you. (Pine trees represent longevity.) In front of the mountain is a beautiful, serene lake on which many lotuses of different colors are floating. The lotuses are green, red, yellow, white, blue, purple, crystal, and rainbow-colored.

A gentle wind is blowing. The sun is rising on the horizon, radiating its golden light all around you. Breathe in the freshness, coolness, and purity of the morning air. Allow it to fill your entire body, from head to toe, skin to bone. Many saints, spiritual fathers and mothers, and Heaven's animals have gathered and are surrounding you.

Sound Power. Chant repeatedly, silently or aloud:

> *Heaven's energy and light come into my abdomen to form my Jin Dan. Thank you.*
> *Heaven's golden light comes into my abdomen to form my Jin Dan. Thank you.*
> *Heaven's rainbow light comes into my abdomen to form my Jin Dan. Thank you.*
> *Heaven's purple light comes into my abdomen to form my Jin Dan. Thank you.*
> *Heaven's crystal light comes into my abdomen to form my Jin Dan. Thank you.*
> *Mother Earth's energy and light come into my abdomen to form my Jin Dan. Thank you.*
> *Mother Earth's mountains' energy and light come into my abdomen to form my Jin Dan. Thank you.*
> *Mother Earth's forests' energy and light come into my abdomen to form my Jin Dan. Thank you.*
> *Mother Earth's oceans' and rivers' energy and light come into my abdomen to form my Jin Dan. Thank you.*
> *Mother Earth's flowers' energy and light come into my abdomen to form my Jin Dan. Thank you.*
> *All energy and light of my spiritual fathers and mothers comes into my abdomen to form my Jin Dan. Thank you.*
> *All energy and light of humanity comes into my abdomen to form my Jin Dan. Thank you.*

All energy and light of Mother Earth comes into my
　　abdomen to form my Jin Dan. Thank you.
All energy and light of countless planets, stars, and galaxies
　　comes into my abdomen to form my Jin Dan. Thank you.
All energy and light of countless universes comes into my
　　abdomen to form my Jin Dan. Thank you.
All energy and light of the Divine comes into my abdomen to
　　form my Jin Dan. Thank you.
All energy and light of Tao comes into my abdomen to form
　　my Jin Dan. Thank you.

Hao! You are extremely blessed.

There is no time limit for this meditation and chanting. The more you repeat it, the more benefits you will receive and the faster you will build your Jin Dan.

Jin Dan Da Tao Shen Xiu Lian Meditation

神

Shen

Soul

天之神	**Tian Zhi Shen**	*tyen jr shun*
	Heaven's soul	
地之神	**Di Zhi Shen**	*dee jr shun*
	Mother Earth's soul	
人之神	**Ren Zhi Shen**	*wren jr shun*
	Humanity's soul	
天地人之神	**Tian Di Ren Zhi Shen**	*tyen dee wren jr shun*
	Heaven's, Mother Earth's, humanity's souls	

万物之神	**Wan Wu Zhi Shen**	*wahn woo jr shun*
	Souls of countless planets, stars, and galaxies	
全宇宙之神	**Quan Yu Zhou Zhi Shen**	*chwen yü joe jr shun*
	Souls of countless universes	
皆是道之神	**Jie Shi Dao Zhi Shen**	*jyeh shr dow jr shun*
	All are Tao's soul	

金丹大道
JIN DAN DA TAO

THE BIG WAY GOLDEN LIGHT BALL

神修炼冥想
SHEN XIU LIAN MING XIANG

SHEN XIU LIAN MEDITATION

Apply the Four Power Techniques:

Body Power. Sit up straight on the floor or on a cushion with legs crossed in the full-lotus position, half-lotus position, or naturally. You may also sit in a chair. Keep your back straight. Put the tip of your tongue as close as you can to the roof of your mouth without touching. Put one palm on your lower abdomen, with your other palm covering this hand.

Soul Power. Say *hello:*

> *Dear Tian Zhi Shen, Heaven's shen,*
> *Dear Di Zhi Shen, Mother Earth's shen,*
> *Dear Ren Zhi Shen, humanity's shen,*

Dear Tian Di Ren Zhi Shen, Heaven's, Mother Earth's,
    and humanity's shen,
Dear Wan Wu Zhi Shen, shen of countless planets, stars,
    and galaxies,
Dear Quan Yu Zhou Zhi Shen, shen of countless universes,
Dear Tao Zhi Shen, Tao's shen,
Dear all spiritual fathers and mothers in all layers of Heaven
    and on Mother Earth,
Dear Divine,
Dear Tao,
I love you all, honor you all, and appreciate you all.
Please come to my lower abdomen to form my Jin Dan.
I am extremely honored.
I cannot thank you enough.

Mind Power. Visualize as follows inside your abdomen:

The pyramids are inside your lower abdomen. There are countless saints inside, above, and around the pyramids. There are countless layers of Heaven's temples above the pyramids. There are countless planets, stars, galaxies, and universes around and above the pyramids. At the top, the Divine and Tao are present.

Your whole abdomen shines with light from all of them. The light has all kinds of colors, visible and invisible. Visible light is yang light. Invisible light is yin light. The power of yang light is great. The power of yin light is beyond imagination.

Feel the power.

Receive the blessings.

Sound Power. Chant repeatedly, silently or aloud:

The souls of all spiritual fathers and mothers in Heaven
   come into my abdomen to form my Jin Dan. Thank you.
The souls of all spiritual fathers and mothers on Mother
   Earth come into my abdomen to form my Jin Dan.
   Thank you.
The souls of humanity come into my abdomen to form my
   Jin Dan. Thank you.
The souls of countless planets, stars, and galaxies come into
   my abdomen to form my Jin Dan. Thank you.
The souls of countless universes come into my abdomen to
   form my Jin Dan. Thank you.
The soul of the Divine comes into my abdomen to form my
   Jin Dan. Thank you.
The soul of Tao comes into my abdomen to form my Jin
   Dan. Thank you.

Hao! You are extremely blessed.

There is no time limit for this meditation and chanting. The more you repeat it, the more benefits you will receive and the faster you will build your Jin Dan.

Jin Dan Da Tao Jin Dan Xiu Lian Meditation

金丹

Jin Dan

Golden Light Ball

天金丹   **Tian Jin Dan**   *tyen jeen dahn*
             Heaven's Jin Dan

地金丹	**Di Jin Dan**	*dee jeen dahn*
	Mother Earth's Jin Dan	
人金丹	**Ren Jin Dan**	*wren jeen dahn*
	Humanity's Jin Dan	
天地人金丹	**Tian Di Ren Jin Dan**	*tyen dee wren jeen*
	Heaven's, Mother Earth's,	*dahn*
	humanity's Jin Dan	
万物金丹	**Wan Wu Jin Dan**	*wahn woo jeen dahn*
	Jin Dan of countless	
	planets, stars, and galaxies	
全宇宙金丹	**Quan Yu Zhou Jin Dan**	*chwen yü joe jeen*
	Jin Dan of countless	*dahn*
	universes	
皆是道金丹	**Jie Shi Dao Jin Dan**	*jyeh shr dow jeen*
	All are Tao's Jin Dan	*dahn*

金丹大道
JIN DAN DA TAO

THE BIG WAY GOLDEN LIGHT BALL

金丹修炼冥想
JIN DAN XIU LIAN MING XIANG

JIN DAN XIU LIAN MEDITATION

Apply the Four Power Techniques:

Body Power. Sit up straight on the floor or on a cushion with legs crossed in the full-lotus position, half-lotus position, or naturally. You may also sit in a chair. Keep your back straight. Put the tip of your tongue as close as you can to the roof of your mouth without touching. Put one palm on your lower abdomen. Put your other palm over this hand.

Soul Power. Say *hello*:

> *Dear Tian Jin Dan, Heaven's Jin Dan,*
> *Dear Di Jin Dan, Mother Earth's Jin Dan,*
> *Dear Ren Jin Dan, humanity's Jin Dan,*
> *Dear Tian Di Ren Jin Dan, Heaven's, Mother Earth's, and*
>   *humanity's Jin Dan,*
> *Dear Wan Wu Jin Dan, Jin Dan of countless planets, stars,*
>   *and galaxies,*
> *Dear Quan Yu Zhou Jin Dan, Jin Dan of countless*
>   *universes,*
> *Dear Tao Jin Dan, Tao's Jin Dan,*
> *Dear all spiritual fathers and mothers in all layers of Heaven*
>   *and on Mother Earth,*
> *Dear Divine,*
> *Dear Tao,*
> *I love you all, honor you all, and appreciate you all.*
> *Please come to my lower abdomen to form my Jin Dan.*
> *I am extremely honored.*
> *I cannot thank you enough.*

Mind Power. Visualize as follows inside your abdomen:

Heaven's soul mountain is inside your abdomen. All layers of Heaven's saints, the Divine, and Tao are doing Xiu Lian on the soul mountain. The soul mountain is named *ling shan* in Chinese. "Ling" means soul. "Shan" means mountain.

Visualize layers and layers of saints in all layers of Heaven around the mountain. They are all in your lower abdomen to form your Jin Dan. Countless souls from Heaven, Mother Earth, and all planets, stars, galaxies, and universes are in your lower abdomen to form your Jin Dan. The Divine and Tao are above the top of the mountain.

The whole mountain shines all kinds of colors of light, as well as invisible light. Heaven's light, Mother Earth's light, humanity's light, the light of countless planets, stars, and galaxies, the light of countless universes, the light of the Divine, and the light of Tao all shine in your lower abdomen. They are forming your Jin Dan. Your whole body shines Tao light from head to toe, skin to bone.

You are extremely blessed beyond words.

Sound Power. Chant repeatedly, silently or aloud:

> *Tian Jin Dan forms my Jin Dan. Thank you.*
> *Di Jin Dan forms my Jin Dan. Thank you.*
> *Ren Jin Dan forms my Jin Dan. Thank you.*
> *Tian Di Ren Jin Dan forms my Jin Dan. Thank you.*
> *Wan Wu Jin Dan forms my Jin Dan. Thank you.*
> *Quan Yu Zhou Jin Dan forms my Jin Dan. Thank you.*
> *All saints' Jin Dan form my Jin Dan. Thank you.*
> *Divine Jin Dan forms my Jin Dan. Thank you.*
> *Tao Jin Dan forms my Jin Dan. Thank you.*
> *Yu Dao He Zhen, meld with Tao.*
> *Tao Jin Dan*
> *Tao Jin Dan*
> *Tao Jin Dan*
> *Tao Tao Tao*

Hao! You are extremely blessed.

There is no time limit for this meditation and chanting. The more you repeat it, the more benefits you will receive and the faster you will build your Jin Dan.

To build a complete Jin Dan takes a long, long time. Jin Dan has layers. Jin Dan has unlimited power and wisdom. To form a complete Jin Dan is to form Tao Dan. To form Tao Dan is to meld with Tao. Therefore, Jin Dan Da Tao Xiu Lian practice is *The Big Way* to reach Tao.

To form Tao Dan means you meld with Tao.

Tao Dan *is* Tao.

To meld with Tao means:

You are Tao. Tao is you.
Tao ke Tao.
Fei chang Tao.

The power of these Jin Dan Da Tao Xiu Lian practices cannot be explained by any words or comprehended by any thought.

Practice.
Practice.
Practice.

Heal.
Heal.
Heal.

Prevent sickness.
Prevent sickness.
Prevent sickness.

Purify soul, heart, mind, and body.
Purify soul, heart, mind, and body.
Purify soul, heart, mind, and body.

Self-clear karma.
Self-clear karma.
Self-clear karma.

Transform relationships, finances, and every aspect of life.
Transform relationships, finances, and every aspect of life.
Transform relationships, finances, and every aspect of life.

Enlighten your soul, heart, mind, and body.
Enlighten your soul, heart, mind, and body.
Enlighten your soul, heart, mind, and body.

Jing Jing Jing
Qi Qi Qi
Shen Shen Shen
Xu Xu Xu
Dao Dao Dao

Jing Qi Shen Xu Dao He Yi
Jing Qi Shen Xu Dao He Yi
Jing Qi Shen Xu Dao He Yi

Jin Dan, Jin Dan
Jin Dan, Jin Dan
Jin Dan, Jin Dan

Yu Dao He Zhen
Yu Dao He Zhen
Yu Dao He Zhen

Zhi Liao Fan Lao Huan Tong Chang Shou Yong Sheng Zhi Dao Tao of Healing, Fan Lao Huan Tong (Rejuvenation), Longevity, and Immortality

E VERY PERSON THROUGHOUT history, whether on the spiritual journey or not, wishes to have good health, rejuvenation, and long life. People do spiritual practices and all other kinds of practices, including physical exercise, diet, taking nutritional supplements, using herbs externally and internally, and more, in order to gain good health, rejuvenation, *fan lao huan tong* (returning to the health and purity of a baby), and longevity.

Millions of people may think about immortality. Immortality could be the best dream and greatest wish but most people instantly think that it is impossible. How can one believe in immortality if one has never seen an immortal person?

In my book *Tao I: The Way of All Life*, published in May 2010 as the sixth book of the Soul Power Series and my first book on Tao, I shared the divine sacred philosophy, wisdom, knowledge, and practical techniques of the two kinds of creation: Tao normal creation and Tao reverse creation.

Recall the process of normal creation of Tao:

Tao sheng yi
Yi sheng er
Er sheng san
San sheng wan wu

Tao creates One.
One creates Two.
Two creates Three.
Three creates all things.

Tao ➔ One ➔ Two ➔ Three ➔ all things
    creates

Recall the process of reverse creation of Tao:

Wan wu gui san
San gui er
Er gui yi
Yi gui Tao

All things return to Three.
Three returns to Two.
Two returns to One.
One returns to Tao.

all things ➔ Three ➔ Two ➔ One ➔ Tao
    return to

Tao is the source of all universes. Tao is The Way of all life. Tao is the universal principles and laws. Tao creates Heaven, Earth, human beings, animals, countless planets, countless stars, countless galaxies, and countless universes.

Humanity is one. Humanity is produced by yin and yang, woman and man.

Every human being is also divisible into yin and yang. For example, the top half of the body above the diaphragm belongs to yang; the bottom half of the body below the diaphragm belongs to yin. The front half of a human being belongs to yin; the back half belongs to yang. The outside of a human being belongs to yang; the inside belongs to yin. These are some of the ways a human being can be divided into yin and yang.

Yin Yang is one of the most important universal laws. Universal laws can explain everything in all universes. Yin Yang is also an ancient philosophy that summarizes everyone and everything—animate and inanimate—in all universes.

The nature of yin and yang is based on the nature of fire and water. Therefore, yin and yang are opposites. Fire is hot, active, excited, and moves upward. Anything that has the fire character belongs to yang. Water is cold, passive, calm, and moves downward. Anything that has the water character belongs to yin.

Yin and yang are interdependent. You cannot explain water without fire, and you cannot explain fire without water. You cannot explain man (yang) without woman (yin), and you cannot explain woman without man. You cannot explain night without day, and you cannot explain day without night. All of these yin-yang pairs are interdependent.

Another example is a battery. A battery has a positive and a negative pole. They are also opposite and interdependent. You cannot have one without the other. The North Pole and South

Pole are also opposite and interdependent. Opposite and interdependent are the two main characteristics of yin and yang.

Yin and yang are interchangeable and transformable. For example, night is yin and day is yang. As night moves to day, yin transforms to yang. As day moves to night, yang transforms to yin.

Yin and yang are infinitely divisible. For example, the kidney is a major yin organ and the urinary bladder is its paired yang organ. The kidney can be divided into kidney yang and kidney yin. The urinary bladder can similarly be divided into urinary bladder yang and urinary bladder yin. One such division is that the structure of the kidneys or urinary bladder belongs to yin, while the function of the kidneys or urinary bladder belongs to yang.

The kidneys and urinary bladder consist of millions of cells. Every cell can also be divided into yin and yang. For example, the structure of a cell belongs to the cell's yin and the function of a cell belongs to the cell's yang.

A cell consists of many cell units, DNA, RNA, spaces, and tiny matter. There is countless tiny matter inside a cell. This tiny matter includes protons, electrons, quarks, leptons, and more. Every tiny matter can also be divided into yin and yang.

The above teaching shows us that a human being demonstrates and follows the normal creation of Tao, which is: Tao creates One. One creates Two. Two creates Three. Three creates all things.

A human being has many systems. Each system has many organs. Each organ has millions and billions of cells. Each cell has countless tiny matter. Tao creates a human being. Human beings follow the normal creation of Tao.

Tao Practices for Healing, Rejuvenation, and Longevity of the Five Elements

Five Elements theory is another important universal law. Heaven and Earth consist of the five elements (Wood, Fire, Earth, Metal, Water). A human being consists of the five elements. Everyone and everything consists of the five elements.

WOOD ELEMENT

The Wood element includes the liver, gallbladder, eyes, tendons, nails, anger in the emotional body, wind, the season of spring, the direction of east, and more.

The liver is the major yin organ that belongs to the Wood element. In the spring, wood grows. Therefore, practice for the liver is vital during the spring and important in any season. I will share a Tao practice to develop your liver power to heal, rejuvenate, and prolong the life of your liver.

Apply the Four Power Techniques:

Body Power. Sit up straight. Put the tip of your tongue near the roof of your mouth without touching. Put your right palm on your abdomen, just below the navel. Put your left palm on your liver area, which is just below the ribs on your right.

Soul Power. Say *hello:*

> *Dear soul mind body of my liver,*
> *I love you, honor you, and appreciate you.*
> *Dear Tao,*
> *Dear Divine,*

Dear Wood element,
Dear all of my spiritual fathers and mothers in the physical
    world and in the spiritual world,
Dear Tao mantra, Tao Shu Gan,[1]
I love you, honor you, and appreciate you.
Please heal my liver, prevent all sickness in my liver,
    rejuvenate and prolong the life of my liver.
Please create my Tao liver.
Thank you.

To create a Tao liver is to create an immortal liver. It takes much dedicated practice, but this is the direction of the Tao teachings in this book.

Mind Power. Visualize Tao light shining in your liver. In order to see Tao light, you must open your Third Eye, which is your spiritual eye. Tao light includes visible light and invisible light. Visible light includes red, golden, rainbow, purple, crystal, and mixed-color light. Invisible light cannot be seen, even with an open Third Eye.

Sound Power. Chant silently or aloud:

Tao shu gan
Tao shu gan
Tao shu gan
Tao shu gan
Tao shu gan

---

1. "Shu" (pronounced *shoo*) means *smooth*. "Gan" (pronounced *gahn*) means *liver*. Therefore, "Tao shu gan" means *Tao smooths the liver.* See pp. 406–408 of *Tao I: The Way of All Life.*

Tao shu gan
Tao shu gan . . .

Chant for three to five minutes per time, three to five times per day. The more you chant, the better. This chant and practice offers unlimited benefits. For chronic and life-threatening conditions of the liver, you must chant a total of two hours or more per day.

⁂

Practical techniques are an important part of all of my books and teachings. As you read this and any of my books, be sure to do the practices. It is like being at a workshop with me. I cannot emphasize enough the significance of practicing. There is an ancient statement:

Zhi yao gong fu shen, tie bang mo cheng zhen

"Zhi yao" means *only if.* "Gong fu" means *time.* "Shen" means *deep and persistent.* "Tie bang" means *iron stick.* "Mo cheng" means *sharpen.* "Zhen" means *needle.* "Zhi yao gong fu shen, tie bang mo cheng zhen" (pronounced *jr yow gawng foo shun, tyeh bahng maw chung jun*) means: *Only if one spends time persistently and continuously can the iron stick be sharpened to a needle.*

This statement tells us that we must practice persistently and consistently if we want to achieve something. For example, if we want to self-heal, we need to spend time to practice. We need to practice persistently and continuously. If we want to rejuvenate, we need to do the same thing. If we want longevity, we need to do even more practice. If we dream of immortality, much more practice is needed.

In this book, you will learn the simplest and most powerful way to do Xiu Lian. "Xiu" means *purification of soul, heart, mind, and body* and "lian" means *practice,* so Xiu Lian is *purification practice.* Xiu Lian is the totality of one's spiritual journey, because the spiritual journey is a purification journey.

Xiu Lian is a special Tao term. To do Xiu Lian is to follow Tao to purify one's soul, heart, mind, and body. Xiu Lian is Tao practice. Xiu Lian is the historical term for Tao practice. To do Xiu Lian is to practice Tao. To practice Tao is to do Xiu Lian.

After you read this book, you will understand that you are doing Xiu Lian in every moment of your life, because Tao is in every aspect of your life. After reading this book, you will understand that you can practice Tao before, while, and after you eat, before sleeping, when you awaken, while you work, during breaks in your work day, and during your times of recreation and leisure. You will know how to follow Tao in everything you do, every word you speak, and every thought you think.

Lao Zi, the author of *Dao De Jing,* said:

Shang shi wen Dao, qin er xi zhi
Zhong shi wen Dao, ruo ji ruo li
Xia shi wen Dao, ha ha da xiao

"Shang shi" means *serious spiritual seeker* or *serious Xiu Lian practitioner.* "Wen" means *hear.* Dao or Tao is The Way. "Qin" means *actively, continuously, and persistently.* "Er" has no specific meaning. "Xi" means *practice.* "Zhi" has no specific meaning. "Shang shi wen Dao, qin er xi zhi" (pronounced *shahng shr wun dow, cheen ur shee jr*) means *the serious Xiu Lian practitioner who hears about Tao, The Way, or the truth, will do serious practice actively, continuously, and persistently.*

"Zhong shi" means *a person who wants to be on the spiritual journey, but is not so serious.* "Ruo ji" means *does the Tao practice.* "Ruo li" means *quits the practice.* "Zhong shi wen Dao, ruo ji ruo li" (pronounced *jawng shr wun dow, rwaw jee rwaw lee*) means *a person who hears about Tao but is not a serious Tao practitioner will practice sometimes, but not seriously, continuously, and persistently.*

"Xia shi" means *a person who is not on the spiritual journey and who does not believe in Tao teaching.* "Ha ha" is the sound of laughter. "Da xiao" means *huge, sarcastic laughter.* "Xia shi wen Dao, ha ha da xiao" (pronounced *shyah shr wun dow, ha ha dah shee-yow*) means *a person who hears about Tao but does not believe in Tao teaching and practice will laugh sarcastically.*

Lao Zi's saying tells us that to practice Tao well, one must be very serious, active, persistent, and dedicated. In one sentence:

Xiu Lian takes the greatest effort.

The purpose of Xiu Lian is to have good health, rejuvenation, and longevity. The final goal is to reach immortality. Why does a person need to live longer? To live longer is to serve humanity better. The Divine and Tao need special servants on Mother Earth to help bring love, peace, and harmony to humanity, Mother Earth, and all universes.

Now let us continue with five elements practices for healing, rejuvenation, and longevity.

FIRE ELEMENT

The Fire element includes the heart, small intestine, tongue, blood vessels, anxiety, and depression in the emotional body, energy, heat, the season of summer, the direction of south, and more.

For example, the body's energy belongs to the Fire element because it has the fire character. In traditional Chinese medicine, inflammation and infection are the result of an excess of yang or fire. Mother Earth has fire issues because it has heat in the form of global warming, "inflammation" in the form of volcanoes, and more.

Practicing to heal and rejuvenate the heart is vital during the summer and important in any season. Let us do a practice to heal, rejuvenate, and prolong the life of the heart.

Apply the Four Power Techniques:

Body Power. Sit up straight. Put the tip of your tongue near the roof of your mouth without touching. Put your right palm just below your navel. Put your left palm on your heart area.

Soul Power. Say *hello:*

> *Dear soul mind body of my heart,*
> *I love you, honor you, and appreciate you.*
> *Dear Tao,*
> *Dear Divine,*
> *Dear Fire element,*
> *Dear all of my spiritual fathers and mothers in the physical world and in the spiritual world,*
> *Dear Tao mantra, Tao Yang Xin,*[2]
> *I love you, honor you, and appreciate you.*
> *Please heal my heart, prevent all sickness in my heart,*
> *rejuvenate and prolong the life of my heart.*

---

2. "Yang" (pronounced *yahng*) means *nourish.* "Xin" (pronounced *sheen*) means *heart.* Therefore, "Tao yang xin" means *Tao nourishes the heart.* See pp. 408–410 of *Tao I: The Way of All Life.*

Please create my Tao heart.
Thank you.

To create a Tao heart is to create an immortal heart.

Mind Power. Visualize Tao light (see p. 74) shining in your heart.

Sound Power. Chant silently or aloud:

Tao yang xin
Tao yang xin
Tao yang xin
Tao yang xin
Tao yang xin
Tao yang xin
Tao yang xin . . .

Chant for three to five minutes per time, three to five times per day. The more you chant, the better. This chant and practice offers unlimited benefits. For chronic and life-threatening conditions of the heart, you must chant a total of two hours or more per day.

EARTH ELEMENT

The Earth element includes the spleen, stomach, mouth and lips, gums and teeth, muscles, worry in the emotional body, dampness, the season of late summer, the central direction, and more.

For example, earth (soil) nourishes and nurtures all things on Mother Earth, including all kinds of plants, flowers, trees, and more. In the body, the spleen and stomach are the major yin and yang Earth element organs, respectively. They digest and absorb all kinds of nutrients from food and liquid to nourish and nurture the body and maintain all of the body's functions.

In any season, but especially in late summer, to heal and rejuvenate the spleen is vital. Let us do a practice to heal, rejuvenate, and prolong the life of the spleen.

Apply the Four Power Techniques:

Body Power. Sit up straight. Put the tip of your tongue near the roof of your mouth without touching. Put your right palm just below your navel. Put your left palm on your spleen area, over your lower left ribs.

Soul Power. Say *hello:*

> *Dear soul mind body of my spleen,*
> *I love you, honor you, and appreciate you.*
> *Dear Tao,*
> *Dear Divine,*
> *Dear Earth element,*
> *Dear all of my spiritual fathers and mothers in the physical*
>   *world and in the spiritual world,*
> *Dear Tao mantra, Tao Jian Pi,[3]*
> *I love you, honor you, and appreciate you.*
> *Please heal my spleen, prevent all sickness in my spleen,*
>   *rejuvenate and prolong the life of my spleen.*
> *Please create my Tao spleen.*
> *Thank you.*

To create a Tao spleen is to create an immortal spleen.

---

3. "Jian" (pronounced *jyen*) means *strengthen.* "Pi" (pronounced *pee*) means *spleen.* Therefore, "Tao jian pi" means *Tao strengthens the spleen.* See pp. 410–412 of *Tao I: The Way of All Life.*

Mind Power. Visualize Tao light (see p. 74) shining in your spleen.

Sound Power. Chant silently or aloud:

> *Tao jian pi*
> *Tao jian pi*
> *Tao jian pi*
> *Tao jian pi*
> *Tao jian pi*
> *Tao jian pi*
> *Tao jian pi . . .*

Chant for three to five minutes per time, three to five times per day. The more you chant, the better. This chant and practice offers unlimited benefits. For chronic and life-threatening conditions of the spleen, you must chant a total of two hours or more per day.

METAL ELEMENT

The Metal element includes the lungs, large intestine, nose, skin, grief and sadness in the emotional body, dryness, the season of autumn, the direction of west, and more.

There are many metal elements in the blood and body, such as iron, sodium, magnesium, zinc, copper, and more.

To heal and rejuvenate the lungs is vital in autumn and important in any season. Let us do a practice to heal, rejuvenate, and prolong the life of the lungs.

Apply the Four Power Techniques:

Body Power. Sit up straight. Put the tip of your tongue near the roof of your mouth without touching. Put your right palm just below your navel. Put your left palm over a lung.

Soul Power. Say *hello*:

> *Dear soul mind body of my lungs,*
> *I love you, honor you, and appreciate you.*
> *Dear Tao,*
> *Dear Divine,*
> *Dear Metal element,*
> *Dear all of my spiritual fathers and mothers in the physical*
> *   world and in the spiritual world,*
> *Dear Tao mantra, Tao Xuan Fei,* [4]
> *I love you, honor you, and appreciate you.*
> *Please heal my lungs, prevent all sickness in my lungs,*
> *   rejuvenate and prolong the life of my lungs.*
> *Please create my Tao lungs.*
> *Thank you.*

To create Tao lungs is to create immortal lungs.

Mind Power. Visualize Tao light (see p. 74) shining in your lungs.

Sound Power. Chant silently or aloud:

---

4. "Xuan" (pronounced *shwen*) means *spread the food essence*. In traditional Chinese medicine, the spleen sends the food essence from the abdomen through the diaphragm to the chest. The lungs then transform and transfer the food essence to the heart to form blood. This is one of the major lung functions, called the function of *xuan fei*. "Fei" means *lungs*. "Tao xuan fei" means *Tao promotes the xuan fei function of the lungs*. See pp. 413–415 of *Tao I: The Way of All Life*.

Tao xuan fei
Tao xuan fei
Tao xuan fei
Tao xuan fei
Tao xuan fei
Tao xuan fei
Tao xuan fei . . .

Chant for three to five minutes per time, three to five times per day. The more you chant, the better. This chant and practice offers unlimited benefits. For chronic and life-threatening conditions of the lungs, you must chant a total of two hours or more per day.

WATER ELEMENT

The Water element includes the kidneys, urinary bladder, ears, bones, fear in the emotional body, cold, the season of winter, the direction of north, and more.

An adult human body is about 60 to 70 percent fluid by weight.

To heal and rejuvenate the kidneys is important at any time; it is especially vital in the winter. Let us do a Tao practice to heal, rejuvenate, and prolong the life of the kidneys.

Apply the Four Power Techniques:

Body Power. Sit up straight. Put the tip of your tongue near the roof of your mouth without touching. Put your right palm over your abdomen, just below your navel. Put your left palm over a kidney.

Soul Power. Say *hello:*

> *Dear soul mind body of my kidneys,*
> *I love you, honor you, and appreciate you.*
> *Dear Tao,*
> *Dear Divine,*
> *Dear Water element,*
> *Dear all of my spiritual fathers and mothers in the physical*
>   *world and in the spiritual world,*
> *Dear Tao mantra, Tao Zhuang Shen,*[5]
> *I love you, honor you, and appreciate you.*
> *Please heal my kidneys, prevent all sickness in my kidneys,*
>   *rejuvenate and prolong the life of my kidneys.*
> *Please create my Tao kidneys.*
> *Thank you.*

To create Tao kidneys is to create immortal kidneys.

Mind Power. Visualize Tao light (see p. 74) radiating in your kidneys.

Sound Power. Chant silently or aloud:

> *Tao zhuang shen*
> *Tao zhuang shen*
> *Tao zhuang shen*
> *Tao zhuang shen*
> *Tao zhuang shen*
> *Tao zhuang shen*
> *Tao zhuang shen . . .*

---

5. "Zhuang" (pronounced *jwahng*) means *strengthen*. "Shen" means *kidneys*. "Tao zhuang shen" means *Tao strengthens the kidneys*. See pp. 415–417 of *Tao I: The Way of All Life.*

Chant for three to five minutes per time, three to five times per day. The more you chant, the better. This chant and practice offers unlimited benefits. For chronic and life-threatening conditions of the kidneys, you must chant a total of two hours or more per day.

Reverse Creation of Tao Is the Total Secret

As I explained earlier in this chapter, yin and yang are infinitely divisible. Therefore, every organ can be subdivided infinitely into yin and yang. This follows the normal creation of Tao. The five elements include every system, every organ, every cell, every DNA and RNA, and every tiny matter in the body. This also follows the normal creation of Tao: Tao creates One. One creates Two. Two creates Three. Three creates all things.

Modern medical research moves to more and more detail. It researches the systems, organs, cells, and further, to the DNA, RNA, and beyond. This movement is from the macrocosm to the microcosm. It follows the normal creation of Tao.

What is the most significant aspect of the reverse creation of Tao? In one sentence:

The reverse creation of Tao is the total secret for healing, prevention of sickness, rejuvenation, and longevity.

In *Dao De Jing*, Lao Zi said, "Zhuan qi zhi rou, neng ying er hu" (pronounced *jwahn chee jr roe, nung ying ur hoo*). This statement means *do Xiu Lian to make the body soft like a baby's.*

Lao Zi also said, "Shang shan ruo shui" (pronounced *shahng shahn rwaw shway*). This statement means *the soft nature of water is close to Tao.* Because Tao cannot be explained in words, Lao Zi used water to try to get people to feel and comprehend Tao.

These two statements from Lao Zi tell the Tao practitioner to practice Tao in order to reach fan lao huan tong; then one can move further to Tao.

Why does a person get sick? In my 2006 book, *Soul Mind Body Medicine*, and in the books of my Soul Power Series, I have shared with my readers and humanity that any sickness is due to soul mind body blockages.

Soul blockages are bad karma. Bad karma is due to the mistakes that a person and his or her ancestors have made to others, in this lifetime and all past lifetimes. These mistakes include killing, harming, cheating, stealing from, and taking advantage of others. When a mistake is made, a spiritual debt is created. This spiritual debt is bad karma. It is a universal law that one has to pay these spiritual debts by learning lessons. The lessons can include sickness and challenges in relationships, finances, business, and any aspect of life.

I have explained karma issues in greater depth in several of my previous books:

- *Soul Mind Body Medicine: A Complete Soul Healing System for Optimum Health and Vitality.* This book shares how to self-heal your sicknesses with the Four Power Techniques.
- *The Power of Soul: The Way to Heal, Rejuvenate, Transform, and Enlighten All Life.*[6] Chapter two of this book is entitled "Karma." There, I explain what

---

6. *The Power of Soul: The Way to Heal, Rejuvenate, Transform, and Enlighten All Life.* (Toronto/New York: Heaven's Library/Atria Books, 2009).

karma is, its significance for one's life, and some practical techniques for self-clearing karma. In this book, I share the key one-sentence secret about karma:

**Karma is the root cause of success and
failure in every aspect of one's life.**

- *Divine Soul Mind Body Healing and Transmission System: The Divine Way to Heal You, Humanity, Mother Earth, and All Universes.*[7] This book teaches that every sickness is due to soul mind body blockages. It explains the different kinds of soul mind body blockages and presents the divine way to clear them. It also teaches practical techniques for self-clearing soul mind body blockages for healing.
- *Tao I: The Way of All Life.* This book teaches divine and Tao secrets for healing, prevention of sickness, rejuvenation, and transformation of relationships and finances. The most important teaching and practice in this book is to chant *Tao Jing* and various Jin Dan chants. Tao Jing is the new "Tao Classic," comprised of seventy-five sacred phrases from the Divine and Tao. Every phrase carries incredible secrets, wisdom, knowledge, and practical techniques. The Jin Dan is the key for healing, prevention of sickness, rejuvenation, longevity, and life transformation. To chant *Tao Jing* and Jin Dan chants is to self-clear karma. The power is beyond words, comprehension, and imagi-

---

7. *Divine Soul Mind Body Healing and Transmission System: The Divine Way to Heal You, Humanity, Mother Earth, and All Universes* (Toronto/New York: Heaven's Library/Atria Books, 2010).

nation. To chant *Tao Jing* and *Jin Dan* is powerful
because it can remove soul mind body blockages in
every aspect of life.

- *Divine Transformation: The Divine Way to Self-clear
  Karma to Transform Your Health, Relationships, Finances, and More.*[8] This book teaches deep wisdom
  about how bad karma blocks every aspect of life. Bad
  karma can even take one's life. Most importantly, this
  book teaches the divine way to self-clear bad karma.
  To transform bad karma is to transform every aspect
  of life, including health, relationships, and finances.

To have long life, one must heal all sicknesses because sickness can take one's life. Life-threatening sicknesses such as heart
attacks, strokes, and serious trauma can take one's life instantly.
Chronic and serious conditions can shorten one's life.

According to *Soul Mind Body Medicine* and the Soul Power
Series, all sickness is due to soul mind body blockages. According to traditional Tao and *Tao I* teachings, "jing" is *matter,* "qi" is
vital energy and life force, and "shen" is *soul.*

In fact, soul mind body are jing qi shen. Jing is the matter of
the body. Qi is the vital energy and life force of the body. Both
jing and qi connect with the mind, but the mind connects mainly
with qi. Soul is shen.

In traditional Chinese medicine, sickness is due to an imbalance of yin and yang. In Tao teaching, sickness exhausts jing qi
shen. A person's vitality and life are like an oil lamp. The jing
qi shen of the whole body is the oil. This oil allows one to shine

---

8. *Divine Transformation: The Divine Way to Self-clear Karma to Transform Your Health, Relationships, Finances, and More* (Toronto/New York: Heaven's Library/Atria Books, 2010).

with energy, stamina, vitality, and immunity. If one is sick, the oil will be depleted, and the "lamp" cannot shine as brightly. If one is very sick, the oil will be depleted even more, and the "lamp" could be very dim.

To study and practice Tao is to add oil to one's lamp, which is to increase jing qi shen. When one's oil lamp is fully replenished, all sicknesses will disappear. The Tao practitioner's body will transform to the baby condition because a baby's lamp is full of fresh oil. When a healthy baby is born, the oil in the lamp is full. As a baby grows and matures, it becomes a child, a teenager, an adult, and a senior. In this process, the oil is gradually exhausted for most human beings. The whole life of a human being can be explained in this way.

At this moment, the Tao is explaining to me that a human being is given approximately one hundred to one hundred forty years of life. Why then do very few people live to the age of one hundred forty? Why is it uncommon for people to live even to the age of one hundred?

Life is just like an oil lamp burning. The major exhaustion of the oil is due to *selfishness*. A selfish person could have very unpleasant desires, such as greed or desire for fame, wealth, and power. If you want to fulfill these kinds of desires, you could easily do something to harm others. You could say something to harm others. You could think something to harm others. This creates bad karma. Bad karma will cause the biggest exhaustion of the oil in one's lamp.

To study and practice Tao, the key is to purify your soul, heart, mind, and body. To purify your soul, heart, mind, and body is to self-clear your bad karma. To purify your soul, heart, mind, and body is also to avoid creating new bad karma. When you practice Tao (Xiu Tao), you are chanting. To chant is to offer service to humanity and to all souls. Heaven will record your service and give you good virtue. Good virtue is expressed in spiritual flowers that can be red, golden, rainbow, purple, crystal, and mixed colors. These spiritual flowers are spiritual currency. They help to pay your spiritual debt. They can also help you avoid creating new bad karma. When bad karma is cleared, the root cause of sickness is removed. Continue to practice. You could then recover from sickness much faster.

A human being's jing qi shen can support a person's life for a maximum of one hundred to one hundred forty years. Not many people live one hundred years or longer because bad karma, sickness, stress, and all kinds of other issues exhaust the oil in one's lamp. As one gets older, the oil is exhausted more and more. When one gets a serious sickness, the oil will be exhausted dramatically.

To practice Tao is to transform the quality of the body. It is to transform jing qi shen. It is to replenish the oil. Even if you are old or sick, if you practice properly your oil will be fulfilled, your sicknesses will be healed, and you could return to a full bottle of oil. This is to reach the baby condition. This is to reach fan lao huan tong.

If you can reach and then maintain the fan lao huan tong condition, you could live a long, long life.

If you can constantly maintain the baby condition, immortality is possible.

To balance jing qi shen and to join jing qi shen as one is to heal, prevent sickness, rejuvenate, and have a long, long life.

The reverse creation of Tao is the process of aligning, balancing, and unifying jing qi shen. Every system has jing qi shen. Every organ has jing qi shen. Every cell has jing qi shen. Every DNA and RNA has jing qi shen. Every tiny matter has jing qi shen. There is countless tiny matter in a single cell. There are millions and billions of cells in a single organ. Aligning the soul mind body of every cell brings healing, rejuvenation, and longevity. To align soul mind body is to align jing qi shen.

The soul mind body or jing qi shen of the countless tiny matter in one cell join as one and the soul mind body or jing qi shen of millions and billions of cells in one organ join as one to follow the reverse creation of Tao: All things return to Three. Three returns to Two. Two returns to One. One returns to Tao.

Soul mind body or jing qi shen of the whole body, including all systems, all organs, all cells, all cell units, all DNA and RNA, all spaces between the cells, and all tiny matter inside the cells, join as one. This is true healing to remove all kinds of soul mind body blockages. This is also to prevent all kinds of sickness. This is to rejuvenate the whole body from head to toe, skin to bone to reach fan lao huan tong. This will further prolong one's life.

If one can maintain fan lao huan tong, one can reach a long, long life. If fan lao huan tong can be maintained forever, that is immortality. Immortality is possible, but it takes incredible effort to do Xiu Lian.

Since creation, millions of spiritual practitioners have searched for good health, rejuvenation, longevity, and immortality. Millions of traditional Tao practitioners have constantly searched for the way of longevity and immortality. The Tao essence of fan lao huan tong, longevity, and immortality that I have just shared comes directly from Tao. I am so honored to present these sacred and secret phrases and practices to you and everyone on Mother Earth who is searching for rejuvenation, longevity, and immortality.

Study.

Practice.

Benefit.

Heal all of your sicknesses.

Heal automatically through the practice of sacred and secret Tao phrases.

Rejuvenate your soul, heart, mind, and body.

Prolong your life.

Move in the direction of immortality.

When you practice, you can heal yourself.

You will gain the confidence to move further.

Continue to practice and rejuvenate yourself. Become younger and younger.

You will gain more confidence to move even further.

Continue to practice and transform your age to the baby state.

You will believe much more.

Continue to practice.

Keep your baby state longer and longer.

Longevity will follow.

You will believe completely.

Continue to practice more.

Immortality is on the way.

To move from healing to rejuvenation to reaching fan lao huan tong to prolonging life and to achieving immortality is a long, long process. A Tao practitioner can only experience it little by little. I always say, "If you want to know if a pear is sweet, taste it. If you want to know if a teaching and practice is powerful, experience it."

To experience it is to gain confidence.

Trust.

Move further.

So much sacred and secret wisdom, knowledge, and practical techniques will be released to serious Tao practitioners.

Millions of people on the spiritual journey could be thirsty for this Divine and Tao liquid and nutrients.

Drink.

I want to emphasize again that one must practice constantly. Every step in the process—from healing to rejuvenation, from rejuvenation to fan lao huan tong, and from fan lao huan tong to longevity—takes very hard purification, discipline, and persistence. The final step, from longevity to immortality, requires much more effort.

You can do it.

I wish the teaching and practices in this book will serve your physical journey and your soul journey.

I wish the teaching and practices in this book will bring good health by healing all sicknesses in your spiritual, mental, emotional, and physical bodies.

I wish the teaching and practices in this book will transform your age to the health and purity of a baby.

I wish the teaching and practices in this book will prolong your life.

I wish the teaching and practices in this book will move your journey to immortality.

I am honored to share and serve.

I love my heart and soul
I love all humanity
Join hearts and souls together
Love, peace and harmony
Love, peace and harmony

Sacred Text of the Tao of Healing, Rejuvenation, Longevity, and Immortality

治疗返老还童长寿永生之道

Zhi Liao Fan Lao Huan Tong Chang Shou Yong Sheng Zhi Dao

(pronounced *jr lee-yow fahn lao hwahn tawng chahng sho yawng shung jr dow*)

1. 上乘妙道 **Shang Cheng Miao Dao** *shahng chung mee-yow dow*
   Highest and most profound Tao

2. 奥秘法门 **Ao Mi Fa Men** *ow mee fah mun*
   The sacred and profound method of entering the gate of rejuvenation, longevity, and immortality

3. 得到真传 **De Dao Zhen Chuan** *duh dow jun chwahn*
   Receive the true secret from the master

4. 修炼有望 **Xiu Lian You Wang** *sheo lyen yoe wahng*
   There is hope to accomplish your Xiu Lian journey

5. 金丹至宝 **Jin Dan Zhi Bao** *jeen dahn jr bao*
   Jin Dan is the highest treasure

6. 修炼根基 **Xiu Lian Gen Ji** *sheo lyen gun jee*
   The root and foundation of Xiu Lian

7. 长寿永生 **Chang Shou Yong Sheng** *chahng sho yawng shung*
Longevity and immortality

8. 不二法门 **Bu Er Fa Men** *boo ur fah mun*
No second way for fan lao huan tong, longevity, and immortality

9. 修炼目的 **Xiu Lian Mu Di** *sheo lyen moo dee*
The purpose of Xiu Lian

10. 祛病健身 **Qu Bing Jian Shen** *chü bing jyen shun*
Remove all sicknesses and strengthen the body

11. 开发智能 **Kai Fa Zhi Neng** *kye fah jr nung*
Develop intelligence

12. 转化人生 **Zhuan Hua Ren Sheng** *jwahn hwah wren shung*
Transform a human being's life

13. 与道合真 **Yu Dao He Zhen** *yü dow huh jun*
Meld with Tao

14. 超乎阴阳 **Chao Hu Yin Yang** *chow hoo yeen yahng*
Go beyond the yin yang world

15. 跳出三界 **Tiao Chu San Jie** *tee-yow choo sahn jyeh*
One is not controlled by the principles of Heaven, Mother Earth, and human beings

16. 无形无拘 **Wu Xing Wu Ju** *woo shing woo jü*
No shape, no control, no restraint from anything

17. 得天地精华 **De Tian Di Jing Hua**
Receive the essence of Heaven and Mother Earth
duh tyen dee jing hwah

18. 与日月同辉 **Yu Ri Yue Tong Hui**
Shine together with the sun and moon
yü rr yoo-eh tawng hway

19. 天地同存 **Tian Di Tong Cun**
Live together with Heaven and Mother Earth
tyen dee tawng tsoon

20. 长寿永生 **Chang Shou Yong Sheng**
Longevity and immortality
chahng sho yawng shung

21. 苦海众生 **Ku Hai Zhong Sheng**
Everyone and everything in the bitter sea, which is the yin yang world
koo hye jawng shung

22. 生老病死 **Sheng Lao Bing Si**
Birth, old age, sickness, death
shung lao bing sz

23. 因果缠身 **Yin Guo Chan Shen**
Karma controls you, no freedom
yeen gwaw chahn shun

24. 反复轮回 **Fan Fu Lun Hui**
Reincarnation continues
fahn foo lwun hway

25. 修仙成道 **Xiu Xian Cheng Dao**
Do Xiu Lian to become a saint in order to become Tao
sheo shyen chung dow

26. 脱出轮回 **Tuo Chu Lun Hui**
Get away from reincarnation
twaw choo lwun hway

27. 人仙地仙　**Ren Xian Di Xian**　*wren shyen dee shyen*
Human saints and Mother Earth saints

28. 上为天仙　**Shang Wei Tian Xian**　*shahng way tyen shyen*
Higher saints are Heaven saints

29. 道仙最上　**Dao Xian Zui Shang**　*dow shyen dzway shahng*
Highest saints are Tao saints

30. 与道合真　**Yu Dao He Zhen**　*yü dow huh jun*
Meld with Tao

31. 和谐宇宙　**He Xie Yu Zhou**　*huh shyeh yü joe*
Harmonize universes

32. 奥妙无穷　**Ao Miao Wu Qiong**　*ow mee-yow woo chyawng*
Profound and mysterious without ending

33. 祛病为先　**Qu Bing Wei Xian**　*chü bing way shyen*
First remove sickness

34. 修善断恶　**Xiu Shan Duan E**　*sheo shahn dwahn uh*
Be kind and stop all evil

35. 除贪嗔痴　**Chu Tan Chen Chi**　*choo tahn chun chee*
Remove greed, anger, and lack of wisdom

36. 修妙明心　**Xiu Miao Ming Xin**　*sheo mee-yow ming sheen*
Purify and enlighten your heart

37. 无私为公　**Wu Si Wei Gong**　*woo sz way gawng*
Serve others selflessly

38. 修炼法要　**Xiu Lian Fa Yao**　*sheo lyen fah yow*
Xiu Lian principles

39.	誓为公仆	**Shi Wei Gong Pu** Vow to be a servant	*shr way gawng poo*
40.	世代服务	**Shi Dai Fu Wu** Serve in all lifetimes	*shr dye foo woo*
41.	服务修炼	**Fu Wu Xiu Lian** Service Xiu Lian	*foo woo sheo lyen*
42.	上乘法门	**Shang Cheng Fa Men** The highest sacred Xiu Lian method	*shahng chung fah mun*
43.	祛除业障	**Qu Chu Ye Zhang** Remove bad karma	*chü choo yuh jahng*
44.	积功累德	**Ji Gong Lei De** Accumulate virtue	*jee gawng lay duh*
45.	元神真灵	**Yuan Shen Zhen Ling** Tao is profound and mysterious	*ywen shun jun ling*
46.	本在心中	**Ben Zai Xin Zhong** Yuan Shen is inside the heart	*bun dzye sheen jawng*
47.	不生不灭	**Bu Sheng Bu Mie** Yuan Shen is not born and does not die	*boo shung boo myeh*
48.	与道同存	**Yu Dao Tong Cun** Yuan Shen and Tao exist together	*yü dow tawng tsoon*
49.	人人皆有	**Ren Ren Jie You** Everyone has Yuan Shen	*wren wren jyeh yoe*
50.	为何不见	**Wei He Bu Jian** Why can't a human being see the Yuan Shen?	*way huh boo jyen*

51. 世俗污浊 **Shi Su Wu Zhuo** *shr soo woo jwaw*
All kinds of pollution
in society

52. 性窍不开 **Xing Qiao Bu Kai** *shing chee-yow boo*
The tunnel of the heart *kye*
is not open

53. 修炼三宝 **Xiu Lian San Bao** *sheo lyen sahn bao*
Practice with the three
treasures of jing qi shen

54. 污浊自化 **Wu Zhuo Zi Hua** *woo jwaw dz hwah*
All of the pollution
self-transforms

55. 明心见性 **Ming Xin Jian Xing** *ming sheen jyen*
Enlighten your heart to *shing*
see your Yuan Shen

56. 元神主宰 **Yuan Shen Zhu Zai** *ywen shun joo dzye*
Yuan Shen is in charge
for your life

57. 内三宝 **Nei San Bao** *nay sahn bao*
Three internal treasures

58. 精气神 **Jing Qi Shen** *jing chee shun*
Matter energy soul

59. 外三宝 **Wai San Bao** *wye sahn bao*
Three external
treasures

60. 耳目口 **Er Mu Kou** *ur moo koe*
Ears eyes mouth

61. 妄视神漏 **Wang Shi Shen Lou** *wahng shr shun loe*
See polluted things,
your soul could get lost

62. 妄听精漏 **Wang Ting Jing Lou** *wahng ting jing loe*
Hear polluted words,
lose your jing

63. 妄言气漏 **Wang Yan Qi Lou** *wahng yahn chee loe*
Speak polluted words,
lose your qi

64. 外三宝漏 **Wai San Bao Lou** *wye sahn bao loe*
Three external treasures
are leaking

65. 目不妄视 **Mu Bu Wang Shi** *moo boo wahng shr*
Do not see polluted things

66. 耳不妄听 **Er Bu Wang Ting** *ur boo wahng ting*
Do not hear polluted
words

67. 口不妄言 **Kou Bu Wang Yan** *koe boo wahng yahn*
Do not speak polluted
words

68. 外三宝 **Wai San Bao Bu Lou** *wye sahn bao boo loe*
不漏 Close your external
treasures, do not leak
your jing qi shen

69. 不视安神 **Bu Shi An Shen Yu Xin** *boo shr ahn shun yü sheen*
于心 Do not see polluted
things to make your
shen reside peacefully
in your heart

70. 不听蓄精 **Bu Ting Xu Jing Yu** *boo ting shü jing yü shun*
于肾 **Shen**
Do not hear polluted
words to increase the
jing in your kidneys

71. 不言孕气   **Bu Yan Yun Qi Dan**   *boo yahn yün chee*
    丹田   **Tian**   *dahn tyen*
             Do not speak polluted
             words to increase the qi
             in the Dan Tian

72. 内三宝   **Nei San Bao Zi He**   *nay sahn bao dz*
    自合   Three internal treasures   *huh*
             join together

73. 外不漏   **Wai Bu Lou**   *wye boo loe*
             Three external treasures
             do not leak

74. 内自合   **Nei Zi He**   *nay dz huh*
             Three internal treasures
             join as one

75. 通天达地   **Tong Tian Da Di**   *tawng tyen dah dee*
             Connect Heaven and
             Mother Earth

76. 逍遥道中   **Xiao Yao Dao Zhong**   *shee-yow yow dow*
             Meld with Tao to   *jawng*
             have true freedom
             and joy

77. 道生一   **Tao Sheng Yi**   *dow shung yee*
             Tao creates One

78. 天一真水   **Tian Yi Zhen Shui**   *tyen yee jun shway*
             Heaven's Oneness
             sacred liquid

79. 金津玉液   **Jin Jin Yu Ye**   *jeen jeen yü yuh*
             Gold liquid, jade liquid

80. 咽入丹田   **Yan Ru Dan Tian**   *yahn roo dahn tyen*
             Swallow into the Lower
             Dan Tian

81. 神气精
    合一
    Shen Qi Jing He Yi
    Join soul energy matter
    as one
    shun chee jing huh yee

82. 天地人
    合一
    Tian Di Ren He Yi
    Join Heaven, Mother
    Earth, human being
    as one
    tyen dee wren huh yee

83. 金丹炼成
    Jin Dan Lian Cheng
    Jin Dan is formed
    jeen dahn lyen chung

84. 抱元守一
    Bao Yuan Shou Yi
    Hold both hands in a
    circle below the navel
    and concentrate on
    the Jin Dan
    bao ywen sho yee

85. 人命如
    灯油
    Ren Ming Ru Deng You
    A human's life is like
    the oil in a lamp
    wren ming roo dung yoe

86. 耗尽命
    归西
    Hao Jin Ming Gui Xi
    When the oil is
    exhausted, life ends
    how jeen ming gway shee

87. 欲健康
    长寿
    **Yu Jian Kang Chang
    Shou**
    Wish to have good
    health and longevity
    yü jyen kahng chahng sho

88. 必添灯油
    Bi Tian Deng You
    Must add oil to the
    lamp
    bee tyen dung yoe

89. 天一真水
    Tian Yi Zhen Shui
    Heaven's Oneness sacred
    liquid
    tyen yee jun shway

90. 金津玉液 **Jin Jin Yu Ye**   *jeen jeen yü yuh*
Gold liquid, jade liquid

91. 犹如添油 **You Ru Tian You**   *yoe roo tyen yoe*
Is just like adding oil
to the lamp

92. 油灯常明 **You Deng Chang Ming**   *yoe dung chahng*
The oil is always   *ming*
burning

93. 修仙之道 **Xiu Xian Zhi Dao**   *sheo shyen jr dow*
The way to become a
saint

94. 性命双修 **Xing Ming Shuang Xiu**   *shing ming*
Do Xiu Lian to develop   *shwahng sheo*
intelligence and body

95. 明心见性 **Ming Xin Jian Xing**   *ming sheen jyen*
Enlighten your heart to   *shing*
see your Yuan Shen

96. 超凡入圣 **Chao Fan Ru Sheng**   *chow fahn roo*
Go beyond an ordinary   *shung*
being and become a
saint

97. 静定慧明 **Jing Ding Hui Ming**   *jing ding hway*
Quiet, still, intelligent,   *ming*
enlightened

98. 静中生定 **Jing Zhong Sheng Ding**   *jing jawng shung*
Stillness comes from   *ding*
quietness

99. 定中生慧 **Ding Zhong Sheng Hui**   *ding jawng shung*
Intelligence comes from   *hway*
stillness

100. 慧中生明 **Hui Zhong Sheng Ming**   *hway jawng shung*
Enlightenment comes   *ming*
from intelligence

101. 跳出欲海 **Tiao Chu Yu Hai**   *tee-yow choo yü hye*
Jump out from the sea
of desire

102. 服务万灵 **Fu Wu Wan Ling**   *foo woo wahn ling*
Serve all souls

103. 抱元守一 **Bao Yuan Shou Yi**   *bao ywen sho yee*
Hold both hands in a
circle below the navel
and concentrate on the
Jin Dan

104. 通体透明 **Tong Ti Tou Ming**   *tawng tee toe ming*
Whole body is
transparent

105. 人之初 **Ren Zhi Chu**   *wren jr choo*
Origin of a human being

106. 精卵化人 **Jing Luan Hua Ren**   *jing lwahn hwah*
Sperm and egg create a   *wren*
human being

107. 内肾先生 **Nei Shen Xian Sheng**   *nay shun shyen*
Kidneys are produced   *shung*
first

108. 渐长两目 **Jian Zhang Liang Mu**   *jyen jahng lyahng*
Gradually grow both   *moo*
eyes

109. 后生外肾 **Hou Sheng Wai Shen**   *hoe shung wye shun*
Grow the urinary system,
including sexual organs

110. 五脏六腑   **Wu Zang Liu Fu**   *woo dzahng leo foo*
Five yin and six yang
organs grow

111. 四肢百骸   **Si Zhi Bai Hai**   *sz jr bye hye*
Four extremities and
skeleton

112. 逐次而生   **Zhu Ci Er Sheng**   *joo tszz ur shung*
Gradually grow one
by one

113. 入静忘我   **Ru Jing Wang Wo**   *roo jing wahng*
Meditate deeply to go   *waw*
into stillness and forget
yourself

114. 刹那悟空   **Cha Na Wu Kong**   *chah nah woo*
Go suddenly into   *kawng*
emptiness and nothingness

115. 恍兮惚兮   **Huang Xi Hu Xi**   *hwahng shee hoo*
Spiritual images appear   *shee*
and disappear

116. 真气从之   **Zhen Qi Cong Zhi**   *jun chee tsawng jr*
Zhen qi, the qi of
Yuan Shen, is
produced

117. 真气升   **Zhen Qi Sheng Ni Wan**   *jun chee shung nee*
泥丸   Zhen qi rises to the Zu   *wahn*
Qiao

118. 化玉液   **Hua Yu Ye**   *hwah yü yuh*
Transforms to jade liquid

119. 入中元   **Ru Zhong Yuan**   *roo jawng ywen*
Swallow into the abdomen

120. 滋润丹田 **Zi Run Dan Tian** *dz rwun dahn tyen*
Nourish the Lower Dan
Tian

121. 何谓坤宫 **He Wei Kun Gong** *huh way kwun*
What is the Kun Temple? *gawng*

122. 肾上心下 **Shen Shang Xin Xia** *shun shahng sheen*
肝左脾右 **Gan Zuo Pi You** *shya gahn dzwaw*
Above the kidneys, *pee yoe*
below the heart, at the
left of the liver, at the
right of the spleen

123. 两肾之前 **Liang Shen Zhi Qian** *lyahng shun jr*
脐轮之后 **Qi Lun Zhi Hou** *chyen chee lwun jr*
In front of both kidneys, *hoe*
behind the navel

124. 中虚之窍 **Zhong Xu Zhi Qiao** *jawng shü jr chee-*
真气产地 **Zhen Qi Chan Di** *yow jun chee chahn*
The space in Kun Temple is *dee*
the land to produce zhen qi

125. 母气坤宫 **Mu Qi Kun Gong** *moo chee kwun*
Kun Temple carries *gawng*
Mother Earth's qi

126. 阴阳交媾 **Yin Yang Jiao Gou** *yeen yahng jee-yow*
Yin yang connect in *goe*
Kun Temple

127. 坤宫意守 **Kun Gong Yi Shou** *kwun gawng yee sho*
Concentrate on Kun
Temple

128. 真火自来 **Zhen Huo Zi Lai** *jun hwaw dz lye*
True fire from Yuan
Shen comes by itself

129. 产药之源 **Chan Yao Zhi Yuan**   *chahn yow jr ywen*
Kun Temple is the source
to create yao (the material
of Jin Dan)

130. 真气自归 **Zhen Qi Zi Gui**   *jun chee dz gway*
Zhen qi comes back to
Kun Temple

131. 天地未判 **Tian Di Wei Pan**   *tyen dee way pahn*
Before Heaven and
Mother Earth existed

132. 清浊未定 **Qing Zhuo Wei Ding**   *ching jwaw way ding*
Clean qi and disturbed
qi have not been
created

133. 混沌一气 **Hun Dun Yi Qi**   *hwun dwun yee chee*
There is only one qi,
which is Tao

134. 时至气化 **Shi Zhi Qi Hua**   *shr jr chee hwah*
When the time comes
for Tao to create

135. 清升为天 **Qing Sheng Wei Tian**   *ching shung way tyen*
Clean qi rises to form
Heaven

136. 浊降为地 **Zhuo Jiang Wei Di**   *jwaw jyahng way dee*
Disturbed qi falls
to form Mother Earth

137. 天地开化 **Tian Di Kai Hua**   *tyen dee kye hwah*
Heaven and Mother
Earth start

138. 地气上升 **Di Qi Shang Sheng**   *dee chee shahng shung*
Mother Earth's qi rises

139. 天气下降　**Tian Qi Xia Jiang**　　*tyen chee shya*
Heaven's qi falls　　　　　*jyahng*

140. 万物孕生　**Wan Wu Yun Sheng**　*wahn woo yün*
Countless things are　　　*shung*
produced

141. 抱元守一　**Bao Yuan Shou Yi**　*bao ywen sho yee*
Hold both hands in a
circle below the navel
and concentrate on the
Jin Dan

142. 真精自固　**Zhen Jing Zi Gu**　　*jun jing dz goo*
Real matter is produced
nonstop

143. 真气自在　**Zhen Qi Zi Zai**　　*jun chee dz dzye*
Real qi continues to be
produced

144. 真神自现　**Zhen Shen Zi Xian**　*jun shun dz shyen*
Yuan Shen appears and
is in charge

145. 抱元守一　**Bao Yuan Shou Yi**　*bao ywen sho yee*
Hold both hands in a
circle below the navel
and concentrate on the
Jin Dan

146. 三宝合一　**San Bao He Yi**　　*sahn bao huh yee*
Three treasures, *jing qi
shen,* join as one

147. 真气自行　**Zhen Qi Zi Xing**　*jun chee dz shing*
Real qi moves by itself

148. 真火自运　**Zhen Huo Zi Yun**　*jun hwaw dz yün*
Real fire moves by itself

149. 百日筑基 **Bai Ri Zhu Ji**   *bye rr joo jee*
Practice for one hundred days to build a foundation for your body

150. 补足漏体 **Bu Zu Lou Ti**   *boo dzoo loe tee*
Completely fulfill your leaky body

151. 抱元守一 **Bao Yuan Shou Yi**   *bao ywen sho yee*
Hold both hands in a circle below the navel and concentrate on the Jin Dan

152. 行走坐卧 **Xing Zou Zuo Wo**   *shing dzoe dzwaw*
不离这个 **Bu Li Zhe Ge**   *waw boo lee juh guh*
Walking, sitting, or lying down, always focus on Jin Dan

153. 千日文 **Qian Ri Wen Wu Huo**   *chyen rr wun woo*
武火 Practice gentle fire and *hwaw*
strong fire for one thousand days

154. 守一咽 **Shou Yi Yan Jin Ye**   *sho yee yahn jeen*
津液 Bao Yuan Shou Yi and *yuh*
swallow jade liquid

155. 性命双修 **Xing Ming Shuang Xiu**   *shing ming*
Do Xiu Lian to develop *shwahng sheo*
intelligence and body together

156. 明心见性 **Ming Xin Jian Xing**   *ming sheen jyen*
Enlighten your heart to *shing*
see your Yuan Shen

157. 穿岁月　**Chuan Sui Yue Wu Xing**　*chwahn sway yoo-*
　　　无形　　Time passes without　　*eh woo shing*
　　　　　　notice

158. 贯金墙　**Guan Jin Qiang Wu Ai**　*gwahn jeen chyahng*
　　　无碍　　Go through the golden　　*woo eye*
　　　　　　wall without blockage

159. 三千日抱　**San Qian Ri Bao Yuan**　*sahn chyen rr bao*
　　　元守一　　**Shou Yi**　　　　　*ywen sho yee*
　　　　　　Practice Bao Yuan Shou
　　　　　　Yi for three thousand days

160. 修得与道　**Xiu De Yu Dao He Zhen**　*sheo duh yü dow*
　　　合真　　Xiu Lian to meld with　　*huh jun*
　　　　　　Tao

161. 天地淡定　**Tian Di Dan Ding**　*tyen dee dahn ding*
　　　　　　Heaven and Mother Earth
　　　　　　have no emotion, no
　　　　　　desire, no attachment

162. 阳升阴降　**Yang Sheng Yin Jiang**　*yahng shung yeen*
　　　　　　Yang qi ascends, yin qi　　*jyahng*
　　　　　　descends

163. 日往月来　**Ri Wang Yue Lai**　*rr wahng yoo-eh lye*
　　　　　　Sun goes, moon comes

164. 万物昌盛　**Wan Wu Chang Sheng**　*wahn woo chahng*
　　　　　　All things flourish　　*shung*

165. 静中至寂　**Jing Zhong Zhi Ji**　*jing jawng jr jee*
　　　　　　Meditate to extreme
　　　　　　quietness where you
　　　　　　forget yourself

166. 神气相抱　**Shen Qi Xiang Bao**　*shun chee shyahng*
　　　　　　Yuan Shen and yuan qi　　*bao*
　　　　　　hold together

167. 气结精凝 **Qi Jie Jing Ning**   *chee jyeh jing ning*
Yuan qi and yuan jing
accumulate and concentrate

168. 结成金丹 **Jie Cheng Jin Dan**   *jyeh chung jeen*
Jing Qi Shen He Yi to   *dahn*
form Jin Dan

169. 丹田温暖 **Dan Tian Wen Nuan**   *dahn tyen wun*
Dan Tian area is warm   *nwahn*

170. 三关升降 **San Guan Sheng Jiang**   *sahn gwahn shung*
Energy ascends and   *jyahng*
descends in three gates

171. 上下冲合 **Shang Xia Chong He**   *shung shya chawng*
Di qi ascends, tian qi   *huh*
descends; yang qi and
yin qi collide and join
in order to balance

172. 醍醐灌顶 **Ti Hu Guan Ding**   *tee hoo gwahn ding*
Suddenly achieve
enlightenment

173. 甘露洒心 **Gan Lu Sa Xin**   *gahn loo sah sheen*
Dew sprays to the heart

174. 玄天妙音 **Xuan Tian Miao Yin**   *shwen tyen mee-*
Hear Heaven's profound   *yow yeen*
sounds

175. 耳中常闻 **Er Zhong Chang Wen**   *ur jawng chahng*
Often hear Heaven's   *wun*
music and voices

176. 至宝玄珠 **Zhi Bao Xuan Zhu**   *jr bao shwen joo*
Jing Qi Shen He Yi
forms the initial Jin
Dan, just like a pearl

177. 真真景象 **Zhen Zhen Jing Xiang** *jun jun jing*
See the real images *shyahng*

178. 永存道中 **Yong Cun Dao Zhong** *yawng tsoon dow*
These images always *jawng*
exist within Tao

179. 犹如灯光 **You Ru Deng Guang** *yoe roo dung*
Just like the lamp *gwahng*
light

180. 长明不熄 **Chang Ming Bu Xi** *chahng ming boo*
The light always shines *shee*
continuously

181. 先天真阳 **Xian Tian Zhen Yang** *shyen tyen jun*
Innate real yang is *yahng*
Yuan Shen

182. 后天真阴 **Hou Tian Zhen Yin** *hoe tyen jun yeen*
After birth, real yin is
Shi Shen plus the body

183. 两气氤氲 **Liang Qi Yin Yun** *lyahng chee yeen*
Yin yang unification *yün*

184. 结成仙胎 **Jie Cheng Xian Tai** *jyeh chung shyen tye*
Form a saint baby

185. 仙胎道胎 **Xian Tai Dao Tai** *shyen tye dow tye*
Saint baby and Tao
Baby

186. 道乳哺养 **Dao Ru Pu Yang** *dow roo poo yahng*
Tao milk feeds the saint
baby and Tao Baby

187. 成长壮大 **Cheng Zhang** *chung jahng*
Zhuang Da *jwahng dah*
Baby grows bigger and
stronger

188. 提高等级 **Ti Gao Deng Ji** *tee gao dung jee*
Your joined Yuan Shen
and Shi Shen are uplifted

189. 十月功成 **Shi Yue Gong Cheng** *shr yoo-eh gawng*
Saint baby or Tao Baby *chung*
takes ten months to grow

190. 脱胎飞升 **Tuo Tai Fei Sheng** *twaw tye fay shung*
Soul baby travels

191. 超乎阴阳 **Chao Hu Yin Yang** *chow hoo yeen*
Go beyond yin yang *yahng*
laws

192. 无形无拘 **Wu Xing Wu Ju** *woo shing woo jü*
No shape, no control, no
restraint from anything

193. 通身浊阴 **Tong Shen Zhuo Yin** *tawng shun jwaw*
Whole body is *yeen*
disturbed yin after birth

194. 尽化纯阳 **Jin Hua Chun Yang** *jeen hwah chwun*
Whole body transforms *yahng*
to pure yang, which is
your Yuan Shen

195. 跳出樊笼 **Tiao Chu Fan Long** *tee-yow choo fahn*
Jump out from the *long*
control of yin, yang,
and San Jie

196. 逍遥无穷 **Xiao Yao Wu Qiong** *shee-yow yow woo*
Freedom and joy are *chyawng*
endless within Tao

197. 炼己炼心 **Lian Ji Lian Xin** *lyen jee lyen sheen*
Xiu Lian for your body
and heart

198. 炼心不动 **Lian Xin Bu Dong** *lyen sheen boo dawng*
The Xiu Lian heart cannot be shaken

199. 离宫修定 **Li Gong Xiu Ding** *lee gawng sheo ding*
Xiu Lian for the heart leads to stillness

200. 定则神和 **Ding Ze Shen He** *ding dzuh shun huh*
Stillness leads to harmonization of Yuan Shen and Shi Shen

201. 和则气安 **He Ze Qi An** *huh dzuh chee ahn*
Harmonization of Yuan Shen and Shi Shen will balance and increase qi and bring true peace in the heart

202. 安则精满 **An Ze Jing Man** *ahn dzuh jing mahn*
Sufficient qi and a peaceful heart will create full jing

203. 满则丹结 **Man Ze Dan Jie** *mahn dzuh dahn jyeh*
Sufficient jing accumulates to form the Jin Dan

204. 结则造化 **Jie Ze Zao Hua** *jyeh dzuh dzow hwah*
Jin Dan forms and follows nature's way

205. 玄珠成象 **Xuan Zhu Cheng Xiang** *shwen joo chung shyahng*
Initial stage of Jin Dan formation like a pearl

206. 太乙含真 **Tai Yi Han Zhen** *tye yee hahn jun*
Everyone has the real
yang of Tao, which is
Yuan Shen

207. 津液炼形 **Jin Ye Lian Xing** *jeen yuh lyen shing*
Tian Yi Zhen Shui and
Jin Jin Yu Ye transform
your body

208. 神形俱妙 **Shen Xing Ju Miao** *shun shing jü mee-*
Xing Gong and Ming *yow*
Gong Xiu Lian have
been accomplished

209. 奋勇精进 **Fen Yong Jing Jin** *fun yawng jing jeen*
Try your greatest best
to do Xiu Lian

210. 舍生忘死 **She Sheng Wang Si** *shuh shung*
Give your life to do *wahng sz*
Xiu Lian

211. 心死神活 **Xin Si Shen Huo** *sheen sz shun hwaw*
Shi Shen gives up the
position, Yuan Shen is
in charge

212. 方可修成 **Fang Ke Xiu Cheng** *fahng kuh sheo*
Xiu Lian can reach Tao *chung*

213. 灵脑身 **Ling Nao Shen Yuan** *ling now shun ywen*
圆满 **Man** *mahn*
Soul mind body
enlightenment

214. 金丹道 **Jin Dan Dao Ti Sheng** *jeen dahn dow tee*
体生 Jin Dan and Tao body *shung*
are produced

215. 海枯石烂	**Hai Ku Shi Lan** The seas run dry and the rocks crumble	*hye koo shr lahn*
216. 道体长存	**Dao Ti Chang Cun** The Tao body lives forever	*dow tee* *chahng tsoon*
217. 阴阳归道	**Yin Yang Gui Dao** Yin yang returns to Tao	*yeen yahng gway* *dow*
218. 与道合真	**Yu Dao He Zhen** Meld with Tao	*yü dow huh jun*
219. 道法自然	**Dao Fa Zi Ran** Follows nature's way	*dow fah dz rahn*
220. 神哉妙哉	**Shen Zai Miao Zai** Miraculous and profound	*shun dzye mee-yow* *dzye*

Sacred and Secret Wisdom, Knowledge, and Practical Techniques of the Tao of Healing, Rejuvenation, Longevity, and Immortality

1
上乘妙道
Shang Cheng Miao Dao

Highest and most profound Tao

"Shang cheng" (pronounced *shahng chung*) means *highest*. "Miao" (pronounced *mee-yow*) means *profound*. Dao (or Tao) is bigger than biggest and smaller than smallest. Tao is The Way. "Shang cheng miao Dao" means *the highest and most profound Tao*.

Since creation, there have been countless ways to study and

practice Tao in order to reach Tao. It is very difficult for the Tao practitioner to find the perfect and best way to study and practice Tao.

What is the best way? The best way is the true way. The best way is the simplest way. The best way is in everyone's heart. You will learn this best, true, and simplest way in the following sacred phrases.

There are countless secrets and wisdom on Mother Earth and in all universes. There is only one absolute truth. Secrets and wisdom are relative. Absolute truth is not relative. If we understand this absolute truth, it will bring humanity good health, true happiness, smooth success in relationships and business, breakthrough development in science and every field, rejuvenation, longevity, and immortality.

Millions of people in history are searching and dreaming for this absolute truth. This absolute truth is shang cheng miao Dao, the highest, most profound, and best Tao.

2

奥秘法门

Ao Mi Fa Men

The sacred and profound method of entering the gate of rejuvenation, longevity, and immortality

"Ao" (pronounced *ow*) means *profound*. "Fa" (pronounced *fah*) means *method*. "Men" (pronounced *mun*) means *gate*. "Ao mi fa men" means *the sacred and profound method of entering the gate of rejuvenation, longevity, and immortality*.

There are countless methods in history for rejuvenation, fan lao huan tong, longevity, and immortality. The founder of Buddhism, Shi Jia Mo Ni Fo, taught 84,000 methods for spiritual practice. Different methods are suitable for different types of people.

In history, millions of spiritual beings have searched for the way of rejuvenation, longevity, and immortality. Millions of people who were not on the spiritual journey have also searched for rejuvenation and longevity. But it is very difficult to find the true way to reach fan lao huan tong (complete rejuvenation), longevity, and immortality. The Tao of Healing, Rejuvenation, Longevity, and Immortality is the true way that will be shared with you shortly in this book.

3
得到真传
De Dao Zhen Chuan

Receive the true secret from the master

"De dao" means *receive*. (This word "dao" is not the same "Dao" as the subject of this book.) "Zhen" means *true*. "Chuan" means *deliver*. "De dao zhen chuan" (pronounced *duh dow jun chwahn*) means *receive the true delivery or secret from the master*.

Millions of people in history have studied Tao and want to reach Tao. It is very difficult to receive the true secrets. Generally speaking, a true master does not deliver the true secrets easily. The master could test a student for thirty years or more before he is ready to deliver the true secrets. Some masters only deliver the true and top secrets just before they die. Sometimes the master dies suddenly and the true secrets are lost. This is such a pity.

I am extremely grateful to Tao and the Divine. They have given me these sacred and secret teachings directly. I am honored to deliver these top secrets to you and to humanity. You may have never met me. You may be reading this for the first time. I am delivering the top secrets to you. You do not need to wait thirty years or more to receive the true sacred and secret teaching from a master. I am honored to deliver these true secrets and, especially, the absolute truth.

Several years ago I met a renowned Indian guru in the San Francisco Bay Area with two world-renowned authors and teachers. I also met a doctor in this meeting. This doctor told me he had quit his job to follow this Indian guru. This guru had a special way to offer healing. He gently touched people's backs with his hands. People received incredible healing.

This doctor wondered how his guru and teacher did this healing. The teacher never explained the method to him. He really wanted to learn the technique, but he was a little afraid to ask the teacher how to do it. In fact, he had asked his teacher a few times but never got any answer. He tried to wait patiently for his teacher to teach him, but he was really concerned and frustrated.

I asked the doctor, "How long have you followed your teacher?" He said, "I quit my job and went to India. I have served my teacher for three years in whatever way my teacher needed. I am just like a servant."

I replied, "Three years are not enough. You have not totally touched your teacher's heart. Your teacher is not ready to pass the secrets to you yet. He may continue to test you. Be patient. If you really respect and admire your teacher's powers and abilities, you have to be patient."

I then shared my personal story with this doctor. When I followed one of my major masters, I had to wait for twelve years to learn the truth of healing from him. At the end of these twelve years, this master told me, "Zhi Gang, I treated you very coldly for twelve years. Sometimes you were hurt because of the way I treated you. You felt I did not care about you. That was my test to you."

My master continued, "I tested your loyalty. I tested your kind heart. I tested your love, care, and compassion. I tested your persistence and determination. I tested you to see if you could carry big responsibilities to offer teaching to humanity about healing, rejuvenation, and longevity. You passed the test. Therefore, I am teaching you the true secret for healing now."

I bowed down to the floor right away. Tears flowed down my face. I was deeply moved and touched. That was my twelve years of persistence in wanting to learn the truth of healing.

There are many profound stories in history about how much a student or disciple wants to learn the truth from a master. One famous example involves the founder of Zen Buddhism, Bodhidharma, known as Daruma in Japan. He traveled to China, where he met the emperor. The emperor told him, "I have built thousands of temples and treated monks very well. Have I gained lots of virtue?" Bodhidharma replied, "No, because your intention was selfish." The emperor was very upset and refused to listen to anything else Bodhidharma had to say.

Bodhidharma left and went to the Shaolin Temple. He lived in a nearby cave where he sat facing a wall for nine years. This is a renowned story in Buddhist history.

Bodhidharma left us many profound teachings. One of his students was Huike, who wanted to become Bodhidharma's disciple. In ancient times, to be a disciple was a great honor. To be a disciple is to have the honor of carrying the teacher's teaching totally, honestly, and persistently. It has never been easy to be accepted as a disciple of a true master.

Bodhidharma asked Huike, "How can you show that you

truly want to learn my teachings?" Huike then cut off his own arm and said, "This is a token of my sincerity that I want to be your disciple to learn from you." Upon seeing this demonstration, Bodhidharma made Huike a disciple and, later, the second-generation Zen Buddhism lineage holder.

This profound story tells us that to learn the truth is not easy. Many masters have given their lives in a search for the truth. Many serious spiritual seekers have followed a master for their entire lives and have still not learned the truth. The master who holds the truth must be willing to deliver the truth to the student. That is how a spiritual seeker learns the truth. There are many stories like this.

I am a servant of humanity and all souls. I have learned from many masters in the physical world. I have learned from many saints in the spiritual world through soul communication. I have learned directly from the Divine and Tao through soul communication.

I am extremely honored to deliver the truth in this book.

This is not simple truth.

This is Da Tao, *The Big Way*. This absolute truth is to lead the Tao practitioner to reach fan lao huan tong (transform old age to the health and purity of the baby state). This is not easy. Fan lao huan tong is a dream state in traditional Tao practice. Not many people have reached fan lao huan tong. In order to reach fan lao huan tong, you must heal your spiritual, mental, emotional, and physical bodies completely.

This absolute truth is to bring you a long, long life and transform your relationships, finances, and every aspect of life.

This absolute truth is to lead you to immortality. It is very difficult to accomplish, but it is possible.

I am honored to deliver the wisdom that I have learned directly from the Divine and Tao. I have learned much from my true masters in the physical world and the spiritual world. I am honored to deliver this absolute truth.

You and every serious spiritual seeker must practice hard after you learn this absolute truth.

I wish for you to succeed.

I wish for you to reach fan lao huan tong.

I wish for you to transform every aspect of your life.

I wish for you to enlighten your soul, heart, mind, and body.

I wish for you to have a long, long life.

I wish for you to move to immortality.

To move to immortality is to meld with Tao.

I wish for you to meld with Tao.

4

修炼有望

Xiu Lian You Wang

There is hope to accomplish your Xiu Lian journey

"Xiu" means *purification*. "Lian" means *practice*. "Xiu lian" means *the totality of one's spiritual journey*. "You" means *has*. "Wang" means *hope*. "Xiu lian you wang" (pronounced *sheo lyen yoe wahng*) connects with the previous sacred phrase, de dao zhen chuan. "Xiu lian you wang" means *if you receive the true delivery from a true master, then you have hope to accomplish your Xiu Lian journey*. To accomplish your Xiu Lian journey is to meld with Tao.

Jin Dan Da Tao Xiu Lian and the Tao of Healing, Rejuvenation, Longevity, and Immortality is Xiu Lian practice to meld with Tao.

5

金丹至宝

Jin Dan Zhi Bao

Jin Dan is the highest treasure

"Jin" means *gold*. "Dan" means *light ball*. "Zhi" means *highest*. "Bao" means *treasure*. "Jin dan zhi bao" (pronounced *jeen dahn jr bao* [rhymes with *now*]) means *Jin Dan is the highest treasure.*

Jin Dan is so important for every aspect of life. There are not enough words to explain the importance of the Jin Dan for healing, prevention of sickness, purification and rejuvenation of the soul, heart, mind, and body, prolonging life, and transforming relationships, finances, and every aspect of life, as well as for enlightening the soul, heart, mind, and body. Jin Dan can help humanity pass through this difficult time of transition and purification on Mother Earth. Jin Dan can help humanity achieve good health, happiness, success, fan lao huan tong, and longevity, and move a human being to immortality.

In the previous chapter, Jin Dan Da Tao Xiu Lian, Jin Dan Da Tao has explained the importance and power of forming a Jin Dan. Jin Dan is the highest treasure in one's Xiu Lian journey.

Jin Dan Da Tao Xiu Lian is the absolute truth.

Jin Dan Da Tao Xiu Lian is to meld with Tao.

6

修炼根基

Xiu Lian Gen Ji

The root and foundation of Xiu Lian

"Xiu" means *purification*. "Lian" means *practice*. "Gen" means *root*. "Ji" means *foundation*. "Xiu lian gen ji" (pronounced *sheo lyen gun jee*) means *the root and foundation of Xiu Lian*.

This sacred phrase is directly connected with the previous sacred phrase, jin dan zhi bao. *Xiu lian gen ji* says that Jin Dan is the highest treasure *and* the root and foundation of Xiu Lian.

There are countless Xiu Lian methods. Jin Dan Da Tao Xiu Lian is the key.

Why?

You must know the importance and power of Jin Dan Da Tao Xiu Lian.

You must know that Jin Dan Da Tao Xiu Lian is the highest Xiu Lian you can practice in your entire life.

You must know that Jin Dan Da Tao Xiu Lian is the absolute truth.

You must know that Jin Dan Da Tao Xiu Lian is the fastest way and the direct way to reach Tao.

You must spend a lot of time reading and doing the practices, including the chanting and meditations in chapter 2, "Jin Dan Da Tao Xiu Lian," again and again.

You must spend a lot of time in your life to practice repeatedly. Every time you practice Jin Dan Da Tao Xiu Lian, you will continue to form your Jin Dan little by little. The more you practice, the faster you will form your complete Jin Dan. If you can form your complete Jin Dan, you will have melded with Tao.

There are no words that can explain enough the importance of Jin Dan Da Tao Xiu Lian.

Jin Dan Da Tao is the highest philosophy. It is also the highest practical treasure. To do Jin Dan Da Tao Xiu Lian is to reach soul mind body enlightenment. To do Jin Dan Da Tao Xiu Lian is to heal, prevent sickness, rejuvenate in order to reach fan lao huan tong, transform relationships, finances, and every aspect of life, have a long, long life, and, finally, move to immortality. Jin Dan Da Tao is the root, foundation, and final destiny of Xiu Lian.

I cannot emphasize enough that to have a complete Jin Dan is to meld with Tao.

To meld with Tao means you are Tao.

Tao is you.

7
长寿永生
Chang Shou Yong Sheng

Longevity and immortality

"Chang shou" means *longevity*. "Yong sheng" means *live forever*. "Chang shou yong sheng" (pronounced *chahng sho yawng shung*) means *longevity and immortality*.

Jin Dan Da Tao is the Tao of longevity and immortality. To study and practice Jin Dan Da Tao Xiu Lian is to reach longevity and immortality. Chapter 2 reveals the highest secrets of Jin Dan Da Tao Xiu Lian.

Now let us spend five minutes to practice Jin Dan Da Tao Xiu Lian one more time.

Apply the Four Power Techniques to prolong your life. This practice is a practice for your whole life. I emphasize this to remind you that you have to do Jin Dan Da Tao Xiu Lian again and again.

Body Power. Sit up straight. Put the tip of your tongue as close as you can to the roof of your mouth without touching. Use the Jin Dan Da Tao Xiu Lian Hand Position. See figure 1 on page 42.

Soul Power. Say *hello:*

> *Dear Tao,*
> *Dear Divine,*
> *Dear soul mind body of countless universes,*
> *Dear soul mind body of countless galaxies, stars, and planets,*
> *Dear soul mind body of Mother Earth,*
> *Dear soul mind body of all humanity,*
> *Dear soul mind body of all animals,*
> *Dear soul mind body of everything in countless planets, stars, galaxies, and universes,*
> *Dear soul mind body of all spiritual fathers and mothers in all layers of Heaven and on Mother Earth,*
> *I love you, honor you, and appreciate you.*
> *Please come to my Jin Dan area to form my Jin Dan, Heaven's Jin Dan, Mother Earth's Jin Dan, humanity's Jin Dan, countless planets', stars', and galaxies' Jin Dan, and countless universes' Jin Dan.*
> *Finally, form Tao Dan.*
> *I am extremely honored and blessed to do this practice to form all kinds of Jin Dan as an unconditional universal servant.*
> *Transform my body to reach fan lao huan tong.*
> *Prolong my life.*
> *Thank you. Thank you. Thank you.*

Mind Power. Visualize the Jin Dan forming in your lower abdomen. It is gathering the *jing qi shen xu dao* of Heaven, Mother Earth, humanity, wan wu (*all things*), including countless planets, stars, and galaxies, and all universes. Focus on the Jin Dan area to observe the countless souls you have invoked. To form the Jin Dan is to prolong your life.

Sound Power. Chant in Chinese, silently or aloud:

精

Jing

Matter

天之精	**Tian Zhi Jing** Heaven's jing	*tyen jr jing*
地之精	**Di Zhi Jing** Mother Earth's jing	*dee jr jing*
人之精	**Ren Zhi Jing** Humanity's jing	*wren jr jing*
天地人之精	**Tian Di Ren Zhi Jing** Heaven's, Mother Earth's, humanity's jing	*tyen dee wren jr jing*
万物之精	**Wan Wu Zhi Jing** Jing of countless planets, stars, and galaxies	*wahn woo jr jing*
全宇宙之精	**Quan Yu Zhou Zhi Jing** Jing of countless universes	*chwen yü joe jr jing*
皆是道之精	**Jie Shi Dao Zhi Jing** All are Tao's jing	*jyeh shr dow jr jing*

气

Qi

Energy

天之气	**Tian Zhi Qi**	*tyen jr chee*
	Heaven's qi	
地之气	**Di Zhi Qi**	*dee jr chee*
	Mother Earth's qi	
人之气	**Ren Zhi Qi**	*wren jr chee*
	Humanity's qi	
天地人之气	**Tian Di Ren Zhi Qi**	*tyen dee wren jr chee*
	Heaven's, Mother Earth's, humanity's qi	
万物之气	**Wan Wu Zhi Qi**	*wahn woo jr chee*
	Qi of countless planets, stars, and galaxies	
全宇宙之气	**Quan Yu Zhou Zhi Qi**	*chwen yü joe jr chee*
	Qi of countless universes	
皆是道之气	**Jie Shi Dao Zhi Qi**	*jyeh shr dow jr chee*
	All are Tao's qi	

神

Shen

Soul

天之神	**Tian Zhi Shen**	*tyen jr shun*
	Heaven's soul	
地之神	**Di Zhi Shen**	*dee jr shun*
	Mother Earth's soul	
人之神	**Ren Zhi Shen**	*wren jr shun*
	Humanity's soul	

天地人之神 **Tian Di Ren Zhi Shen** *tyen dee wren jr shun*
Heaven's, Mother Earth's,
humanity's souls

万物之神 **Wan Wu Zhi Shen** *wahn woo jr shun*
Souls of countless planets,
stars, and galaxies

全宇宙之神 **Quan Yu Zhou Zhi Shen** *chwen yü joe jr shun*
Souls of countless universes

皆是道之神 **Jie Shi Dao Zhi Shen** *jyeh shr dow jr shun*
All are Tao's soul

虚
Xu

Emptiness

天之虚 **Tian Zhi Xu** *tyen jr shü*
Heaven's emptiness

地之虚 **Di Zhi Xu** *dee jr shü*
Mother Earth's emptiness

人之虚 **Ren Zhi Xu** *wren jr shü*
Humanity's emptiness

天地人之虚 **Tian Di Ren Zhi Xu** *tyen dee wren jr shü*
Heaven's, Mother Earth's,
humanity's emptiness

万物之虚 **Wan Wu Zhi Xu** *wahn woo jr shü*
Emptiness of countless
planets, stars, and galaxies

全宇宙之虚 **Quan Yu Zhou Zhi Xu** *chwen yü joe jr shü*
Emptiness of countless
universes

皆是道之虚 **Jie Shi Dao Zhi Xu** *jyeh shr dow jr shü*
All are Tao's emptiness

道
Dao

Complete Emptiness

天之道	**Tian Zhi Dao** Heaven's Tao	*tyen jr dow*
地之道	**Di Zhi Dao** Mother Earth's Tao	*dee jr dow*
人之道	**Ren Zhi Dao** Humanity's Tao	*wren jr dow*
天地人之道	**Tian Di Ren Zhi Dao** Heaven's, Mother Earth's, humanity's Tao	*tyen dee wren jr dow*
万物之道	**Wan Wu Zhi Dao** Tao of countless planets, stars, and galaxies	*wahn woo jr dow*
全宇宙之道	**Quan Yu Zhou Zhi Dao** Tao of countless universes	*chwen yü joe jr dow*
皆是大道	**Jie Shi Da Dao** All are Big Tao	*jyeh shr dah dow*

精气神虚道合一
Jing Qi Shen Xu Dao He Yi

Matter Energy Soul Emptiness Tao Join as One

天精气神虚 道合一	**Tian Jing Qi Shen Xu** **Dao He Yi** Heaven's matter energy soul emptiness Tao join as one	*tyen jing chee shun* *shü dow huh yee*

地精气神虚 道合一	**Di Jing Qi Shen Xu** **Dao He Yi** Mother Earth's matter energy soul emptiness Tao join as one	*dee jing chee shun* *shü dow huh yee*
人精气神虚 道合一	**Ren Jing Qi Shen Xu** **Dao He Yi** Humanity's matter energy soul emptiness Tao join as one	*wren jing chee* *shun shü dow* *huh yee*
天地人精气 神虚道合一	**Tian Di Ren Jing Qi** **Shen Xu Dao He Yi** Heaven's, Mother Earth's, humanity's matter energy soul emptiness Tao join as one	*tyen dee wren jing* *chee shun shü dow* *huh yee*
万物精气神 虚道合一	**Wan Wu Jing Qi Shen** **Xu Dao He Yi** Matter energy soul emptiness Tao of countless planets, stars, and galaxies join as one	*wahn woo jing chee* *shun shü dow huh yee*
全宇宙精气 神虚道合一	**Quan Yu Zhou Jing Qi** **Shen Xu Dao He Yi** Matter energy soul emptiness Tao of countless universes join as one	*chwen yü joe jing chee* *shun shü dow huh yee*
皆是与道 合一	**Jie Shi Yu Dao He Yi** All are joining as one with Tao	*jyeh shr yü dow huh* *yee*

金丹
Jin Dan

Golden Light Ball

天金丹   **Tian Jin Dan**   *tyen jeen dahn*
Heaven's Jin Dan

地金丹   **Di Jin Dan**   *dee jeen dahn*
Mother Earth's Jin Dan

人金丹   **Ren Jin Dan**   *wren jeen dahn*
Humanity's Jin Dan

天地人金丹   **Tian Di Ren Jin Dan**   *tyen dee wren jeen*
Heaven's, Mother Earth's,   *dahn*
humanity's Jin Dan

万物金丹   **Wan Wu Jin Dan**   *wahn woo jeen dahn*
Jin Dan of countless
planets, stars, and galaxies

全宇宙金丹   **Quan Yu Zhou Jin Dan**   *chwen yü joe jeen*
Jin Dan of countless   *dahn*
universes

皆是道金丹   **Jie Shi Dao Jin Dan**   *jyeh shr dow jeen*
All are Tao's Jin Dan   *dahn*

与道合真
Yu Dao He Zhen

Meld with Tao

天与道合真   **Tian Yu Dao He Zhen**   *tyen yü dow huh jun*
Heaven melds with Tao

地与道合真   **Di Yu Dao He Zhen**   *dee yü dow huh jun*
Mother Earth melds
with Tao

人与道合真	**Ren Yu Dao He Zhen**	*wren yü dow huh jun*
	Humanity melds with Tao	
天地人与道合真	**Tian Di Ren Yu Dao He Zhen**	*tyen dee wren yü dow huh jun*
	Heaven, Mother Earth, humanity meld with Tao	
万物与道合真	**Wan Wu Yu Dao He Zhen**	*wahn woo yü dow huh jun*
	Countless planets, stars, and galaxies meld with Tao	
全宇宙与道合真	**Quan Yu Zhou Yu Dao He Zhen**	*chwen yü joe yü dow huh jun*
	Countless universes meld with Tao	
皆是与道合真	**Jie Shi Yu Dao He Zhen**	*jyeh shr yü dow huh jun*
	All meld with Tao	

This practice is the homework for your life. There is no time limit. Do the practice right away whenever you are in any of the following conditions:

- you are tired
- you have pain
- you have any emotional imbalance
- you have mental confusion
- you have any unhealthy condition
- you want to open your heart and soul
- you want to boost your energy, stamina, vitality, and immunity

- you want to heal any sickness
- you do *not* suffer from any of the above conditions
- you want to prevent sickness in your spiritual, mental, emotional, or physical body
- you want to rejuvenate your soul, heart, mind, and body
- you want to prolong your life
- you want to purify your soul, heart, mind, and body
- you want to enlighten your soul, heart, mind, and body
- you want to transform your relationships
- you want to transform your finances
- you want to move to immortality

Then you can do Jin Dan Da Tao Xiu Lian.

The more you do it, the more benefits you will receive.

The more you do it, the more you will want to do it.

Why? Because the results will inspire you to do more.

8
不二法门
Bu Er Fa Men

No second way for fan lao huan tong, longevity, and immortality

"Bu" means *no*. "Er" means *two* or *second*. "Fa" means *method*. "Men" means *gate*. "Bu er fa men" (pronounced *boo ur fah mun*) means there is *no second way for fan lao huan tong, longevity, and immortality.*

This phrase connects with and completes the three previous phrases:

Jin Dan Zhi Bao   *Jin Dan is the highest treasure*
Xiu Lian Gen Ji   *The root and foundation of Xiu Lian*
Chang Shou Yong Sheng *Longevity and immortality*

Together with Bu Er Fa Men, these phrases tell us that Jin Dan is the highest treasure in Xiu Lian, Jin Dan Da Tao Xiu Lian is the root and foundation of Xiu Lian, and Jin Dan Da Tao is the only way for fan lao huan tong, longevity, and immortality.

Jin Dan is *jing qi shen he yi* (matter, energy, and souls join as one). A normal human being does not have a Jin Dan. One must practice in order to join *jing qi shen* as one. To join jing qi shen as one is not enough. One must join the *jing qi shen* of Heaven, Mother Earth, humanity, and countless planets, stars, galaxies, and universes to complete the Jin Dan. To form this kind of Jin Dan is to form Tao Dan.

In *Tao I: The Way of All Life*, I shared how to form your Jin Dan. Chapter 3 of that book, "Jin Dan—Tao Practice in Daily Life," shares the sacred and secret wisdom, knowledge, and practical techniques to form your Jin Dan, which is a human Jin Dan.

In chapter 2 of this book, "Jin Dan Da Tao Xiu Lian," I share with you and humanity how to form Tao Dan.

Ancient Tao practitioners took thirty to fifty years, and even an entire lifetime, of dedicated practice to form their Jin Dans. In 2009, the Divine started to offer Divine Jin Dan Soul Mind Body Transplants to ready ones. A few years later, Tao will offer Tao Jin Dan Soul Mind Body Transplants to students in my ten-year Tao training program. These Jin Dan treasures are extremely sacred and profound. I only can offer these highest treasures from the Divine and Tao to Tao students in my ten-day (or longer) Tao Retreats.

I started my ten-year Tao training program with my first Tao Retreat in Ramsau, Austria, in May 2010. Every year, people will have the opportunity to begin the first year of training. Every year, advanced Tao students and practitioners will move further and further. *Tao I: The Way of All Life* is the foundation for your Tao journey. My Tao teaching is not traditional Taoism. My Tao training is training that comes directly from the Divine and Tao.

If you want to heal yourself, if you want to rejuvenate and reach fan lao huan tong, if you want longevity, if you want to move in the direction of immortality, read *Tao I* as soon as possible in addition to this book.

Now, Tao has created Jin Dan Da Tao training. For thousands of years, millions of Tao practitioners have dreamed of forming a Jin Dan to reach fan lao huan tong and longevity. To reach fan lao huan tong is not easy at all.

Jin Dan is the only way to reach fan lao huan tong, which is to transform old age to the health and purity of the baby state. Think about it. There are billions of people on Mother Earth, but how many people can transform their old age to the baby state? It is very rare.

Therefore, Jin Dan Da Tao is the highest treasure to guide everyone who is dreaming of reaching fan lao huan tong. The secret is released now. To have a long, long life is more difficult. To reach immortality . . . nobody has seen that. People think immortality is impossible. You may not know that immortals do not want to tell anyone because people will not believe them. If they tell the truth, people will think they are crazy.

Immortals have the highest wisdom. They are the most humble servants. Even if you find out that they are special, they may not admit it. They appear to be so young that you would never imagine that they have lived such a long, long life.

Those who reach immortality are completely humble servants. They do not have even a thought of a "show off" attitude. By the time they reach immortality, they have gained extraordinary abilities. They have melded with Tao. They can disappear in front of your eyes. They can move instantly from one place to another. They can go through walls.

Many of you have heard or read fairy tales about extraordinary beings. For example, the Count of St. Germain was known as the "Wonderman of Europe" in the 1700s. His appearance did not change for one hundred years. He could speak every language. He traveled by thought, fed the poor, and worked for peace.

The abilities described in fairy tales are abilities of the saints who have melded with Tao.

To imagine the abilities of those who reach immortality is not enough.

To comprehend the abilities of those who reach immortality is not enough.

The absolute truth is given now: Jin Dan Da Tao Xiu Lian.

Can you grab it?

It depends on your spiritual standing and your readiness.

You may not realize it, but the treasure is in front of you. You hold the key to this greatest treasure. You may not recognize the treasure, and then you may miss it.

How can you avoid missing this golden opportunity? Let me share one sentence with you:

If you want to know if a pear is sweet, taste it;
if you want to know if Jin Dan Da Tao works, experience it.

You are blessed.

Humanity is blessed.

Mother Earth is blessed.

Countless planets, stars, galaxies, and universes are blessed.

I present Jin Dan Da Tao in the simplest way. It has never been presented in this way before.

I am your unconditional servant. I am an unconditional servant of humanity and all souls.

I wish for you to grab this absolute truth and highest treasure for fan lao huan tong, longevity, and immortality.

I wish for you to practice seriously.

I wish for you to reach fan lao huan tong as soon as possible.

I wish for you to have a long, long life.

Finally, I wish for you to reach immortality.

9
修炼目的
Xiu Lian Mu Di

The purpose of Xiu Lian

"Xiu" means *purification*. "Lian" means *practice*. "Mu di" means *purpose*. "Xiu lian mu di" (pronounced *sheo lyen moo dee*) means *the purpose of Xiu Lian*.

Xiu Lian is a special term in Tao practice. In fact, Xiu Lian is a term that can be used for every spiritual practice.

Millions of people are on the spiritual journey. There are many serious spiritual seekers who are searching for the absolute truth.

Xiu Lian has layers. Shi Jia Mo Ni Fo taught 84,000 spiritual methods. There are different methods for different layers of spiritual practice.

Some people do Xiu Lian because they want to heal their sicknesses, including chronic and life-threatening conditions.

Some people do Xiu Lian because they want to boost their energy, stamina, vitality, and immunity.

Some people do Xiu Lian because they want to purify their souls, hearts, minds, and bodies.

Some people do Xiu Lian because they want to rejuvenate.

Some people do Xiu Lian because they want to transform their relationships.

Some people do Xiu Lian because they want to transform their finances.

Some people do Xiu Lian because they want to have a long life.

Advanced spiritual seekers do Xiu Lian because they want to reach fan lao huan tong, longevity, and immortality in order to be better servants.

10
祛病健身
Qu Bing Jian Shen

Remove all sicknesses and strengthen the body

"Qu" means *remove*. "Bing" means *sicknesses*. "Jian" means *strengthen*. "Shen" means *body*. "Qu bing jian shen" (pronounced *chü bing jyen shun*) means *remove all sicknesses and strengthen the body* for good health.

In several of my earlier books, I have shared the key teachings about sickness:

- Any sickness is due to soul mind body blockages.
  - o Soul blockages are bad karma.

- Mind blockages include negative mind-sets, negative beliefs, negative attitudes, attachments, ego, and more.
- Body blockages are energy and matter blockages.
- To heal any sickness is to remove soul mind body blockages.
- Use the Four Power Techniques (Body Power, Soul Power, Mind Power, Sound Power) to self-heal.

In Tao teaching, all sicknesses are due to the misalignment and imbalance of jing qi shen.

Jing is matter. Every cell consists of matter. Qi is energy. Every cell vibrates, breathes in and out, contracts and expands. Matter is inside the cells. Energy is outside of the cells. When cells contract, they "exhale." Matter inside the cells radiates and transforms to energy outside of the cells. When cells expand, they "inhale." Energy outside of the cells transforms to matter inside the cells. This transformation between matter inside the cells and energy outside of the cells should be in relative balance. When this balance is broken, sickness occurs.

Matter and energy are both carriers of message. Message is shen, which is soul. Shen, soul, or message directs the transformation between the matter inside the cells and energy outside of the cells. Remember one of the most important one-sentence secrets of the Soul Power Series:

**Heal the soul first; then healing of the
mind and body will follow.**

Now I will lead you to practice Jin Dan Da Tao to heal all kinds of sickness. Jin Dan Da Tao Xiu Lian can heal all kinds of sickness because the practitioner receives jing qi shen xu dao he yi from Heaven, Mother Earth, humanity, countless planets, stars, and galaxies, all universes, the Divine, and Tao.

It may take weeks or months to recover from a chronic or life-threatening condition. You may have suffered with a condition for twenty or thirty years or more. Therefore, be patient and be persistent in your practice. Healing is waiting for you.

The healing power of Jin Dan Da Tao is beyond comprehension. Do it and you will understand.

Apply the Four Power Techniques:

Body Power. Sit up straight. Put the tip of your tongue as close as you can to the roof of your mouth without touching. Use the Jin Dan Da Tao Xiu Lian Hand Position. See figure 1 on page 42.

Soul Power. Say *hello:*

> *Dear Tao,*
> *Dear Divine,*
> *Dear soul mind body of countless universes,*
> *Dear soul mind body of countless galaxies, stars, and planets,*
> *Dear soul mind body of Mother Earth,*
> *Dear soul mind body of all humanity,*
> *Dear soul mind body of all animals,*
> *Dear soul mind body of everything in countless planets, stars,*
>   *galaxies, and universes,*
> *Dear soul mind body of all spiritual fathers and mothers in*
>   *all layers of Heaven and on Mother Earth,*
> *I love you, honor you, and appreciate you.*
> *Please heal* _____ (request the healing you wish for
>   your spiritual, mental, emotional, and physical bodies).

I am very grateful.
Thank you. Thank you. Thank you.

Mind Power. Visualize golden light shining in your sickness area.
Visualize golden light shining from head to toe, skin to bone.

Sound Power. Chant silently or aloud:

Tian Zhi Jing	*tyen jr jing*
Di Zhi Jing	*dee jr jing*
Ren Zhi Jing	*wren jr jing*
Tian Di Ren Zhi Jing	*tyen dee wren jr jing*
Wan Wu Zhi Jing	*wahn woo jr jing*
Quan Yu Zhou Zhi Jing	*chwen yü joe jr jing*
Jie Shi Dao Zhi Jing	*jyeh shr dow jr jing*
Tian Zhi Qi	*tyen jr chee*
Di Zhi Qi	*dee jr chee*
Ren Zhi Qi	*wren jr chee*
Tian Di Ren Zhi Qi	*tyen dee wren jr chee*
Wan Wu Zhi Qi	*wahn woo jr chee*
Quan Yu Zhou Zhi Qi	*chwen yü joe jr chee*
Jie Shi Dao Zhi Qi	*jyeh shr dow jr chee*
Tian Zhi Shen	*tyen jr shun*
Di Zhi Shen	*dee jr shun*
Ren Zhi Shen	*wren jr shun*
Tian Di Ren Zhi Shen	*tyen dee wren jr shun*
Wan Wu Zhi Shen	*wahn woo jr shun*
Quan Yu Zhou Zhi Shen	*chwen yü joe jr shun*
Jie Shi Dao Zhi Shen	*jyeh shr dow jr shun*

Tian Zhi Xu	tyen jr shü
Di Zhi Xu	dee jr shü
Ren Zhi Xu	wren jr shü
Tian Di Ren Zhi Xu	tyen dee wren jr shü
Wan Wu Zhi Xu	wahn woo jr shü
Quan Yu Zhou Zhi Xu	chwen yü joe jr shü
Jie Shi Dao Zhi Xu	jyeh shr dow jr shü
Tian Zhi Dao	tyen jr dow
Di Zhi Dao	dee jr dow
Ren Zhi Dao	wren jr dow
Tian Di Ren Zhi Dao	tyen dee wren jr dow
Wan Wu Zhi Dao	wahn woo jr dow
Quan Yu Zhou Zhi Dao	chwen yü joe jr dow
Jie Shi Da Dao	jyeh shr dah dow
Tian Jing Qi Shen Xu Dao He Yi	tyen jing chee shun shü dow huh yee
Di Jing Qi Shen Xu Dao He Yi	dee jing chee shun shü dow huh yee
Ren Jing Qi Shen Xu Dao He Yi	wren jing chee shun shü dow huh yee
Tian Di Ren Jing Qi Shen Xu Dao He Yi	tyen dee wren jing chee shun shü dow huh yee
Wan Wu Jing Qi Shen Xu Dao He Yi	wahn woo jing chee shun shü dow huh yee
Quan Yu Zhou Jing Qi Shen Xu Dao He Yi	chwen yü joe jing chee shun shü dow huh yee
Jie Shi Yu Dao He Yi	jyeh shr yü dow huh yee
Tian Jin Dan	tyen jeen dahn
Di Jin Dan	dee jeen dahn

Ren Jin Dan	*wren jeen dahn*
Tian Di Ren Jin Dan	*tyen dee wren jeen dahn*
Wan Wu Jin Dan	*wahn woo jeen dahn*
Quan Yu Zhou Jin Dan	*chwen yü joe jeen dahn*
Jie Shi Dao Jin Dan	*jyeh shr dow jeen dahn*
Tian Yu Dao He Zhen	*tyen yü dow huh jun*
Di Yu Dao He Zhen	*dee yü dow huh jun*
Ren Yu Dao He Zhen	*wren yü dow huh jun*
Tian Di Ren Yu Dao He Zhen	*tyen dee wren yü dow huh jun*
Wan Wu Yu Dao He Zhen	*wahn woo yü dow huh jun*
Quan Yu Zhou Yu Dao He Zhen	*chwen yü joe yü dow huh jun*
Jie Shi Yu Dao He Zhen	*jyeh shr yü dow huh jun*

Chant Jin Dan Da Tao one time. You could receive great benefits. The more times you chant, the more benefits you will receive.

Jin Dan Da Tao Xiu Lian is the highest spiritual treasure to self-heal. Chant Jin Dan Da Tao with me on the CD or audio download that is included in this book. My frequency and vibration will serve you for a faster recovery.

11

开发智能

Kai Fa Zhi Neng

Develop intelligence

"Kai fa" means *develop*. "Zhi neng" means *intelligence*. "Kai fa zhi neng" (pronounced *kye fah jr nung*) means *develop intelligence*.

A human being has different intelligences. The first intelligence is mind intelligence. Mind means consciousness. Mind intelligence comes mainly from the brain. It also comes from the different systems, organs, and cells, because everything has consciousness. Since you were born (and maybe even before), your parents taught you. Through kindergarten, elementary school, middle school, high school, and university, one continues to learn all kinds of knowledge and develop mind intelligence.

The second intelligence is heart intelligence. Five thousand years ago, *The Yellow Emperor's Internal Classic*, the authority book of traditional Chinese medicine, stated that *the heart houses the mind and soul*. The heart is the key for intelligence. If a person has heart disease or other heart conditions, it could seriously affect his or her intelligence.

The third intelligence is soul intelligence. I have focused on the intelligence of one's body soul. Your body soul reincarnates. It carries all of your lifetimes of wisdom. To develop your body soul intelligence is vital. For example, after you develop your soul intelligence, you may suddenly be able to write a book that you could not have written before. Or, perhaps you can suddenly sing without receiving any training. You have developed your soul intelligence.

Now, I will introduce the fourth major intelligence. I have not explained it in any of my previous books. This intelligence comes from *Yuan Shen*.

What is Yuan Shen (pronounced *ywen shun*)? When a man's sperm and a woman's egg join as one, Tao will respond instantly by sending a Yuan Shen to the new embryo.

Yuan Shen will hide in your heart. Yuan Shen is the true emperor for a human being, but it does not appear to most human beings. Only the serious spiritual practitioner who has reached soul enlightenment is able to see his or her Yuan Shen.

Shi Jia Mo Ni Fo, the founder of Buddhism, said, "Ming xin jian xing." "Ming" means *enlighten*. "Xin" means *heart*. "Jian" means *see*. "Xing" means *Yuan Shen*, which is your true self. Therefore, "ming xin jian xing" (pronounced *ming sheen jyen shing*) means *enlighten your heart to see your Yuan Shen*.

Before you reach ming xin jian xing, your original soul (your body soul who has reincarnated from life to life) is in charge. Your original soul is your original emperor but it is not your true emperor. Your body soul is named Shi Shen (pronounced *shr shun*). This old emperor finds it very difficult to give up its position, because of the karma your original soul carries from lifetime to lifetime. Therefore, when you clear your karma, your original soul is delighted to call your Yuan Shen to take over in the emperor position.

After reaching soul enlightenment, which is ming xin jian xing, your Yuan Shen is in charge. Yuan Shen is Tao. Yuan Shen will transform every aspect of your life. Yuan Shen will guide Shi Shen. Little by little, Shi Shen will meld with Yuan Shen. It takes time for Shi Shen to completely meld with Yuan Shen. This process is a long one. If your Shi Shen completely melds with your Yuan Shen, you are melded with Tao.

Many people have reached ming xin jian xing or soul enlightenment. It does not mean that many of these people have melded with Tao. It could take many, many lifetimes to move from ming xin jian xing to melding with Tao. Many spiritual beings who have reached ming xin jian xing were not able to meld with Tao. After their physical lives ended, their original souls continued to reincarnate.

After Shi Shen reincarnates again, Yuan Shen will be with you again. You (in your new incarnation) must reach ming xin jian xing again. But because Shi Shen reached ming xin jian xing in the previous lifetime, the original soul will more easily reach ming xin jian xing in the new lifetime. After reaching ming xin jian xing again, Yuan Shen will continue to guide Shi Shen. Shi Shen will further meld with Yuan Shen.

It could take lifetime after lifetime to finally meld with Tao. Tao is The Way. Tao is the source of all planets, stars, galaxies, and universes. Tao is the creator of everyone and everything. Tao creates One. One creates Two. Two is Heaven and Mother Earth. Heaven is yang. Mother Earth is yin. Heaven and Mother Earth interact to create all things.

Tao has unlimited wisdom. After soul enlightenment or ming xin jian xing, Yuan Shen guides you to gain Tao wisdom.

12

转化人生

Zhuan Hua Ren Sheng

Transform a human being's life

"Zhuan hua" means *transform*. "Ren sheng" means *human's life*. "Zhuan hua ren sheng" (pronounced *jwahn hwah wren shung*) means *transform a human being's life*.

If Yuan Shen guides your Shi Shen as the boss or emperor,

Tao will guide your life. However, your Shi Shen, which is your original soul, will not always listen completely to your Yuan Shen. Therefore, there can be many struggles on one's spiritual path and journey.

There are many spiritual tests. Why are there so many struggles and so much testing? Because your Shi Shen will not listen to your Yuan Shen completely. Your Yuan Shen will give lessons, teachings, and testing to your Shi Shen. Your Shi Shen will transform little by little.

To reach ming xin jian xing means your Yuan Shen becomes the boss. This is the key for life transformation. Every aspect of your life will be transformed.

13
与道合真
Yu Dao He Zhen

Meld with Tao

"Yu" means *with*. Dao or Tao is The Way. "He" means *join*. "Zhen" means *truth of Tao*. "Yu Dao he zhen" (pronounced *yü dow huh jun*) means *meld with Tao*.

I have just explained ming xin jian xing. When you reach ming xin jian xing, your soul has just realized the greatness of Tao. Ming xin jian xing is to start to see Tao. Shi Shen has not melded with Tao yet. How can you meld with Tao? Let me reveal the four sacred stages:

Stage 1

百日筑基
Bai Ri Zhu Ji

Practice for one hundred days to build a foundation for your body

"Bai" means *hundred*. "Ri" means *day*. "Zhu" means *build*. "Ji" means *foundation*. "Bai ri zhu ji" (pronounced *bye rr joo jee*) means *practice for one hundred days to build a foundation for your body*.

Almost every human being has imbalances in the body. In Tao practice, any sickness is named *lou ti*. "Lou" means *leak*. "Ti" means *body*. "Lou ti" (pronounced *loe tee*) means *leaky body*.

In Tao teaching, a human body consists of jing qi shen. Jing qi shen are three treasures. Later in this chapter I will reveal many special teachings for jing qi shen.

"Jing" means *matter*. Sixty to seventy percent of the human body consists of fluid. Fluid is matter. Every system, every organ, and every cell and tissue is made of matter.

"Qi" means *vital energy and life force*. Every system, every organ, and every cell has its own qi or energy.

"Shen" means *soul*, including the body soul and the souls of systems, organs, cells, cell units, DNA, RNA, spaces between the cells, and tiny matter inside the cells.

To have lou ti, a leaky body, means that the jing qi shen is deficient because of sickness, old age, selfishness, greed for wealth or power, impure desires, and more. All of these exhaust jing qi shen, which has "leaked out."

As I shared earlier, a life is like an oil lamp. When a baby is born, the lamp is full of oil. The baby grows, becomes a teenager, then an adult, and finally a senior. Age exhausts the oil in one's lamp. Sickness exhausts the oil. Bad karma exhausts the most oil.

To spend one hundred days to build the foundation of the body is to spend one hundred days to fulfill the oil in one's lamp. There are many ways to fulfill the oil. The fastest way is Jin Dan Da Tao Xiu Lian.

Remember, I said that I will mention Jin Dan Da Tao Xiu Lian again and again. I will lead you to practice Jin Dan Da Tao Xiu Lian again and again. I am bringing my workshop, retreat, and special training to you within this book. Practice Jin Dan Da Tao Xiu Lian with me now. Do not think you know it already. Do not feel that this is repetitive. You have to repeat this practice hundreds of times, thousands of times, but hundreds and thousands of times are not enough. If you can practice Jin Dan Da Tao Xiu Lian from morning to night, that is the top secret. That is the fastest way to heal, rejuvenate, reach fan lao huan tong, have long life, and move to immortality. Chant Jin Dan Da Tao nonstop.

Why is Jin Dan Da Tao Xiu Lian most important? Because Jin Dan Da Tao will fulfill your jing qi shen, which is the oil in your lamp. Your body will become energized and very strong, and younger and younger. When your jing qi shen is fulfilled, your jing qi shen will come into alignment and all sicknesses will disappear automatically.

To align jing qi shen is to build the Jin Dan. Jing qi shen are three internal treasures of a human being. Jin Dan Da Tao Xiu Lian invokes jing qi shen from Heaven, Mother Earth, countless planets, stars, galaxies, and universes, and the Divine and Tao to form your Jin Dan.

If your Jin Dan is formed, your sicknesses will start to disappear. If you can form your complete Jin Dan, all sicknesses will disappear and you will become younger. You will have a long, long life and then you will move toward immortality.

Let us do Jin Dan Da Tao Xiu Lian again right now. We cannot do it enough. Do it seriously. Do not think that you know it already. You need to practice Jin Dan Da Tao constantly. Then you will be able to feel that the more practice you do, the more benefits you can receive. You will be inspired to do it all the time. If you can do it all the time by yourself naturally, you are significantly closer to Tao. That is a big sign that you can move your Tao journey much faster.

To complete your Jin Dan is to meld with Tao. I emphasize again that to meld with Tao means you are Tao and Tao is you. It is hard to comprehend but it is true.

Apply the Four Power Techniques:

Body Power. Sit up straight. Put the tip of your tongue as close as you can to the roof of your mouth without touching. Use the Jin Dan Da Tao Xiu Lian Hand Position. See figure 1 on page 42.

Soul Power. Say *hello:*

> *Dear Tao,*
> *Dear Divine,*
> *Dear soul mind body of countless universes,*
> *Dear soul mind body of countless galaxies, stars, and planets,*
> *Dear soul mind body of Mother Earth,*
> *Dear soul mind body of all humanity,*
> *Dear soul mind body of all animals,*

Dear soul mind body of everything in countless planets, stars,
*   galaxies, and universes,*
Dear soul mind body of all spiritual fathers and mothers in
*   all layers of Heaven and on Mother Earth,*
I love you, honor you, and appreciate you.
Please fulfill my jing qi shen to balance and restore my
*   lou ti.*
I am very grateful.
Thank you. Thank you. Thank you.

Mind Power. Visualize your Jin Dan in your lower abdomen getting bigger and bigger. Your jing qi shen is fulfilled. Your oil lamp is filled.

Sound Power. Chant silently or aloud:

Tian Zhi Jing
Di Zhi Jing
Ren Zhi Jing
Tian Di Ren Zhi Jing
Wan Wu Zhi Jing
Quan Yu Zhou Zhi Jing
Jie Shi Dao Zhi Jing

Tian Zhi Qi
Di Zhi Qi
Ren Zhi Qi
Tian Di Ren Zhi Qi
Wan Wu Zhi Qi
Quan Yu Zhou Zhi Qi
Jie Shi Dao Zhi Qi

Tian Zhi Shen
Di Zhi Shen
Ren Zhi Shen
Tian Di Ren Zhi Shen
Wan Wu Zhi Shen
Quan Yu Zhou Zhi Shen
Jie Shi Dao Zhi Shen

Tian Zhi Xu
Di Zhi Xu
Ren Zhi Xu
Tian Di Ren Zhi Xu
Wan Wu Zhi Xu
Quan Yu Zhou Zhi Xu
Jie Shi Dao Zhi Xu

Tian Zhi Dao
Di Zhi Dao
Ren Zhi Dao
Tian Di Ren Zhi Dao
Wan Wu Zhi Dao
Quan Yu Zhou Zhi Dao
Jie Shi Da Dao

Tian Jing Qi Shen Xu Dao He Yi
Di Jing Qi Shen Xu Dao He Yi
Ren Jing Qi Shen Xu Dao He Yi
Tian Di Ren Jing Qi Shen Xu Dao He Yi
Wan Wu Jing Qi Shen Xu Dao He Yi
Quan Yu Zhou Jing Qi Shen Xu Dao He Yi
Jie Shi Yu Dao He Yi

Tian Jin Dan
Di Jin Dan
Ren Jin Dan
Tian Di Ren Jin Dan
Wan Wu Jin Dan
Quan Yu Zhou Jin Dan
Jie Shi Tao Jin Dan

Tian Yu Dao He Zhen
Di Yu Dao He Zhen
Ren Yu Dao He Zhen
Tian Di Ren Yu Dao He Zhen
Wan Wu Yu Dao He Zhen
Quan Yu Zhou Yu Dao He Zhen
Jie Shi Yu Dao He Zhen

Now I will reveal the second sacred stage to meld with Tao.

Stage 2

俱足形

Ju Zu Xing

Your body is fulfilled with sufficient jing qi shen to reach the baby state

"Ju" means *all*. "Zu" means *sufficient*. "Xing" means *body*. "Ju zu xing" (pronounced *jü dzoo shing*) means *your body is fulfilled with sufficient jing qi shen to reach the baby state.*

To fulfill your Jin Dan is to fulfill your jing qi shen. To fulfill your jing qi shen is to have a full lamp of jing qi shen. To have a full lamp of jing qi shen is to reach the baby state.

Let us do the practice for forming the Jin Dan that I revealed and explained in pages 390–397 of *Tao I: The Way of All Life*.

Apply the Four Power Techniques:

Body Power. Sit up straight. Put the tip of your tongue as close as you can to the roof of your mouth without touching. Place both palms on your lower abdomen, one over the other.

Soul Power. Say *hello:*

> *Dear Tao,*
> *Dear Divine,*
> *Dear soul mind body of countless universes,*
> *Dear soul mind body of countless planets, stars, and galaxies,*
> *Dear soul mind body of Mother Earth,*
> *Dear soul mind body of all humanity,*
> *Dear soul mind body of all spiritual fathers and mothers in*
> *   all layers of Heaven and on Mother Earth,*
> *I love you, honor you, and appreciate you.*
> *Please form my Jin Dan.*
> *I am very grateful.*
> *Thank you. Thank you. Thank you.*

Mind Power. Visualize your Jin Dan forming. This special golden light ball is getting bigger and bigger in your lower abdomen.

Sound Power. Chant repeatedly, silently or aloud:

> *Tao sheng yi*
> *Tian yi zhen shui*

Jin jin yu ye
Yan ru dan tian
Shen qi jing he yi
Tian di ren he yi
Jin dan lian cheng . . .

"Tao sheng yi" (pronounced *dow shung yee*) means *Tao creates One*. Tao is The Way. Tao is the source of all universes. "Sheng" means *create*. "Yi" means *one*.

"Tian yi zhen shui" (pronounced *tyen yee jun shway*) means *Heaven's unique sacred liquid*. "Tian" means *Heaven*. "Yi" means *unique* or *one*. "Zhen" means *true* or *sacred*. "Shui" means *liquid*. Tian yi zhen shui comes from Heaven into your head, and then through your palate to your mouth.

"Jin jin yu ye" (pronounced *jeen jeen yü yuh*) means *gold liquid, jade liquid*. The first "jin" means *gold*. The second "jin" means *liquid*. "Yu" means *jade*. "Ye" means *liquid*. Gold and jade express the preciousness of jin jin yu ye, which comes from Mother Earth. The sacred qi of Mother Earth rises through your feet, up your legs, and through your trunk to come to your mouth, where it then transforms to liquid. Therefore, jin jin yu ye is sacred liquid from Mother Earth. Tian yi zhen shui and jin jin yu ye join together in your mouth.

"Yan ru dan tian" (pronounced *yahn roo dahn tyen*) means *swallow the sacred liquid from Heaven and Mother Earth into your Lower Dan Tian*. "Yan" means *swallow*. "Ru" means *go into*. "Dan tian" is the Lower Dan Tian in your lower abdomen.

"Shen qi jing he yi" (pronounced *shun chee jing huh yee*) means *souls energy matter join as one*. "Shen" means *soul*. It includes your body soul and the souls of all of your systems, organs, cells, cell units, DNA, RNA, spaces between the cells, and tiny matter inside the cells.

"Qi" means *vital energy and life force*. It includes the qi of all of your systems, organs, cells, and more.

"Jing" means *matter*. It includes the matter of all your systems, organs, and cells, from head to toe and from skin to bone.

Shen qi jing he yi is to join all souls, all energy, all matter of a human being from head to toe, skin to bone as one in the lower abdomen to form the Jin Dan.

"Tian di ren he yi" means *Heaven, Mother Earth, and human beings join as one*. "Tian" means *Heaven*. "Di" means *Mother Earth*. "Ren" means *humanity*. "He" means *join*. "Yi" means *one*.

Heaven has soul, energy, and matter. Mother Earth has soul, energy, and matter. Humanity has soul, energy, and matter. Tian di ren he yi is to join the soul, energy, and matter of Heaven, Mother Earth, and humanity as one in your abdomen to form the Jin Dan.

"Jin dan lian cheng" (pronounced *jeen dahn lyen chung*) means *Jin Dan is formed*. "Jin" means *golden*. "Dan" means *light ball*. "Lian" means *cooked*. "Cheng" means *done*.

Together, tian yi zhen shui, jin jin yu ye, shen qi jing he yi, and tian di ren he yi form your Jin Dan.

Let us chant more:

Tao sheng yi	*dow shung yee*
Tian yi zhen shui	*tyen yee jun shway*
Jin jin yu ye	*jeen jeen yü yuh*
Yan ru dan tian	*yahn roo dahn tyen*
Shen qi jing he yi	*shun chee jing huh yee*

Tian di ren he yi   *tyen dee wren huh yee*
Jin dan lian cheng   *jeen dahn lyen chung*

Tao sheng yi
Tian yi zhen shui
Jin jin yu ye
Yan ru dan tian
Shen qi jing he yi
Tian di ren he yi
Jin dan lian cheng

Tao sheng yi
Tian yi zhen shui
Jin jin yu ye
Yan ru dan tian
Shen qi jing he yi
Tian di ren he yi
Jin dan lian cheng

Tao sheng yi
Tian yi zhen shui
Jin jin yu ye
Yan ru dan tian
Shen qi jing he yi
Tian di ren he yi
Jin dan lian cheng . . .

Chant as much as you can. There is no time limit. The more you chant, the faster you will form your Jin Dan.

There are two more sacred stages to meld with Tao.

Stage 3

明心见性
Ming Xin Jian Xing

Enlighten your heart to see your Yuan Shen

"Ming" means *enlighten*. "Xin" means *heart*. "Jian" means *see*. "Xing" means *your true self, which is your Yuan Shen*. To reach "Ming xin jian xing" (pronounced *ming sheen jyen shing*) is to enlighten your heart to see your Yuan Shen.

Earlier in this chapter, I explained Yuan Shen, which is Tao.

When the sperm of a man and the egg of a woman join as one, Tao responds instantly at that moment to give Yuan Shen to the embryo.

Your Yuan Shen will be with you for your entire life. After you see your Yuan Shen, it is on duty as the true emperor. Yuan Shen will lead and guide your Shi Shen, your "body soul" who reincarnates lifetime after lifetime. Little by little, your Shi Shen will meld with your Yuan Shen.

Complete melding of your Shi Shen with your Yuan Shen takes time. After ming xin jian xing, your Shi Shen still will not follow your Yuan Shen completely. The Shi Shen still has its own view of the world. Yuan Shen is the Tao. Shi Shen is in the yin yang world. Yuan Shen and Shi Shen could have far different views of the world. Therefore, it can really take a lot of time for Shi Shen to completely meld with Yuan Shen.

After ming xin jian xing, Yuan Shen will guide your Xiu Lian. Yuan Shen will transform your Shi Shen little by little. The transformation of your soul, heart, mind, and body continues.

Jin Dan is jing qi shen he yi (matter, energy, souls join as one). Ming xin jian xing is to see your Yuan Shen. Yuan Shen is also jing qi shen he yi. Therefore, to form the Jin Dan and to see your Yuan Shen are the same thing.

Jin Dan has layers. To see your Yuan Shen also has layers. You cannot form a complete Jin Dan right away. Similarly, you cannot completely see your Yuan Shen right away either. In one sentence:

To form a complete Jin Dan is to meld with Yuan Shen, which is to meld with Tao.

To see your Yuan Shen is Xing Gong. "Xing" means *big intelligence*. "Gong" means *practice*. "Xing Gong" (pronounced *shing gawng*) is *Xiu Lian practice to develop big intelligence*. Big intelligence is Tao intelligence.

To form your Jin Dan is Ming Gong. "Ming" means *the foundation of the body*. "Gong" again means *practice*. "Ming Gong" (pronounced *ming gawng*) is *Xiu Lian practice for good health*.

To reach ming xin jian xing is to form the Jin Dan. To form the Jin Dan is to reach ming xin jian xing. This means that your Xing Gong and Ming Gong have been developed together. You have big intelligence and a healthy body together.

To reach ming xin jian xing or to form the Jin Dan does not mean that you have melded with Tao. To move from ming xin jian xing or forming the Jin Dan to melding with Tao is to move from the process of transformation of quantity to the process of transformation of quality.

It takes continuous purification and practice to meld with Tao, because it takes time for one's Shi Shen to be fully guided by one's Yuan Shen. In other words, it takes time for one's Shi Shen to completely meld with one's Yuan Shen. The practitioner will face many challenges during this process. There will also be a lot of spiritual testing.

Every spiritual seeker and practitioner must understand this wisdom. For example, if you reach ming xin jian xing, it does not mean that you will not get sick anymore. It does not mean that you will not have difficulties in your relationships and finances anymore. It does not mean that your bad karma has been completely cleared. You have to continue to purify your soul, heart, mind, and body. You have to continue to practice with your Jin Dan. Your bad karma will be cleared little by little. Your body will be transformed further and further. Your dedication to do spiritual Xiu Lian will be deeper and deeper. The more you do Jin Dan practice, the more love, forgiveness, and compassion you will have, and the more you will want to be an unconditional universal servant.

To achieve ming xin jian xing or to form a Jin Dan is just to see or feel Tao. To meld with Tao has to take a long, long time. The key is to transform your Shi Shen's view of the world.

The Xiu Tao practitioner must continue to practice Jin Dan to become stronger and stronger in the body. To practice Jin Dan is to heal all sicknesses. To practice Jin Dan is to reach fan lao huan tong. To practice Jin Dan is to have longevity. If you do not have good health and longevity, it is very hard to meld with Tao. Many spiritual practitioners transition before they can meld with Tao. Their physical body cannot last long enough for them to meld with Tao because they have not practiced Jin Dan enough.

For a Tao Xiu Lian practitioner, the most significant thing is to remove all of the bad karma from all past lives. Then it will be possible to achieve yu Dao he zhen, which means meld with Tao. When this happens, reincarnation stops. You then become the Tao. The benefits cannot be explained by words.

Stage 4

与道合真
Yu Dao He Zhen

Meld with Tao

"Yu" means *with*. Dao or Tao is The Way. "He" means *join*. "Zhen" means *the truth of Tao*. "Yu Dao He Zhen" (pronounced *yü dow huh jun*) means *meld with Tao*.

To practice Tao, one must practice both Ming Gong (body practice) and Xing Gong (intelligence practice). In fact, Jin Dan Xiu Lian is the Xiu Lian of Ming Gong and Xing Gong together.

I emphasize again that the Jin Dan has layers. There are different layers of Heaven. There are different layers of Jin Dan. Tao creates Heaven and Mother Earth. To reach yu Dao he zhen is to form the Tao Dan.

Forming the Tao Dan is not easy at all. Follow the sacred teachings in this book. Do the Jin Dan Da Tao Xiu Lian practices and all of the sacred practices I have shared. Then you will have the possibility and opportunity to form your Tao Dan.

Remember Tao normal creation and Tao reverse creation. Earlier in this book, I shared that to do Xiu Lian is to do Tao reverse creation. To do Xiu Lian is to accelerate Tao reverse creation. Consider the Yin Yang symbol in figure 2 below.

Figure 2. Yin Yang Symbol

The right side, which is mostly white, is yang. The left side, which is mostly black, is yin. The center of the yin yang circle is Tao Zhong. "Tao Zhong" (pronounced *dow jawng*) means *the core of Tao*.

Tao plus yin and yang is Three. Three produces everything. Move clockwise around the circle from the tip of the tail of the black fish at the top. You will go through the white fish to the tip of its tail at the bottom of the circle. Then you will come back up through the black fish to return to the tip of the tail of the black fish. This is one complete circle. This clockwise circle is Tao normal creation: Tao produces One. One produces Two. Two produces Three. Three produces all things.

From the same point at the top of the circle (the tip of the tail of the black fish), you can go down the vertical midline of the circle directly to Tao Zhong at the center of the circle. This movement is in a counterclockwise direction. When you follow this path, you reach the center in a very short distance. This is Tao reverse creation. The distance is much shorter than the clockwise circle that is Tao normal creation. This illustrates and demonstrates why you need to do Tao reverse creation practice.

A human's life is very limited. For a human being to meld with Tao in one short lifetime is very, very difficult because a human being carries karma. To self-clear karma is very difficult. Someone who carries heavy bad karma could take fifty, one hundred, or even more lifetimes to self-clear his or her karma. Therefore, it is much more difficult for a person who carries heavy karma to reach ming xin jian xing and to form a Jin Dan.

Jin Dan Da Tao practice is Tao reverse creation. Jin Dan is the unity of jing qi shen. The human being is made of jing qi shen. Jin Dan is to join jing qi shen as one. Three returns to One. Therefore, Jin Dan Da Tao practice is Tao reverse creation.

To meld with Tao is not only to completely meld your Shi Shen with your Yuan Shen; it is also to meld your physical body with Tao. To meld your physical body with Tao is to reach immortality.

Now sit up straight. Put both of your palms over your lower abdomen, below the navel. Chant Jin Dan Da Tao one more time to continue to form your Jin Dan. Visualize the Jin Dan golden light ball forming in your lower abdomen.

Chant now:

Tian Zhi Jing
Di Zhi Jing
Ren Zhi Jing
Tian Di Ren Zhi Jing
Wan Wu Zhi Jing
Quan Yu Zhou Zhi Jing
Jie Shi Dao Zhi Jing

Tian Zhi Qi
Di Zhi Qi
Ren Zhi Qi
Tian Di Ren Zhi Qi
Wan Wu Zhi Qi
Quan Yu Zhou Zhi Qi
Jie Shi Dao Zhi Qi

Tian Zhi Shen
Di Zhi Shen
Ren Zhi Shen
Tian Di Ren Zhi Shen
Wan Wu Zhi Shen

Quan Yu Zhou Zhi Shen
Jie Shi Dao Zhi Shen

Tian Zhi Xu
Di Zhi Xu
Ren Zhi Xu
Tian Di Ren Zhi Xu
Wan Wu Zhi Xu
Quan Yu Zhou Zhi Xu
Jie Shi Dao Zhi Xu

Tian Zhi Dao
Di Zhi Dao
Ren Zhi Dao
Tian Di Ren Zhi Dao
Wan Wu Zhi Dao
Quan Yu Zhou Zhi Dao
Jie Shi Da Dao

Tian Jing Qi Shen Xu Dao He Yi
Di Jing Qi Shen Xu Dao He Yi
Ren Jing Qi Shen Xu Dao He Yi
Tian Di Ren Jing Qi Shen Xu Dao He Yi
Wan Wu Jing Qi Shen Xu Dao He Yi
Quan Yu Zhou Jing Qi Shen Xu Dao He Yi
Jie Shi Yu Dao He Yi

Tian Jin Dan
Di Jin Dan
Ren Jin Dan
Tian Di Ren Jin Dan

Wan Wu Jin Dan
Quan Yu Zhou Jin Dan
Jie Shi Dao Jin Dan

Tian Yu Dao He Zhen
Di Yu Dao He Zhen
Ren Yu Dao He Zhen
Tian Di Ren Yu Dao He Zhen
Wan Wu Yu Dao He Zhen
Quan Yu Zhou Yu Dao He Zhen
Jie Shi Yu Dao He Zhen

Practice Jin Dan Da Tao Xiu Lian all the time. There is no limitation.

I have revealed the four sacred and most profound stages to meld with Tao:

Bai Ri Zhu Ji	*Practice one hundred days to build a foundation for your body.*
Ju Zu Xing	*Your body is fulfilled with sufficient jing qi shen to reach the baby state.*
Ming Xin Jian Xing	*Enlighten your heart to see your Yuan Shen.*
Yu Dao He Zhen	*Meld with Tao.*

The Tao of fan lao huan tong (rejuvenation to the baby state) and chang shou yong sheng (longevity and immortality) is to meld with Tao. When you meld with Tao, you have achieved fan lao huan tong, longevity, and immortality.

Yu Dao he zhen is the ultimate goal and answer.

Jin Dan Da Tao Xiu Lian is the process to reach yu Dao he zhen.

The most profound, absolute truth for fan lao huan tong, longevity, and immortality has been presented in front of you now.

What are you going to do?

Grab it.

Practice seriously and persistently.

I wish for you to reach fan lao huan tong sooner.

I wish for you to prolong your life.

I wish for you to move in the direction of immortality.

You could meld with Tao.

14
超乎阴阳
Chao Hu Yin Yang

Go beyond the yin yang world

"Chao hu" means *go beyond.* "Yin yang" means *yin yang world.* "Chao hu yin yang" (pronounced *chow hoo yeen yahng*) means *go beyond the yin yang world.*

Tao creates One. One creates Two. Two creates Three. Three creates everything. Two is Heaven and Mother Earth, yang and yin. Tao created Heaven and Mother Earth. Humanity lives in the yin yang world.

The yin yang world is the *you world.* "You" (pronounced *yoe*) means *existence.* Tao is the *wu world.* "Wu" (pronounced *woo*) means *emptiness and nothingness.* Tao creates Heaven and Mother Earth and yin and yang. *Wu* creates *you.* Nothingness creates existence.

Chao hu yin yang connects directly with the previous sacred phrase, yu Dao he zhen. After you meld with Tao, because you become Tao, you are not controlled by yin yang anymore. Tao creates yin yang. There are not enough words to explain your condition after you have become Tao.

When you practice Jin Dan Da Tao Xiu Lian, you are transforming your jing qi shen from three to two to one to Tao. Tao creates all things. When you are Tao, Heaven and Mother Earth, yin and yang, can no longer control you because they are two.

You will gain big wisdom and knowledge. You can use Tao wisdom to deal with every aspect of your life. For example, you will deal with your relationship with your partner in a different way. You will deal with your colleagues in a different way. You will develop your business in a different way, for example, by introducing new strategies.

In one sentence:

Your Yuan Shen, which is Tao, will guide you to deal with every aspect of your life by following Tao.

Many things that are bothersome and disturbing will be removed. You will have inner joy and inner peace. To have inner joy and inner peace is very important for one's life. Every aspect of your life is in the yin yang world. They are controlled by the principles of yin and yang. After you meld with Tao, you can use Tao wisdom to deal with the yin yang world. That will be the big difference.

Another deeper meaning that could be beyond the normal person's comprehension is that after you reach yu Dao he zhen, yin yang cannot control you anymore. You will receive special blessings and protection from Tao, the Divine, and saints. You could gain saint's extraordinary abilities that could include abilities to lift your body off of the ground, walk on water, manifest food, water, and many objects, move instantly from one place to another without a vehicle, and much more. This kind of training will not be explained in this book.

15
跳出三界
Tiao Chu San Jie

One is not controlled by the principles of Heaven, Mother Earth, and human beings

"Tiao chu" means *jump out*. "San jie" means *Heaven, Mother Earth, and human beings*. "Tiao chu san jie" (pronounced *tee-yow choo sahn jyeh*) means *you are not controlled by the principles of Heaven, Mother Earth, and human beings*.

This sacred phrase is directly connected with yu Dao he zhen. After yu Dao he zhen, you are beyond the control of the yin yang world, as I explained in connection with the previous sacred phrase, chao hu yin yang. You also are not controlled by the principles of Heaven, Mother Earth, and human beings, because they all belong to the yin yang world. This sacred phrase, tiao chu san jie, further explains how powerful it is to reach yu Dao he zhen. All kinds of saint's extraordinary abilities, including those I mentioned above and even more, can manifest.

16
无形无拘
Wu Xing Wu Ju

No shape, no control, no restraint from anything

"Wu" means *no*. "Xing" means *shape*. "Ju" means *control*. "Wu xing wu ju" (pronounced *woo shing woo jü*) means *no shape, no control, no restraint from anything*.

This sacred phrase explains further that when one melds with Tao, Tao has no shape, no restraint. Tao creates yin yang. Therefore, the principles of yin yang cannot restrain you anymore.

There is a renowned statement in *The Yellow Emperor's Internal Classic*: "Ju zhe cheng xing, san zhe cheng qi."

"Ju zhe cheng xing" (pronounced *jü juh chung shing*) means *accumulate energy to become a shape*. This is Tao creation. Tao creates all things. "San zhe cheng qi" (pronounced *sahn juh chung chee*) means *dissipation of energy becomes qi*. When you meld with Tao, you can perform ju zhe cheng xing, san zhe cheng qi. Therefore, wu xing and wu ju will apply to you.

17
得天地精华
De Tian Di Jing Hua

Receive the essence of Heaven and Mother Earth

"De" means *receive*. "Tian" means *Heaven*. "Di" means *Mother Earth*. "Jing hua" means *essence*. "De tian di jing hua" (pronounced *duh tyen dee jing hwah*) means *receive the essence of Heaven and Mother Earth*.

When Xiu Tao practitioners do Jin Dan Da Tao Xiu Lian, the essence of Heaven, Mother Earth, and human beings, as well as of countless planets, stars, galaxies, and universes, will pour into the practitioner's soul, heart, mind, and body. The essence from all of them will join as one in the practitioner's Jin Dan to form and develop the Jin Dan.

To receive the essence of Heaven and Mother Earth and of countless planets, stars, galaxies, and universes is Jin Dan Da Tao Xiu Lian. The purpose of Jin Dan Da Tao Xiu Lian is to meld with Tao.

18
与日月同辉
Yu Ri Yue Tong Hui

Shine together with the sun and moon

"Yu" means *with*. "Ri" means *sun*. "Yue" means *moon*. "Tong hui" means *shine together*. "Yu ri yue tong hui" (pronounced *yü rr yoo-eh tawng hway*) means *shine together with the sun and moon*.

After you reach yu Dao he zhen, you meld with the sun and the moon. You meld with countless planets, stars, galaxies, and universes. You shine the light of all of them. In particular, you join with the sun and the moon, you become one with the sun and the moon, and your light is the light of the sun and the moon. This is yu ri yue tong hui.

19
天地同存
Tian Di Tong Cun

Live together with Heaven and Mother Earth

"Tian" means *Heaven*. "Di" means *Mother Earth*. "Tong" means *together*. "Cun" means *existence*. "Tian di tong cun" (pronounced *tyen dee tawng tsoon*) means *live together with Heaven and Mother Earth*.

This sacred phrase explains that when one reaches yu Dao he zhen, one's life is as long as Heaven's and Mother Earth's.

Compared to Heaven and Mother Earth, a human being's life is limited; the lives of Heaven and Mother Earth are unlimited. Compared to Tao, the lives of Heaven and Mother Earth are limited; the life of Tao is unlimited.

Human beings cannot predict how long Heaven and Mother Earth can live. We may think that the lives of Heaven and Mother Earth are unlimited. To live together with Heaven and Mother Earth is to say that how long Heaven and Mother Earth can live is how long you can live. It is to live forever.

20
长寿永生
Chang Shou Yong Sheng

Longevity and immortality

"Chang shou" means *longevity.* "Yong sheng" means *immortality.* "Chang shou yong sheng" (pronounced *chahng sho yawng shung*) means *longevity and immortality.*

I have already revealed the absolute truth, including the highest wisdom and the highest practice. Jin Dan Da Tao Xiu Lian is the highest wisdom and highest practice. Earlier in this chapter, I explained the sacred phrase, yu Dao he zhen, and the four sacred stages to meld with Tao. These are the most important teachings of this book.

Practice Jin Dan Da Tao Xiu Lian as much as you can in your life. I will lead you to practice one more time now.

Apply the Four Power Techniques:

Body Power. Sit up straight. Put the tip of your tongue as close as you can to the roof of your mouth without touching. Grip your left thumb with the fingers of your right hand and make a fist. Your right hand should grasp your left thumb with 70 to 80 percent of your maximum strength. Wrap all four fingers of the left hand over the right hand. This is the Yin Yang Palm Hand (Body Power) Position. See figure 3.

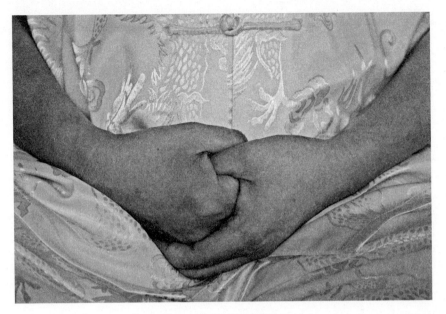

Figure 3. Yin Yang Palm

Place your Yin Yang Palm over your lower abdomen.

Soul Power. Say *hello:*

> *Dear Tao,*
> *Dear Divine,*
> *Dear soul mind body of countless universes,*
> *Dear soul mind body of countless galaxies, stars, and*
> *   planets,*
> *Dear soul mind body of Mother Earth,*
> *Dear soul mind body of all humanity,*
> *Dear soul mind body of all animals,*
> *Dear soul mind body of everything in countless planets, stars,*
> *   galaxies, and universes,*
> *Dear soul mind body of all spiritual fathers and mothers in*
> *   all layers of Heaven and on Mother Earth,*

I love you, honor you, and appreciate you.
Please fully develop my Jin Dan.
Please heal all of my sicknesses in the spiritual, mental,
    emotional, and physical bodies.
Please help me to rejuvenate and reach fan lao huan tong.
Please prolong my life.
Please move me in the direction of immortality.
I am very grateful.
Thank you. Thank you. Thank you.

Mind Power. Visualize golden light shining in your areas of sickness. Visualize golden light shining from head to toe, skin to bone.

Sound Power. Chant silently or aloud:

Tian Zhi Jing
Di Zhi Jing
Ren Zhi Jing
Tian Di Ren Zhi Jing
Wan Wu Zhi Jing
Quan Yu Zhou Zhi Jing
Jie Shi Dao Zhi Jing

Tian Zhi Qi
Di Zhi Qi
Ren Zhi Qi
Tian Di Ren Zhi Qi
Wan Wu Zhi Qi
Quan Yu Zhou Zhi Qi
Jie Shi Dao Zhi Qi

Tian Zhi Shen
Di Zhi Shen
Ren Zhi Shen
Tian Di Ren Zhi Shen
Wan Wu Zhi Shen
Quan Yu Zhou Zhi Shen
Jie Shi Dao Zhi Shen

Tian Zhi Xu
Di Zhi Xu
Ren Zhi Xu
Tian Di Ren Zhi Xu
Wan Wu Zhi Xu
Quan Yu Zhou Zhi Xu
Jie Shi Dao Zhi Xu

Tian Zhi Dao
Di Zhi Dao
Ren Zhi Dao
Tian Di Ren Zhi Dao
Wan Wu Zhi Dao
Quan Yu Zhou Zhi Dao
Jie Shi Da Dao

Tian Jing Qi Shen Xu Dao He Yi
Di Jing Qi Shen Xu Dao He Yi
Ren Jing Qi Shen Xu Dao He Yi
Tian Di Ren Jing Qi Shen Xu Dao He Yi
Wan Wu Jing Qi Shen Xu Dao He Yi
Quan Yu Zhou Jing Qi Shen Xu Dao He Yi
Jie Shi Yu Dao He Yi

Tian Jin Dan
Di Jin Dan
Ren Jin Dan
Tian Di Ren Jin Dan
Wan Wu Jin Dan
Quan Yu Zhou Jin Dan
Jie Shi Dao Jin Dan

Tian Yu Dao He Zhen
Di Yu Dao He Zhen
Ren Yu Dao He Zhen
Tian Di Ren Yu Dao He Zhen
Wan Wu Yu Dao He Zhen
Quan Yu Zhou Yu Dao He Zhen
Jie Shi Yu Dao He Zhen

Chant one time. You could receive great benefits. The more times you chant, the more benefits you will receive.

I cannot emphasize Jin Dan Da Tao Xiu Lian enough. Jin Dan Da Tao Xiu Lian is the Xiu Lian of chang shou yong sheng. Jin Dan Da Tao Xiu Lian is the Xiu Lian of yu Dao he zhen. There are no other words. This is the highest practice.

Why do I emphasize this again and again? It is to tell you that you must do it. You must practice again and again. There is no time limit. You must receive an "aha!" moment again and again. You must receive a "wow!" moment again and again.

The power, the joy, the purification, the healing, the rejuvenation, the life transformation, the fan lao huan tong, the longevity, and the immortality are waiting for you after you practice Jin Dan Da Tao Xiu Lian.

I wish for you to speed your process to reach the final destiny, yu Dao he zhen.

21
苦海众生
Ku Hai Zhong Sheng

**Everyone and everything in the bitter sea,
which is the yin yang world**

22
生老病死
Sheng Lao Bing Si

Birth, old age, sickness, death

23
因果缠身
Yin Guo Chan Shen

Karma controls you, no freedom

24
反复轮回
Fan Fu Lun Hui

Reincarnation continues

Let me explain these four sacred phrases together:

Ku Hai Zhong Sheng. "Ku" means *bitter.* "Hai" means *sea.*
"Zhong sheng" means *everyone and everything in the yin yang world.* "Ku hai zhong sheng" (pronounced *koo hye jawng shung*)
means *everyone and everything in the bitter sea, which is the yin yang world.*

Sheng Lao Bing Si. "Sheng" means *birth*. "Lao" means *old age*. "Bing" means *sickness*. "Si" means *death*. "Sheng lao bing si" (pronounced *shung lao bing sz*) means *birth, old age, sickness, death*.

Yin Guo Chan Shen. "Yin" means *cause*. "Guo" means *effect*. "Yin guo" means *karma*, which is the universal law of cause and effect. "Chan" means *wrap around*. "Shen" means *body*. "Yin guo chan shen" (pronounced *yeen gwaw chahn shun*) means *karma controls you and gives you no freedom*.

Fan Fu Lun Hui. "Fan fu" means *repeat*. "Lun hui" means *reincarnation*. "Fan fu lun hui" (pronounced *fahn foo lwun hway*) means *reincarnation continues*.

Heaven and Mother Earth are yin and yang. Heaven and Mother Earth are within the yin yang world. Heaven and Mother Earth are created by Tao. Tao creates One. One creates Two. Two is Heaven and Mother Earth. Heaven and Mother Earth have to follow Tao.

For example, in some countries in the winter time the temperature can be −40° C. A human being must wear enough clothes before going outside in this weather. If a person wears shorts outside, the cold weather could easily kill that person.

There are many laws and principles to follow in Heaven and on Mother Earth. Every country has laws. The spiritual world has laws also. Spiritual law is named *ling fa* (pronounced *ling fah*). In one sentence:

> **Everyone and everything in the yin yang world must be controlled and restricted by the laws and principles of yin and yang.**

A human being is an example. A human being has sheng lao bing si. Why? Because in the yin yang world this is the normal process of a human being's life.

To study Tao and to do Jin Dan Da Tao Xiu Lian is to reach fan lao huan tong. This does not follow sheng lao bing si (birth, old age, sickness, death). This moves backward. It is the reverse creation of Tao: All things return to Three. Three returns to Two. Two returns to One. One returns to Tao.

Why does a person get sick? Why does a person find it difficult to live more than one hundred years? The root cause is karma. Yin guo chan shen means karma is with a person like a bandage wrapped tightly around the body. The person has no freedom.

Most people carry karma. Some people carry very heavy karma. In my last ten years of personal observation, I have witnessed people suddenly having heart attacks, dying from cancer, seriously injured in car accidents, suffering from broken relationships, and becoming bankrupt.

The root cause of all of these challenges and disasters is bad karma. Bad karma means one has made mistakes in previous lifetimes and in this lifetime by taking advantage of, harming, hurting, cheating, stealing from, even killing others, and more. Karma is a spiritual law. When one has made a mistake, one must learn lessons in this lifetime and in future lifetimes. The lessons can include sickness, challenges in finances or relationships, and more. If one has made serious mistakes, one must learn serious lessons.

Karma is divided into good karma and bad karma. Good karma means that one has served others with love, care, compassion, sincerity, honesty, generosity, kindness, and more in previous lifetimes and in this lifetime. This one will receive rewards from Heaven. The rewards can include good health, longevity, blessed relationships and finances, and more.

A person with bad karma will learn lessons in this lifetime and in future lifetimes. A person with bad karma does not have freedom. When the time is ready, bad karma will attack the person. Dark souls will come to this person to teach him or her the karmic lessons.

Here is an example of how dark souls can come to one who has bad karma. For example, you may have been a general in a past lifetime. You could have killed many people in war. When those people were killed, their physical bodies died, but their souls survived. Most of those souls will move on in their spiritual journey. However, ten to twenty percent of those souls may have been so upset that they made a vow to come back for revenge.

For the souls who made a vow to come back to follow you to give you lessons, Heaven does not disapprove. As long as you have the bad karma, these dark souls follow you lifetime after lifetime. Spiritual law allows for this.

In ancient spiritual teaching, these dark souls are named *yuan jia zhai zhu* (pronounced *ywen jya jye joo*). "Yuan jia" refers to the souls that you and your ancestors killed, harmed, hurt, took advantage of, cheated, stole from, and more, and who are committed to exact revenge on you. Some of these souls may have committed themselves to the Dark Side to harm you lifetime after lifetime. "Zhai zhu" means *owner*. When you borrow money from a bank, you owe the bank. The bank is the owner or zhai zhu. In this case of bad karma, you owe the souls you have hurt or harmed. Therefore, they are your zhai zhu. "Yuan jia zhai zhu" means that you and your ancestors owe those souls you harmed and took advantage of. Some of them have committed to become your enemy and cause disasters in your life. This is one aspect of how karma works. Karma is the universal law of cause and effect.

Doing a forgiveness practice regularly is vital for self-clearing karma. I am giving you the wisdom and practical technique now. I have taught hundreds of thousands of people worldwide how to do this forgiveness practice to self-clear karma. This is the way to do it:

Forgiveness Practice

Say *hello:*

> *Dear all dark souls who are in my body,*
> *Dear all souls that I have harmed and my ancestors have*
>   *harmed in any of our lifetimes,*
> *I call you.*
> *I deeply apologize for what my ancestors and I have done*
>   *to you.*
> *I sincerely ask for forgiveness from all of you.*
> *Please forgive me.*
> *Please forgive my ancestors.*
> *We have learned our lessons.*
> *We will not make the same mistakes again.*
> *Let us sing the Divine Soul Song* Love, Peace and
>   Harmony *together.*

Sing the Divine Soul Song *Love, Peace and Harmony* repeatedly:

> *I love my heart and soul*
> *I love all humanity*
> *Join hearts and souls together*
> *Love, peace and harmony*
> *Love, peace and harmony . . .*

Generally speaking, do the forgiveness practice a minimum of five minutes per time, three times per day. This will help your healing and life transformation tremendously.

After you speak with the souls you have hurt or harmed, sing *Love, Peace and Harmony* for several minutes. The longer you sing, the better.

Reincarnation is a law in the yin yang world. Therefore, fan fu lun hui (reincarnation continues) is a fact.

To Xiu Tao is to practice Tao. Jin Dan Da Tao Xiu Lian is to meld with Tao. Jin Dan Da Tao Xiu Lian is to stop reincarnation. If you meld with Tao, then you have gone beyond yin and yang. You have returned from Two to One and from One to Tao. This is the reverse creation of Tao.

25
修仙成道
Xiu Xian Cheng Dao

Do Xiu Lian to become a saint in order to become Tao

26
脱出轮回
Tuo Chu Lun Hui

Get away from reincarnation

Xiu Xian Cheng Tao. "Xiu" means *Xiu Lian*. "Xian" means *saint*. "Cheng" means *become*. Dao or Tao is The Way. "Xiu xian cheng Dao" (pronounced *sheo shyen chung dow*) means *do Xiu Lian to become a saint in order to become Tao*.

Millions of people in history have done Xiu Lian. Many have

been successful. On the Xiu Lian journey, the successful ones are named "xian." "Xian" means *saint*. Saints have developed unconditional love, forgiveness, and compassion. Saints have gained higher wisdom. Saints have layers. I will explain this over the next few sacred phrases.

Tuo Chu Lun Hui. "Tuo chu" means *get away from*. "Lun hui" means *reincarnation*. "Tuo chu lun hui" (pronounced *twaw choo lwun hway*) means *get away from reincarnation*.

To do Jin Dan Da Tao Xiu Lian, the first purpose and step is to remove all sickness. The key to remove all sickness is to self-clear karma. This first step of Jin Dan Da Tao Xiu Lian is exactly the same as stage one of yu Dao he zhen. As explained earlier in this chapter, stage one of yu Dao he zhen is bai ri zhu ji—practice one hundred days to build a foundation for your body.

The second purpose and step of Jin Dan Da Tao Xiu Lian is to reach fan lao huan tong. This is exactly the same as stage two of yu Dao he zhen, which as explained earlier is ju zu xing—your body is fulfilled with sufficient jing qi shen to reach the baby state.

The third purpose and step of Jin Dan Da Tao Xiu Lian is to have longevity. To reach longevity, one has to reach ming xin jian xing, and then your Yuan Shen can start to guide your body to do Xiu Lian. Finally, your Shi Shen, which is your body soul, will completely meld with Yuan Shen. When you have reached this stage, you will have a long, long life.

Recall that stage three of yu Dao he zhen is ming xin jian xing—enlighten your heart to see your Yuan Shen. The final goal of ming xin jian xing is to have longevity and move to immortality.

The fourth and ultimate purpose and step of Jin Dan Da Tao Xiu Lian is to become Tao. To become Tao is to meld with Tao.

This is exactly the same as stage four of yu Dao he zhen, which is yu Dao he zhen—meld with Tao.

As you can see, the four steps of Jin Dan Da Tao Xiu Lian and the four stages of yu Dao he zhen are exactly the same. Jin Dan Da Tao Xiu Lian is the process of yu Dao he zhen. The final goal of Jin Dan Da Tao Xiu Lian is to reach yu Dao he zhen.

If you reach yu Dao he zhen, you are absolutely tuo chu lun hui, which means to get away from reincarnation. Yu Dao he zhen is much more than stopping reincarnation.

Yu Dao he zhen means that you are Tao, Tao is you. What Tao can do, you can do. You and Tao are one. Tao creates everything in countless planets, stars, galaxies, and all universes. You meld with Tao. You are Tao. You are immortal.

I explain yu Dao he zhen again and again. It is to share with you and every reader that yu Dao he zhen is possible. Of course, it takes a long, long, time for every Tao practitioner to reach an "aha!" or "wow!" moment many times in order to really understand yu Dao he zhen. Remember, I shared earlier that to realize yu Dao he zhen takes steps.

Practice Jin Dan Da Tao. Heal yourself first. Then you will believe more.

Continue to do Jin Dan Da Tao Xiu Lian. Rejuvenate your body next. If you really become younger, you will believe much more.

Continue Xiu Tao practice of Jin Dan Da Tao until you have achieved a long, long life. Then you may not have any doubt anymore.

Continue to do Jin Dan Da Tao Xiu Lian. You are moving to immortality.

27
人仙地仙
Ren Xian Di Xian

Human saints and Mother Earth saints

28
上为天仙
Shang Wei Tian Xian

Higher saints are Heaven saints

29
道仙最上
Dao Xian Zui Shang

Highest saints are Tao saints

30
与道合真
Yu Dao He Zhen

Meld with Tao

31
和谐宇宙
He Xie Yu Zhou

Harmonize universes

32
奥妙无穷
Ao Miao Wu Qiong

Profound and mysterious without ending

Ren Xian Di Xian. "Ren" means *human being*. "Xian" means *saints*. "Di" means *Mother Earth*. "Ren xian di xian" (pronounced *wren shyen dee shyen*) means *Human Being saints and Mother Earth saints*.

Shang Wei Tian Xian. "Shang" means *higher*. "Wei" means *is*. "Tian" means *Heaven*. "Xian" means *saints*. "Shang wei tian xian" (pronounced *shahng way tyen shyen*) means *higher saints are Heaven saints*.

Dao Xian Zui Shang. Dao or Tao is The Way. "Xian" means *saints*. "Zui shang" means *highest*. "Tao xian zui shang" (pronounced *dow shyen dzway shahng*) means *the highest saints are Tao saints*. Tao saints are the saints who have melded with Tao.

Human Being saints (or simply Human saints), Mother Earth saints, Heaven Saints, and Tao saints are different layers of saints. They are given different Divine and Tao abilities to serve humanity and all souls in all universes. Each layer carries unique abilities that will allow the saints in that layer to serve in their special way.

Human Being saints will have the ability to offer divine soul healing, divine soul transformation, divine manifestation, and divine creation to humanity. They will be primarily servants of humanity to offer this type of service to humanity.

In addition, Human Being saints will also develop unique divine abilities, such as the abilities to lift off of the ground, walk through walls, and manifest physical objects such as food. This will allow them to serve better in disasters during Mother Earth's transition. Human Being saints are like generals who will go out to the world to spread soul healing and enlightenment to humanity. That is their main role and responsibility.

Mother Earth saints will receive higher divine abilities than Human Being saints. Mother Earth saints will have the ability to lessen or even stop disasters that will occur during Mother Earth's transition, such as floods, hurricanes, tornadoes, and earthquakes on Mother Earth. To receive these abilities from the Divine and Tao, Mother Earth saints must have a pure heart.

Like Human Being saints, Mother Earth saints will also be leaders in spreading soul healing and enlightenment to humanity, but will have further divine abilities, including the abilities to fly and to move from one place to another instantly. Mother Earth saints will be very special servants for humanity and the number of people who will reach this level will be much less than the number of Human Being saints.

Heaven saints are very special servants who will have the ability to restructure the layers of Heaven and to offer soul healing, soul transformation, and soul enlightenment to the Soul World. They will also help bring Heaven to Mother Earth.

Heaven saints will be very special servants of humanity and will be recognized worldwide as some of the highest level servants for humanity. They will bring Heaven to Earth in a special way through their divine and Tao channels. They will be the major spiritual leaders on Mother Earth.

In addition, Heaven saints will have the ability to do soul travel in Heaven to receive Heaven's teachings, wisdom, and knowledge and as well to offer teachings to the saints in Heaven. Very few people will have the ability to do soul travel in this special way. Heaven saints will also develop the special divine abilities mentioned before, but on a much higher level. The number of people who will reach this level will be much less than the number of Mother Earth saints.

There will be very few who will reach the Tao saint level. Tao saints will have the ability to completely meld with Tao and serve all that exists. They will be able to harmonize all universes, all souls, and all layers of Heaven in a most special way that has never occurred before. This type of servant will be very special. Tao saints will be the top leaders in the Soul Light Era.

This book gives the absolute truth to humanity. It does not mean you can reach the Tao saint level easily. It is very difficult. It takes absolute total effort for a Tao practitioner to meld with Tao.

To meld with Tao is to reach immortality. To read this book, to read *Tao I: The Way of All Life,* and to read all other books in my Soul Power Series is important. A serious Tao practitioner must understand the sacred wisdom, knowledge, and practical techniques I offer in the Soul Power Series. At the same time, the practitioner must practice persistently and continuously.

You will reach yu Dao he zhen in four stages. At every stage, your confidence will increase. You will move your spiritual journey beyond comprehension.

Practice. Practice. Practice.

⋇

On page 30 of my book, *Tao I,* I gave the five steps to reach Tao. In this book, *Tao II,* I have shared the four major stages to meld with Tao. The essence is the same. The Divine and Tao have asked me to offer a ten-year Tao training program to accomplish these steps and stages. In *Tao I*, I described some details of what you need to do for the training. Study it. Joining my ten-year Tao training program is vital to help you to meld with Tao.

The first two years of the program emphasize removing all sicknesses. There will be a ten-day Tao Retreat each year. These retreats will be available by live webcast as well as in person at a physical venue. The training started in May 2010 with my first International Tao Retreat in Ramsau, Austria. Every year, this first-year Tao training will be offered to those who wish to become new students.

The third and fourth years of the program focus on fan lao huan tong. To reach fan lao huan tong is to become a Human Being saint. There will be a fifteen-day Tao Retreat each year for those who have successfully completed the first two years of the program. These retreats will also be available by live webcast.

The fifth and sixth years of training will train Mother Earth saints. There will be a twenty-day Tao Retreat each year for those who have successfully completed the first four years of training. These retreats will not be available by webcast. Every student at this level must gather together at the physical venue.

The seventh and eighth years are to train to become a Heaven saint. The formal training is for twenty-five days each year. Every student must gather together at the physical venue for this training.

The ninth and tenth years are to train to become a Tao saint. The formal training is for thirty days each year. Every student must gather together at the physical venue for this training.

Now, I will continue to explain the sacred phrases:

Yu Dao He Zhen. "Yu" means *with*. Dao or Tao is The Way. "He" means *join together*. "Zhen" means *absolute truth, which is*

Tao. "Yu Dao he zhen" (pronounced *yü dow huh jun*) means *meld with Tao.*

When you reach yu Dao he zhen, you have become Tao. You are Tao and Tao is you. This sacred phrase has been explained very well earlier in this chapter. Please re-read those explanations. Every time you do, you will gain deeper insight. You could have another "aha!" moment.

He Xie Yu Zhou. "He xie" means *harmonize.* "Yu zhou" means *universes.* "He xie yu zhou" (pronounced *huh shyeh yü joe*) means *harmonize universes.*

Tao creates One. One creates Two. Two creates Three. Three creates wan wu (all things). Wan wu includes countless planets, stars, galaxies, and universes. When you reach the Tao saint level, you have melded with Tao. When you meld with Tao, you are given Tao abilities to harmonize countless universes. This sacred phrase tells us that Tao can serve countless universes, countless galaxies, countless stars, and countless planets.

Ao Miao Wu Qiong. "Ao miao" means *profound and mysterious.* "Wu qiong" means *no ending.* "Ao miao wu qiong" (pronounced *ow mee-yow woo chyawng*) means *profound and mysterious without ending.*

If you practice Tao to become a Tao saint, you are completely melded with Tao. Remember the Tao I teaching. The first two sacred phrases of Tao Jing are:

Tao ke Tao, fei chang Tao

"Tao ke Tao" (pronounced *dow kuh dow*) means *Tao that can be explained by words or comprehended by thoughts.* "Fei chang Tao" (pronounced *fay chahng dow*) means *is not the true Tao or eternal Tao.*

Tao is extremely profound and mysterious. The normal creation of Tao and the reverse creation of Tao are examples. Tao normal creation is: Tao creates One. One creates Two. Two creates Three. Three creates all things. Tao reverse creation is: All things return to Three. Three returns to Two. Two returns to One. One returns to Tao.

Although I experienced and shared Tao normal creation and Tao reverse creation in *Tao I,* in order to truly understand Tao normal creation and Tao reverse creation, you must do Tao Xiu Lian practice. You must go into the emptiness and nothingness condition. To go into the emptiness and nothingness condition is to go into the Tao condition. To go into the Tao condition is to receive direct Tao teaching. Tao will teach and show you more about Tao normal creation and Tao reverse creation.

Since July 2003, the Divine and Tao have been teaching me every day. I continually receive new secrets, wisdom, knowledge, and practical techniques for healing, preventing sickness, purifying and rejuvenating soul, heart, mind, and body, prolonging life, and more.

I have realized that Heaven, the Divine, and Tao have unlimited secrets, wisdom, knowledge, and practical techniques. I always guide my students to "ask for and learn wisdom directly from Heaven, the Divine, and Tao."

How can you learn directly from Heaven, the Divine, and Tao? Open your spiritual channels. In the second book of my Soul Power Series, *Soul Communication: Opening Your Spiritual Channels for Success and Fulfillment,*[9] I have shared practical tech-

---

9. *Soul Communication: Opening Your Spiritual Channels for Success and Fulfillment* (Toronto/New York: Heaven's Library/Atria Books, 2008).

niques to open a human being's four major spiritual channels, which are:

- Soul Language Channel (use your soul's language to communicate with the Divine, Tao, the spiritual world, and all universes)
- Direct Soul Communication Channel (have direct conversations with the Divine, Tao, the spiritual world, and all universes)
- Third Eye Channel (see spiritual images of Heaven and the universe with your spiritual eye to better understand the truth of the universe)
- Direct Knowing Channel (directly know the truth and answers to your questions)

After opening and developing your spiritual channels, you can learn wisdom and practical techniques directly from the Divine and Tao, as well as from the saints, buddhas, and other spiritual fathers and mothers in Heaven. They will show you the wisdom in your Third Eye or they will directly teach you the wisdom through conversation. They will give you an "aha!" moment or a "wow!" moment. There are all kinds of ways that they can teach you.

After melding with Tao, you are Tao. You absolutely understand everything in countless planets, stars, and galaxies, and in all universes. Tao created all of them. Tao has guided all of them. You can do things that are beyond any words, any comprehension, and any imagination. It is profound and beyond words and limits to meld with Tao.

33
祛病为先
Qu Bing Wei Xian

First remove sickness

34
修善断恶
Xiu Shan Duan E

Be kind and stop all evil

35
除贪嗔痴
Chu Tan Chen Chi

Remove greed, anger, and lack of wisdom

36
修妙明心
Xiu Miao Ming Xin

Purify and enlighten your heart

37
无私为公
Wu Si Wei Gong

Serve others selflessly

38
修炼法要
Xiu Lian Fa Yao

Xiu Lian principles

39
誓为公仆
Shi Wei Gong Pu

Vow to be a servant

40
世代服务
Shi Dai Fu Wu

Serve in all lifetimes

41
服务修炼
Fu Wu Xiu Lian

Service Xiu Lian

42
上乘法门
Shang Cheng Fa Men

The highest sacred Xiu Lian method

43

祛除业障

Qu Chu Ye Zhang

Remove bad karma

44

积功累德

Ji Gong Lei De

Accumulate virtue

Qu Bing Wei Xian. "Qu" means *remove.* "Bing" means *sickness.* "Wei xian" means *first.* "Qu bing wei xian" (pronounced *chü bing way shyen*) means *first remove sickness.*

Jin Dan Da Tao Xiu Lian practice is to reach fan lao huan tong, longevity, and immortality. A Tao practitioner and any spiritual practitioner cannot reach fan lao huan tong with sickness. Sickness will block the Tao journey and any spiritual journey.

Millions of people on the spiritual journey cannot live a long life. They may chant and meditate very hard for thirty to fifty years or even for their entire lives. Why can they not prolong their lives? The key is bad karma. Bad karma is the root cause of sickness. If a person carries heavy karma, then even with very hard practice, although some karma would be self-cleared, it is very difficult to completely self-clear heavy bad karma. Therefore, bad karma takes people's lives away.

To self-clear karma is to remove sickness. How do you self-clear karma? You can do it with the Jin Dan Da Tao Xiu Lian practice. The reason is extremely simple. The Jin Dan Da Tao Xiu Lian practice is Tao practice. Tao is the source of everything.

You are practicing Tao and you are learning absolute truth.

The purpose of practicing Jin Dan Da Tao Xiu Lian is to meld with Tao. To meld with Tao is to serve humanity and countless planets, stars, galaxies, and universes better. Therefore, in one sentence:

Practicing Jin Dan Da Tao Xiu Lian is the fastest way to self-clear karma.

Practicing Jin Dan Da Tao Xiu Lian is invoking the jing qi shen xu dao of Heaven, Mother Earth, human beings, and wan wu, which includes countless planets, stars, galaxies, and universes, to join as one to meld with Tao. This is the biggest service. Therefore, it is the fastest way to self-clear your bad karma. But remember that it still does not mean you can self-clear your bad karma right away. It still does take some time. You must be aware of this.

Quite a few of my students in the last few years have mistakenly thought they should recover right away from their sicknesses after receiving Divine Karma Cleansing. Divine Karma Cleansing is a Divine Order to Heaven's generals and soldiers and to the leaders and workers of the Akashic Records to forgive one's bad karma. This Divine Order opens Heaven's virtue bank. Divine virtue pays one's spiritual debt or one's ancestors' spiritual debts. Then this one is forgiven. Divine Karma Cleansing is not free for Heaven. The Divine has to pay virtue to forgive the recipient of Divine Karma Cleansing and his or her ancestors.

I have offered thousands of Divine Karma Cleansings worldwide. In 2010, my Worldwide Representatives, who are new divine channels, have also begun to receive the authority and ability to offer Divine Karma Cleansings. I have received thousands of heart-touching and moving stories about karma cleansing.

Some people do not believe in karma. You have an absolute choice and right to keep your belief system. I am honored to share my insights. If the teaching fits your belief system, grab it. If you do not believe it, I do not have any intention to transform your belief system. I am honored to have the opportunity to share my personal insights. Thank you for the opportunity to share.

I have received numerous stories of instant miracles after Divine Karma Cleansing. However, I have always offered the clear teaching that to receive Divine Karma Cleansing and Divine Soul Mind Body Transplants does not mean you are recovered. To receive Divine Karma Cleansing does mean you are forgiven. To receive Divine Soul Mind Body Transplants does mean you have received permanent divine treasures. However, sickness has already damaged your systems, organs, and cells.

People do not understand that if you have bad karma, dark souls have come into your body. These dark souls eat your body. They damage your systems, organs, tissues, and cells. After receiving Divine Karma Cleansing, you are forgiven. The dark souls leave you, but to restore your health, you need to chant or meditate. You need to apply the Four Power Techniques to do Xiu Lian practice. It takes time to recover completelty.

I shared a very special story in my previous book, *Divine Transformation*. I would like to share this heart-touching story again because it is a very good example for every person who has a chronic or life-threatening condition. It really shows that you must understand the importance of practice.

I met a lady from Switzerland who came to one of my workshops in Germany. She suffered from a rare condition that was like multiple sclerosis. It was very severe. She had suffered for many years. She had to go to the hospital a few times a year to have her excruciating pain managed. Every time, she had to be given morphine injections to control the pain. She would stay in the hospital for one to two weeks at a time just to manage and control the pain. There was no solution for her sickness.

After receiving personal and ancestral Divine Karma Cleansings and all kinds of Divine Soul Mind Body Transplants, she still was not able to get better. But she remembered my teaching: *To receive Divine Karma Cleansing and Divine Soul Mind Body Transplants does not mean that you are recovered. It means that you are forgiven and you are given divine treasures to self-heal. You must practice. For chronic and life-threatening conditions, you must practice two hours or more a day.*

She started to practice after the workshop. She did practice at least two hours a day. Weekends, she spent five to seven hours a day chanting. She practiced dedicatedly like this for about three months and then her pain suddenly stopped. Now, more than one year later, the pain has not returned. She was extremely grateful. She could not appreciate enough the Divine Karma Cleansings and Divine Soul Mind Body Transplants.

At this moment, I formally release that the top secret for self-clearing karma is to practice Jin Dan Da Tao Xiu Lian. Make sure that you practice Jin Dan Da Tao Xiu Lian a lot. The power of practicing Jin Dan Da Tao Xiu Lian to heal your sicknesses is unlimited and unpredictable.

Let us practice Jin Dan Da Tao Xiu Lian now.

Apply the Four Power Techniques to self-clear bad karma and to self-heal:

Body Power. Sit up straight. Put both of your palms over your lower abdomen, below the navel.

Soul Power. Say *hello:*

> *Dear soul mind body of Jin Dan Da Tao Xiu Lian,*
> *I love you, honor you, and appreciate you.*
> *You have the power to forgive my mistakes and my ancestors'*
>   *mistakes.*
> *Dear all dark souls who are in my body,*
> *I sincerely apologize for the mistakes that my ancestors and*
>   *I have made in all of our lifetimes.*
> *Please forgive us.*
> *We are extremely grateful.*
> *We have learned our lessons.*
> *We will serve humanity and all souls unconditionally.*
> *Dear Divine,*
> *Dear Tao,*
> *I am very grateful that I can request your forgiveness.*
> *I will become an unconditional universal servant.*
> *Please forgive my bad karma and my ancestors' bad karma.*
> *I am extremely honored and blessed.*
> *Thank you.*

Mind Power. Visualize your Jin Dan rotating in your lower abdomen. Your bad karma is forgiven. You are receiving healing and blessings.

Sound Power. Chant Jin Dan Da Tao Xiu Lian now:

> *Tian Zhi Jing*
> *Di Zhi Jing*
> *Ren Zhi Jing*
> *Tian Di Ren Zhi Jing*

Wan Wu Zhi Jing
Quan Yu Zhou Zhi Jing
Jie Shi Dao Zhi Jing

Tian Zhi Qi
Di Zhi Qi
Ren Zhi Qi
Tian Di Ren Zhi Qi
Wan Wu Zhi Qi
Quan Yu Zhou Zhi Qi
Jie Shi Dao Zhi Qi

Tian Zhi Shen
Di Zhi Shen
Ren Zhi Shen
Tian Di Ren Zhi Shen
Wan Wu Zhi Shen
Quan Yu Zhou Zhi Shen
Jie Shi Dao Zhi Shen

Tian Zhi Xu
Di Zhi Xu
Ren Zhi Xu
Tian Di Ren Zhi Xu
Wan Wu Zhi Xu
Quan Yu Zhou Zhi Xu
Jie Shi Dao Zhi Xu

Tian Zhi Dao
Di Zhi Dao
Ren Zhi Dao

Tian Di Ren Zhi Dao
Wan Wu Zhi Dao
Quan Yu Zhou Zhi Dao
Jie Shi Da Dao

Tian Jing Qi Shen Xu Dao He Yi
Di Jing Qi Shen Xu Dao He Yi
Ren Jing Qi Shen Xu Dao He Yi
Tian Di Ren Jing Qi Shen Xu Dao He Yi
Wan Wu Jing Qi Shen Xu Dao He Yi
Quan Yu Zhou Jing Qi Shen Xu Dao He Yi
Jie Shi Yu Dao He Yi

Tian Jin Dan
Di Jin Dan
Ren Jin Dan
Tian Di Ren Jin Dan
Wan Wu Jin Dan
Quan Yu Zhou Jin Dan
Jie Shi Dao Jin Dan

Tian Yu Dao He Zhen
Di Yu Dao He Zhen
Ren Yu Dao He Zhen
Tian Di Ren Yu Dao He Zhen
Wan Wu Yu Dao He Zhen
Quan Yu Zhou Yu Dao He Zhen
Jie Shi Yu Dao He Zhen

Practice Jin Dan Da Tao Xiu Lian more. You could receive instant results. You are extremely happy, honored, and blessed.

Some of you could feel more pain after practicing Jin Dan Da Tao Xiu Lian. It may seem like you are getting worse. Remember that you are *not* getting worse. You could be experiencing fighting from a dark soul or it could be fighting of the energy blockage being removed.

Your feeling worse could also be spiritual testing from Heaven. Do you trust? Do you believe in the forgiveness and the Jin Dan Da Tao Xiu Lian practice? This is the test. You may receive a little testing, but you may not be aware that it is a test. You may start to complain and say, "This does not work," or "Why am I getting worse?"

Please understand that this spiritual testing can come from Heaven, from the Divine, or from Tao. Every single one of my thousands of students worldwide has experienced spiritual testing. My advanced students and my high-level teachers have experienced serious spiritual testing. Spiritual testing is a "must" step for every spiritual being. It can come with any spiritual healing. Be aware of this truth. It is very important for every spiritual seeker and practitioner.

Continue to practice. Do more forgiveness practice. Chant Jin Dan Da Tao Xiu Lian more. Do not be afraid. You are doing Tao practice, but you may have to go through these challenges. You cannot think that the Divine and Tao are making you worse. Any challenge, any spiritual testing, is part of your purification process. It is very important to know this wisdom.

Xiu Shan Duan E. "Xiu shan" means *practice kindness.* "Duan e" means *stop evil.* "Xiu shan duan e" (pronounced *sheo shahn dwahn uh*) means *be kind and stop all evil.*

To practice kindness is to have total love, forgiveness, and compassion. It can be difficult to do, especially when some people have harmed you, taken advantage of you, or hurt you. Can you forgive them? To have total love, forgiveness, and compassion is vital.

Always offer unconditional love, forgiveness, compassion, generosity, integrity, sincerity, and honesty to others, to society, to your city, to your country, to Mother Earth, to humanity, and to all souls in all universes. To offer all of this is to offer kindness.

To remove evil, the key is to remove selfishness. If one is selfish, all kinds of evil could follow, such as jealousy, meanness, vengefulness, hatred, anger, and more. To remove evil is to purify the heart. To purify the heart is to have total love, forgiveness, and compassion.

The opposite of selfishness is selflessness. To be selfless is to be a servant. The purpose of life is to serve. To be a servant is to make others happier and healthier. To be a servant is to create love, peace, and harmony for humanity, Mother Earth, and all universes.

Chu Tan Chen Chi. "Chu" means *remove*. "Tan" means *greed*. "Chen" means *anger*. "Chi" means *no intelligence to distinguish kindness from evil*. "Chu tan chen chi" (pronounced *choo tahn chun chee*) means *remove greed, anger, and lack of wisdom*.

This is a typical Buddhist teaching. Although I am teaching Tao in this book, at the highest level, Tao and Buddhist teaching are the same. I am just sharing the spiritual wisdom.

Greed has many facets. For example, there is greed for money, greed for power, greed for material possessions, and more. Greed is an extreme desire for something that can never be satisfied. Greed also includes being stingy. Stinginess means a person could have an abundance of something, but does not want to share any of it. In one sentence:

Greed is the source of all evil.

If a person is very greedy and cannot get what he or she wants, he or she could become angry.

Chi, which is lack of wisdom, means that one cannot distinguish between right and wrong or between kindness and evil. A person who lacks this wisdom will often think the wrong thing is a good thing, or think a good thing is a wrong thing. Such a person is very confused.

In order to transform greed, anger, and lack of wisdom, the key is to purify the heart. In Buddhist teaching, it is ming xin jian xing, *enlighten your heart to see your true self.* In Tao teaching, *to purify and enlighten the heart is to see your Yuan Shen.*

Xiu Miao Ming Xin. "Xiu" means *Xiu Lian.* Xiu Lian is purification. "Miao" means *profound.* "Ming" means *enlighten.* "Xin" means *heart.* "Xiu miao ming xin" (pronounced *sheo mee-yow ming sheen*) means *purify and enlighten your heart.*

Tao creates all things in all universes. Tao is quiet and calm. Tao is pure and profound. Tao has no attachment. Tao flows naturally. To study Tao and to purify the heart, it is very important to follow nature's way.

The Divine gave me a Soul Song, *God Gives His Heart to Me.* This Divine Soul Song is an absolute treasure for purifying the heart. Let me lead you in a practice to purify the heart.

Apply the Four Power Techniques:

Body Power. Put your left palm over your Message Center. Also known as the heart chakra, the Message Center is a fist-sized energy center located in the center of your chest, behind the sternum. The Message Center is very important for developing soul communication abilities and for healing. It is also the love center, forgiveness center, karma center, emotional center, life transformation center, soul enlightenment center, and more. Put your right hand in the traditional prayer position.

Soul Power. Say *hello:*

> *Dear Divine Soul Song,* God Gives His Heart to Me,
> *I love you, honor you, and appreciate you.*
> *Please purify my heart and transform my heart to be pure,*
> *profound, sincere, and to have unconditional love,*
> *forgiveness, and compassion.*
> *I am very grateful.*
> *Thank you.*

Mind Power. Visualize your Jin Dan rotating in your lower abdomen. In every practice from now on, you can apply Mind Power in the same way. This way is to focus on the Jin Dan. It does not matter in which part of the body you want to receive healing or rejuvenation. To focus on the Jin Dan is to focus on Tao.

Jin Dan Da Tao Xiu Lian practice is Tao practice. There is only one place to focus: the Jin Dan. The teaching is so simple. It is too simple to believe. Remember Da Tao zhi jian, *The Big Tao is extremely simple.*

Sound Power. Sing or chant the lyrics:

> *God gives his heart to me*
> *God gives his love to me*
> *My heart melds with his heart*
> *My love melds with his love*

Lu La Lu La La Li
Lu La Lu La La Li
Lu La Lu La Li
Lu La Lu La Li

God gives his heart to me
God gives his love to me
My heart melds with his heart
My love melds with his love

Lu La Lu La La Li
Lu La Lu La La Li
Lu La Lu La Li
Lu La Lu La Li

God gives his heart to me
God gives his love to me
My heart melds with his heart
My love melds with his love

Lu La Lu La La Li
Lu La Lu La La Li
Lu La Lu La Li
Lu La Lu La Li

God gives his heart to me
God gives his love to me
My heart melds with his heart
My love melds with his love

Lu La Lu La La Li
Lu La Lu La La Li
Lu La Lu La Li
Lu La Lu La Li . . .

Chant or sing for at least three to five minutes, three to five times per day. Purifying the heart is the key for Tao practice. Purifying the heart is the key for all spiritual practices. There is no limitation for this practice. The more you practice, the more your heart will purify. The benefits are unlimited.

Wu Si Wei Gong. "Wu si" means *no selfishness.* "Wei gong" means *for others.* "Wu si wei gong" (pronounced *woo sz way gawng*) means *serve others selflessly.*

Karma is the root cause of success and failure in every aspect of life. People may ask, "How do I know if I have created bad karma?" or "How do I know if I have created good karma?"

The answer is straightforward. You and everyone relates to the world in three ways, through:

- action—what you do
- speech—what you say
- thought—what you think

In one sentence:

If what you do, say, or think is only for you, you create bad karma; if what you do, say, or think is for others, you create good karma.

To have no selfishness is to avoid creating bad karma. To serve others selflessly is to create good karma. Discipline your actions, your words, and your thoughts. You will advance much faster on your spiritual journey and your physical journey.

Xiu Lian Fa Yao. "Xiu Lian" means *purification practice.* "Fa yao" means *principles.* "Xiu lian fa yao" (pronounced *sheo lyen fah yow*) means *Xiu Lian principles.*

The previous sacred phrase, wu si wei gong, is a good example of a Xiu Lian principle. When you do Jin Dan Da Tao Xiu Lian, you are creating Jin Dan. To practice Jin Dan is to meld with Tao. If you meld with Tao then you serve *wan ling.* Wan ling is all souls—countless souls in all planets, stars, galaxies, and universes. Therefore, to practice Jin Dan Da Tao Xiu Lian is the biggest service for others. You will create huge amounts of virtue.

If you are doing self-healing, the ultimate purpose is to meld with Tao. To meld with Tao, you have to heal yourself. Otherwise, how can you reach fan lao huan tong? If you cannot reach fan lao huan tong, your physical body will transition. To meld with Tao is to go beyond fan lao huan tong. To meld with Tao is to live forever. Therefore, self-healing is Tao practice. You are creating virtue for self-healing.

I give this teaching to make sure that you do not misunderstand the one-sentence secret I just shared:

> **If what you do, say, or think is only for you,**
> **you create bad karma; if what you do, say, or**
> **think is for others, you create good karma.**

This is one of the highest and most important Xiu Lian principles.

Shi Wei Gong Pu. "Shi" means *vow*. "Wei" means *to be*. "Gong pu" means *servant*. "Shi wei gong pu" (pronounced *shr way gawng poo*) means *vow to be a servant*.

This is the eighth book of my Soul Power Series. Every book begins with a section on the Soul Power Series. The first paragraph states:

The purpose of life is to serve. I have committed my life to this purpose. Service is my life mission.

My total mission is to transform the consciousness of all souls in all universes and enlighten them in order to create love, peace, and harmony for humanity, Mother Earth, and all universes.

A human being has a physical journey and a spiritual journey. The physical journey is limited because a human being's life is limited. The soul journey is eternal.

In your physical life, if you commit yourself to be a servant to others, you are connecting with Tao. Tao creates all things. Tao serves all. Tao serves unconditionally. It does not matter if you are a good and kind person or a selfish and mean person. Tao serves all. The sun and the moon shine for everyone. Mother Earth holds everyone.

Tao creates Heaven. Tao creates the sun, the moon, Mother Earth, and countless planets, stars, galaxies, and universes. *Tao serves all.* Understand this simple truth and your heart could open much wider. You could offer unconditional love and forgiveness to everyone and everything. This kind of love and forgiveness is the love and forgiveness of Tao.

Shi Dai Fu Wu. "Shi dai" means *all lives*. "Fu wu" means *service*. "Shi dai fu wu" (pronounced *shr dye foo woo*) means *serve in all lifetimes*.

The purpose of life is to serve. The purpose of one's physical life is to serve one's soul journey. The soul journey is to reach enlightenment. The final goal of the soul journey is to meld with Tao.

Soul enlightenment has layers. We are staying in Jiu Tian, the nine layers of Heaven. ("Jiu" means *nine*. "Tian" means *Heaven*.) At this time, there are approximately 6.8 billion people in Mother Earth. Mother Earth is in the Jiu Tian (pronounced *jeo tyen*) realm. The souls in this realm must reincarnate. It does not matter whether you would love to come back again or not. You have to come back. This is the rule of Jiu Tian.

To uplift the soul to Tian Wai Tian is a major accomplishment. "Wai" means *beyond*. "Tian Wai Tian" (pronounced *tyen wye tyen*) means *Heaven beyond Heaven*. The Divine stays in Tian Wai Tian. If a soul is uplifted to Tian Wai Tian, the soul stops reincarnation.

If the soul stops reincarnation, this soul will continue to serve. For example, you can call the Divine. You can call a major buddha or saint who has been uplifted to Tian Wai Tian. They will come to serve you right away. They serve you in soul form. They can offer healing and transformation for your life. They can protect you to avoid disasters. They are great servants.

If one melds with Tao, one becomes Tao. Tao creates all things. Tao is the true source and creator of Heaven, Mother Earth, humanity, countless planets, stars, galaxies, and universes. Tao serves everyone and everything. Tao is an unconditional servant.

We study and practice Tao. We are unconditional servants also.

Fu Wu Xiu Lian. "Fu wu" means *service*. "Xiu lian" means *totality of the spiritual journey*. "Fu wu xiu lian" means *Service Xiu Lian*.

I introduced Service Xiu Lian in my previous book, *Divine Transformation: The Divine Way to Self-clear Karma to Transform Your Health, Relationships, Finances, and More*. I will give you the essence of Fu Wu Xiu Lian here.

Fu Wu Xiu Lian means that whenever you do spiritual practices (xiu lian), you are also serving (fu wu) through your practice. For example, when you sing the Divine Soul Song *Love, Peace and Harmony*:

> *I love my heart and soul*
> *I love all humanity*
> *Join hearts and souls together*
> *Love, peace and harmony*
> *Love, peace and harmony*

you are serving humanity and all souls to create love, peace, and harmony for humanity, Mother Earth, and all universes.

When you chant the Tao Song:

> *Tian di ren he yi*
> *Tian di ren he yi*
> *Tian di ren he yi*
> *Tian di ren he yi . . .*

you are serving humanity, Mother Earth, and Heaven. You are also doing spiritual practice. The spiritual practice is to serve. This is Service Xiu Lian.

The big example you have learned earlier in this book is that when you practice Jin Dan Da Tao Xiu Lian, you are offering universal service. You are serving Heaven, Mother Earth, humanity, countless planets, stars, galaxies, and universes. You are serving Tao.

Shang Cheng Fa Men. "Shang cheng" means *highest*. "Fa men" means *sacred method*. "Shang cheng fa men" (pronounced *shahng chung fah mun*) means *the highest sacred Xiu Lian method*.

Shang cheng fa men is full and complete Xiu Lian. This full and complete Xiu Lian is, in fact, Tao Xiu Lian. Tao creates wan ling, every soul and everything in countless planets, stars, galaxies, and universes. To serve wan ling is to serve Tao.

Jin Dan Da Tao Xiu Lian is Fu Wu Xiu Lian, which is the highest Xiu Lian method. Jin Dan Da Tao Xiu Lian gathers *jing qi shen xu dao* of Heaven, Mother Earth, and wan wu, including countless planets, stars, galaxies, and universes, to form the Jin Dan of all of them. Finally, Tao Dan is formed.

To form the Tao Dan is to meld with Tao. They are the same thing, but with different words. They are one.

Qu Chu Ye Zhang. "Qu chu" means *remove*. "Ye zhang" means *bad karma*. "Qu chu ye zhang" (pronounced *chü choo yuh jahng*) means *remove bad karma*.

Fu Wu Xiu Lian and Jin Dan Da Tao Xiu Lian are one. Jin Dan Da Tao Xiu Lian can remove bad karma. This is because to practice Tao is to serve all souls. When you serve all souls, you can be given countless virtue. To receive virtue is to be forgiven. Therefore, Xiu Lian itself is to self-clear karma.

Let us do the Jin Dan Da Tao Xiu Lian practice to self-clear bad karma again. To self-clear bad karma is to transform all life. We cannot do Jin Dan Da Tao Xiu Lian enough.

Every time I lead you in this practice, do it seriously. Do not skip or rush quickly through this practice to read further. You will miss a lot. This is just like being in a Tao Retreat with me. If I lead every participant to practice, no one can read a book. Everyone has to practice.

I want to emphasize again:

To practice Jin Dan Da Tao Xiu Lian is to self-clear bad karma.

To practice Jin Dan Da Tao Xiu Lian is to heal.

To practice Jin Dan Da Tao Xiu Lian is to reach fan lao huan tong.

To practice Jin Dan Da Tao Xiu Lian is to achieve longevity.

To practice Jin Dan Da Tao Xiu Lian is to move in the direction of immortality.

Immortality is to meld with Tao.

Use the CD or audio MP3 downloads offered as part of this book. Even if you have never met me, you can chant with me.

Let us practice Jin Dan Da Tao Xiu Lian now.

Apply the Four Power Techniques to self-clear bad karma and to heal:

Body Power. Sit up straight. Put both of your palms over your lower abdomen, below the navel.

Soul Power. Say *hello:*

> *Dear soul mind body of Jin Dan Da Tao Xiu Lian,*
> *I love you, honor you, and appreciate you.*
> *You have the power to forgive my mistakes and the mistakes*
> *of my ancestors.*
> *Dear all dark souls who are in my body,*
> *I sincerely apologize for the mistakes that my ancestors and*
> *I have made in all of our lifetimes.*
> *Please forgive us.*
> *We are extremely grateful.*
> *We have learned our lessons.*

We will serve humanity and all souls unconditionally.
Dear Divine,
Dear Tao,
I am so grateful that I can request forgiveness.
I will become an unconditional universal servant.
Please forgive my bad karma and my ancestors' bad karma.
I am extremely honored and blessed.
Thank you.

Mind Power. Visualize your Jin Dan rotating in your abdomen. Your bad karma is forgiven. You are receiving healing and blessings.

Sound Power. Chant Jin Dan Da Tao Xiu Lian now:

Tian Zhi Jing
Di Zhi Jing
Ren Zhi Jing
Tian Di Ren Zhi Jing
Wan Wu Zhi Jing
Quan Yu Zhou Zhi Jing
Jie Shi Dao Zhi Jing

Tian Zhi Qi
Di Zhi Qi
Ren Zhi Qi
Tian Di Ren Zhi Qi
Wan Wu Zhi Qi
Quan Yu Zhou Zhi Qi
Jie Shi Dao Zhi Qi

Tian Zhi Shen
Di Zhi Shen
Ren Zhi Shen
Tian Di Ren Zhi Shen
Wan Wu Zhi Shen
Quan Yu Zhou Zhi Shen
Jie Shi Dao Zhi Shen

Tian Zhi Xu
Di Zhi Xu
Ren Zhi Xu
Tian Di Ren Zhi Xu
Wan Wu Zhi Xu
Quan Yu Zhou Zhi Xu
Jie Shi Dao Zhi Xu

Tian Zhi Dao
Di Zhi Dao
Ren Zhi Dao
Tian Di Ren Zhi Dao
Wan Wu Zhi Dao
Quan Yu Zhou Zhi Dao
Jie Shi Da Dao

Tian Jing Qi Shen Xu Dao He Yi
Di Jing Qi Shen Xu Dao He Yi
Ren Jing Qi Shen Xu Dao He Yi
Tian Di Ren Jing Qi Shen Xu Dao He Yi
Wan Wu Jing Qi Shen Xu Dao He Yi
Quan Yu Zhou Jing Qi Shen Xu Dao He Yi
Jie Shi Yu Dao He Yi

Tian Jin Dan
Di Jin Dan
Ren Jin Dan
Tian Di Ren Jin Dan
Wan Wu Jin Dan
Quan Yu Zhou Jin Dan
Jie Shi Dao Jin Dan

Tian Yu Dao He Zhen
Di Yu Dao He Zhen
Ren Yu Dao He Zhen
Tian Di Ren Yu Dao He Zhen
Wan Wu Yu Dao He Zhen
Quan Yu Zhou Yu Dao He Zhen
Jie Shi Yu Dao He Zhen

You have just practiced with me. Suddenly you could feel, "Oh, my pain feels better" or you could realize, "Wow! My pain has disappeared." Suddenly you could have more energy. Suddenly you could feel very clear in your mind. You do not need to make a request for everything, but everything is transforming.

If you are a beginner on the spiritual journey, when you do any practice, I teach you to use the Four Power Techniques. I have always taught that the most important power is Soul Power, which is Say Hello Healing and Blessing. Say *hello* and request what you need for healing, blessing, and transformation of your life. To request healing, blessing, and transformation of your life is the process to meld with Tao. To meld with Tao is to serve the soul mind body of countless planets, stars, galaxies, and universes. To serve is to self-clear bad karma. To serve is to receive healing, blessing, and transformation for every aspect of life.

The top secret of Xiu Lian is *not to request anything.* For example, if you want to self-clear bad karma or to heal your back, your shoulder, your depression, or your cancer; if you want to transform your relationships or your finances, just do Jin Dan Da Tao Xiu Lian.

Tao knows your problems. You do not need to tell Tao. You do the job and Tao will bless you. Therefore, every aspect of life can suddenly be transformed, including your health, relationships, and finances.

Just start to do Jin Dan Da Tao Xiu Lian anytime, anywhere. Chant it aloud or silently. Put your mind on your lower abdomen and just do it. Remember this top secret: **Just do it!** You do not need to ask for anything.

Sit up straight. Put both of your palms on your lower abdomen. Put your mind on your lower abdomen. Then start to chant:

> *Tian Zhi Jing*
> *Di Zhi Jing*
> *Ren Zhi Jing*
> *Tian Di Ren Zhi Jing*
> *Wan Wu Zhi Jing*
> *Quan Yu Zhou Zhi Jing*
> *Jie Shi Dao Zhi Jing*
>
> *Tian Zhi Qi*
> *Di Zhi Qi*
> *Ren Zhi Qi*
> *Tian Di Ren Zhi Qi*
> *Wan Wu Zhi Qi*
> *Quan Yu Zhou Zhi Qi*
> *Jie Shi Dao Zhi Qi*

Tian Zhi Shen
Di Zhi Shen
Ren Zhi Shen
Tian Di Ren Zhi Shen
Wan Wu Zhi Shen
Quan Yu Zhou Zhi Shen
Jie Shi Dao Zhi Shen

Tian Zhi Xu
Di Zhi Xu
Ren Zhi Xu
Tian Di Ren Zhi Xu
Wan Wu Zhi Xu
Quan Yu Zhou Zhi Xu
Jie Shi Dao Zhi Xu

Tian Zhi Dao
Di Zhi Dao
Ren Zhi Dao
Tian Di Ren Zhi Dao
Wan Wu Zhi Dao
Quan Yu Zhou Zhi Dao
Jie Shi Da Dao

Tian Jing Qi Shen Xu Dao He Yi
Di Jing Qi Shen Xu Dao He Yi
Ren Jing Qi Shen Xu Dao He Yi
Tian Di Ren Jing Qi Shen Xu Dao He Yi
Wan Wu Jing Qi Shen Xu Dao He Yi
Quan Yu Zhou Jing Qi Shen Xu Dao He Yi
Jie Shi Yu Dao He Yi

Tian Jin Dan
Di Jin Dan
Ren Jin Dan
Tian Di Ren Jin Dan
Wan Wu Jin Dan
Quan Yu Zhou Jin Dan
Jie Shi Dao Jin Dan

Tian Yu Dao He Zhen
Di Yu Dao He Zhen
Ren Yu Dao He Zhen
Tian Di Ren Yu Dao He Zhen
Wan Wu Yu Dao He Zhen
Quan Yu Zhou Yu Dao He Zhen
Jie Shi Yu Dao He Zhen

Practice more and more. Jin Dan Da Tao Xiu Lian is the fastest way to meld with Tao. Words are not enough to explain the benefits. Karma issues, health issues, relationship issues, and finance issues will be transformed just by practicing Jin Dan Da Tao Xiu Lian.

Ji Gong Lei De. "Ji" and "Lei" mean *accumulation.* "Gong de" means *virtue.* "Ji gong lei de" (pronounced *jee gawng lay duh*) means *accumulate virtue.*

I offered this teaching in my earlier books. I will give the essence again.

On Mother Earth, you work. It does not matter if you are an employee or a boss or you work for yourself. You are gaining money. Money is the reward for your work. Money is the energy to support your family and to serve others.

In the spiritual world, do saints earn money? Yes! Every soul in the spiritual world also earns spiritual money. Spiritual money is virtue. In the physical world, money is expressed in coins, paper bills, and more. In the spiritual world, virtue is expressed in colored dots and flowers. Generally speaking, the colors are red, golden, rainbow, purple, crystal, and all kinds of mixed colors.

Ten small colored dots form one small flower. Ten small flowers form a big flower. When a soul serves, red or other colored dots are given. If a soul serves in a big way, all kinds of colored flowers are given. Every soul must serve in order to receive virtue.

To serve is to earn and gain virtue. To gain virtue is to uplift one's soul standing. To uplift soul standing is to move toward yu Dao he zhen—melding with Tao.

To serve is to accumulate virtue. To do Fu Wu Xiu Lian or Jin Dan Da Tao Xiu Lian is the biggest service that a spiritual being can offer.

To do Jin Dan Da Tao Xiu Lian is to accumulate virtue.

45
元神真灵
Yuan Shen Zhen Ling

Tao is profound and mysterious

46
本在心中
Ben Zai Xin Zhong

Yuan Shen is inside the heart

47
不生不灭
Bu Sheng Bu Mie

Yuan Shen is not born and does not die

48
与道同存
Yu Dao Tong Cun

Yuan Shen and Tao exist together

49
人人皆有
Ren Ren Jie You

Everyone has Yuan Shen

50
为何不见
Wei He Bu Jian

Why can't a human being see the Yuan Shen?

51
世俗污浊
Shi Su Wu Zhuo

All kinds of pollution in society

52
性窍不开
Xing Qiao Bu Kai

The tunnel of the heart is not open

53
修炼三宝
Xiu Lian San Bao

Practice with the three treasures of jing qi shen

54
污浊自化
Wu Zhuo Zi Hua

All of the pollution self-transforms

55
明心见性
Ming Xin Jian Xing

Enlighten your heart to see your Yuan Shen

56
元神主宰
Yuan Shen Zhu Zai

Yuan Shen is in charge for your life

Yuan Shen Zhen Ling. "Yuan shen" means *Tao*. "Zhen" means *real*. "Ling" means *profound and mysterious*. "Yuan shen zhen ling" (pronounced *ywen shun jun ling*) means *Tao is profound and mysterious.*

A human being is in the yin yang world. The yin yang world is the *you* world. "You" means *existence.* Tao is emptiness and *nothingness.* Tao is the *wu* world. "Wu" means nothingness. The *wu* world creates the you world. Tao creates everything.

When the father's sperm and mother's egg join as one to create an embryo, this is *yin yang xiang jiao.* "Xiang jiao" (pronounced *shyahng jee-yow*) means *connect together.* Yin and yang connect together. At the moment the sperm and egg join as one, Tao responds instantly. Tao will send Yuan Shen to the embryo. Yuan Shen is Tao. Because Yuan Shen is Tao, Yuan Shen knows everything. Yuan Shen does not need to study. It hides inside one's body until one can find his or her Yuan Shen.

After a baby is born, Shi Shen is in charge. Shi Shen is the body soul who reincarnates again and again. After birth, everyone has to study. Your Shi Shen is in charge of the study. For all of the wisdom you have learned, your Shi Shen is the boss. But your Shi Shen is not your true emperor. Yuan Shen is your true emperor. One can find Yuan Shen only through spiritual practice.

Ben Zai Xin Zhong. "Ben" means *originally.* "Zai" means *locate.* "Xin zhong" means *inside the heart.* "Ben zai xin zhong" (pronounced *bun dzye sheen jawng*) means *Yuan Shen is inside the heart.* Yuan Shen is Tao. It is sent from Tao to you. It is hidden in your heart.

Bu Sheng Bu Mie. "Bu" means *no.* "Sheng" means *birth.* "Mie" means *die.* "Bu sheng bu mie" (pronounced *boo shung boo myeh*) means *Yuan Shen is not born and does not die.* Yuan Shen is Tao. Tao is not born and does not die. Tao is permanent.

Yu Dao Tong Cun. "Yu" means *with*. Dao or Tao is The Way. "Tong cun" means *exist together*. "Yu Dao tong cun" (pronounced *yü dow tawng tsoon*) means *Yuan Shen and Tao exist together*.

Ren Ren Jie You. "Ren ren" means *everyone*. "Jie" means *all*. "You" means *has*. "Ren ren jie you" (pronounced *wren wren jyeh yoe*) means *everyone has a Yuan Shen*. Tao gives everybody a Yuan Shen. Tao treats everybody equally. Tao has no preferences.

Wei He Bu Jian. "Wei he" means *why*. "Bu jian" means *cannot see*. "Wei he bu jian" (pronounced *way huh boo jyen*) means *why can't a human being see the Yuan Shen?*

Shi Su Wu Zhuo. "Shi su" means *society*. "Wu zhuo" means *all kinds of pollution*. "Shi su wu zhuo" (pronounced *shr soo woo jwaw*) means *all kinds of pollution in society*. The pollution includes greed, anger, lack of wisdom, hatred, jealousy, war, harming, taking advantage, cheating, stealing, and more.

Xing Qiao Bu Kai. "Xing qiao" means *tunnel of the heart*. "Bu kai" means *not open*. "Xing qiao bu kai" (pronounced *shing chee-yow boo kye*) means *the tunnel of the heart is not open*.

All kinds of pollution on Mother Earth block the tunnel of the heart. Then, a person cannot see the Yuan Shen or Tao.

Xiu Lian San Bao. "Xiu lian" means *purification practice*. "San bao" means *three treasures*. "Xiu lian san bao" (pronounced *sheo lyen sahn bao* [rhymes with *now*]) means *practice three treasures*. The three treasures are jing qi shen. "Jing" means *matter*. "Qi" means *energy*. "Shen" means *soul*. I will explain this much more in the following sacred phrases.

Wu Zhuo Zi Hua. "Wu zhuo" means *all of the pollution*. "Zi hua" means *self transformation*. "Wu zhuo zi hua" (pronounced *woo jwaw dz hwah*) means *all of the pollution self-transforms*.

This sacred phrase is directly connected with the previous phrase, xiu lian san bao. If one does the Xiu Lian practice of San Bao, which are jing qi shen, all pollution will self-transform.

Ming Xin Jian Xing. "Ming" means *enlighten*. "Xin" means *heart*. "Jian" means *see*. "Xing" means *Yuan Shen*. "Ming xin jian xing" (pronounced *ming sheen jyen shing*) means *enlighten your heart to see your Yuan Shen*.

I explained ming xin jian xing earlier in conjunction with the sacred phrase, yu Dao he zhen (line 13). Go back to read the explanation of this sacred phrase again on pages 148–167. You will understand much further this time.

Only through Xiu Lian can you see your Yuan Shen. The key for Xiu Lian is to purify your heart. To purify your heart is to remove all types of pollution. After removing all kinds of pollution, you will see your Yuan Shen. Your true emperor will be the leader. Shi Shen, your original soul, will start to listen to Yuan Shen. Shi Shen will gradually meld with your Yuan Shen.

It takes time for Yuan Shen to guide and lead Shi Shen. Finally, your Shi Shen will completely meld with Yuan Shen. It will take the greatest effort.

In ancient times, serious Tao practitioners practiced Tao for ten years, thirty years, or an entire lifetime. Ten years are enough for complete Tao practice in my Tao training program, but before melding with Tao, one must first reach ming xin jian xing.

Yuan Shen Zhu Zai. "Yuan shen" means *Tao*. "Zhu zai" means *in charge*. "Yuan shen zhu zai" (pronounced *ywen shun joo dzye*) means *Yuan Shen is in charge for your life.*

After ming xin jian xing, you are enlightened. If you reach enlightenment, Yuan Shen appears. Your Yuan Shen becomes the true boss of your life. Your Yuan Shen will then guide you for your entire life to deal with every aspect of your life and to move your journey of yu Dao he zhen.

57
内三宝
Nei San Bao

Three internal treasures

58
精气神
Jing Qi Shen

Matter energy soul

59
外三宝
Wai San Bao

Three external treasures

60
耳目口
Er Mu Kou

Ears eyes mouth

61
妄视神漏
Wang Shi Shen Lou

See polluted things, your soul could get lost

62
妄听精漏
Wang Ting Jing Lou

Hear polluted words, lose your jing

63
妄言气漏
Wang Yan Qi Lou

Speak polluted words, lose your qi

64
外三宝漏
Wai San Bao Lou

Three external treasures are leaking

65

目不妄视

Mu Bu Wang Shi

Do not see polluted things

66

耳不妄听

Er Bu Wang Ting

Do not hear polluted words

67

口不妄言

Kou Bu Wang Yan

Do not speak polluted words

68

外三宝不漏

Wai San Bao Bu Lou

**Close your external treasures,
do not leak your *jing qi shen***

69

不视安神于心

Bu Shi An Shen Yu Xin

**Do not see polluted things to make your
shen reside peacefully in your heart**

70
不听蓄精于肾

Bu Ting Xu Jing Yu Shen

**Do not hear polluted words to increase
the jing in your kidneys**

71
不言孕气丹田

Bu Yan Yun Qi Dan Tian

**Do not speak polluted words to increase
the qi in the Dan Tian**

72
内三宝自合

Nei San Bao Zi He

Three internal treasures join together

73
外不漏

Wai Bu Lou

Three external treasures do not leak

74
内自合

Nei Zi He

Three internal treasures join as one

75
通天达地
Tong Tian Da Di

Connect Heaven and Mother Earth

76
逍遥道中
Xiao Yao Dao Zhong

Meld with Tao to have true freedom and joy

Nei San Bao. "Nei" means *internal*. "San" means *three*. "Bao" means *treasures*. "Nei san bao" (pronounced *nay sahn bao* [rhymes with *now*]) means *three internal treasures*.

Jing Qi Shen. "Jing" means *matter*. "Qi" means *vital energy and life force*. "Shen" means *soul*. "Jing qi shen" (pronounced *jing chee shun*) means *matter energy soul*. Jing qi shen are the three internal treasures.

A human body is made of matter. A system, an organ, and a cell are made of matter. Everything in the universe is made of matter. In Tao teaching, jing represents the whole body's jing, including the jing of all systems, organs, and cells.

Matter vibrates. Energy radiates out from matter. Matter has shape. Qi has no shape. *The Yellow Emperor's Internal Classic*, the authority book of traditional Chinese medicine, states: "Qi ju ze cheng xing, qi san ze chang feng" (pronounced *chee jü dzuh chung shing, chee sahn dzuh chahng fung*). This means *accumulation of qi forms a shape, dissipation of qi is just like the wind flowing away*. The wind is qi. In Tao teaching, qi represents the whole body's qi, including the qi of all systems, organs, and cells.

"Shen" means *souls*, including the souls of the body, systems, organs, and cells.

Jing qi shen represents the matter, energy, and souls of the whole body. They are the three internal treasures of a human being. A human's life is based on jing qi shen. When jing qi shen is not aligned and in balance, or when one lacks sufficient jing qi shen, then one becomes sick. To heal is to align, balance, and nourish jing qi shen. To heal is to fulfill one's jing qi shen.

Wai San Bao. "Wai" means *external*. "San" means *three*. "Bao" means *treasures*. "Wai san bao" (pronounced *wye sahn bao*) means *three external treasures*.

Er Mu Kou. "Er" means *ears*. "Mu" means *eyes*. "Kou" means *mouth*. "Er mu kou" (pronounced *ur moo koe*) means *ears, eyes, mouth*. These are the three external treasures.

Wang Shi Shen Lou. "Wang shi" means *see polluted things*. "Shen lou" means *soul gets lost*. "Wang shi shen lou" (pronounced *wahng shr shun loe*) means *if you see polluted things, your soul could get lost*.

For example, if you see people who are greedy for money and power, people who are selfish, people who are mean, people who are cheating or stealing, or people who are upset and angry, these polluted things could affect you.

Mother Earth is a polluted place. Mother Earth is just like red dust. Mother Earth is just like the bitter sea. Human beings live in a polluted environment. This polluted environment could make your soul get lost.

In ancient spiritual teaching, eyes are the windows of the heart and the soul. If you see polluted things, your heart and soul will be affected. Therefore, to see polluted things could make your heart and soul get lost.

Wang shi shen lou is to remind us not to see these polluted things and, if we do, not to let them affect our heart and soul. The key is still to purify the heart.

Wang Ting Jing Lou. "Wang ting" means *hear polluted things.* "Jing" means *matter.* "Lou" literally means *leak.* "Wang ting jing lou" (pronounced *wahng ting jing loe*) means *if you hear polluted words, you could lose your jing.*

On Mother Earth there are many words and voices that are not clean. For example, many people love to complain. Some people complain too much. If you keep quiet when you hear complaining, you will lose your jing. Complaining is not right. If you keep quiet, you are silently supporting the complaining. At the least, say, "Sorry, I do not like to hear this." Or you can say, "Please do not continue." Or straightforwardly say, "You are complaining. Please stop."

Hearing polluted voices and polluted words will cause you to lose your matter. Hearing is connected with the kidneys. Kidneys produce jing. To hear polluted things will hurt your kidneys. Therefore, to hear polluted things will cause you to lose jing. This is how hearing and matter (jing) are connected.

This sacred phrase is to remind us to stop hearing polluted words or voices. This is also part of the purification process for each person.

Wang Yan Qi Lou. "Wang yan" means *speak polluted words.* "Qi" means *vital energy and life force.* "Lou" means *leak.* "Wang yan qi lou" (pronounced *wahng yahn chee loe*) means *if you speak polluted words, you could lose your qi.*

For example, a person who is very angry, yelling, and saying bad words will lose qi. After you speak a lot, you may have experienced feeling tired. When you are upset, you are so excited that you lose even more energy.

There is a renowned ancient spiritual teaching: *Huo shao gong de lin.* "Huo" means *anger, just like fire.* "Shao" means *burn.* "Gong de lin" means *the virtue forest.* "Huo shao gong de lin" (pronounced *hwaw shao gawng duh leen*) means *anger burns your virtue.*

When two people, "A" and "B," are arguing, and A is upset, yelling and yelling, what happens if B keeps quiet? A continues to throw his virtue to B. B gains a lot. Virtue is spiritual currency. Virtue blesses every aspect of your life. Losing virtue is serious.

Another ancient spiritual teaching is *Huo rong kou chu.* "Huo" means *disaster.* "Rong" means *from.* "Kou" means *mouth.* "Chu" means *come out.* "Huo rong kou chu" (pronounced *hwaw rawng koe choo*) means *disasters come from speech.*

These teachings and the sacred phrase wang yan qi lou remind us that we have to be careful of our speech. We have to purify and discipline our speech. Polluted speech will cause us to lose qi and virtue.

Wai San Bao Lou. "Wai" means *external.* "San" means *three.* "Bao" means *treasures.* "Lou" means *leak.* "Wai san bao lou" (pronounced *wye sahn bao loe*) means *three external treasures are leaking.*

The previous three sacred phrases, wang shi shen lou, wang ting jing lou, and wang yan qi lou are wai san bao lou. When your eyes, ears, and mouth see, hear, and speak polluted things, you lose your jing qi shen. This is the "leaking" of your jing qi shen. Therefore, on the spiritual journey, it is very important for every spiritual being to avoid pollution. Everyone must purify. How do you purify? Avoid polluted things first.

In a renowned spiritual teaching, there are three sentences

with the same essence of the Tao teaching here: *see no evil, hear no evil, speak no evil.* This famous statement is also depicted by three monkeys: Mizaru, covering his eyes, who sees no evil; Kikazaru, covering his ears, who hears no evil; and Iwazaru, covering his mouth, who speaks no evil.

Mu Bu Wang Shi. "Mu" means *eye.* "Bu" means *not.* "Wang shi" means *see polluted things.* "Mu bu wang shi" (pronounced *moo boo wahng shr*) means *do not see polluted things.*

We just learned that to see polluted things could make your heart and soul get lost. Therefore, this phrase directly teaches everyone not to see polluted things. Then your heart and soul will not get lost.

Er Bu Wang Ting. "Er" means *ears.* "Bu" means *not.* "Wang ting" means *hear polluted words.* "Er bu wang ting" (pronounced *ur boo wahng ting*) means *do not hear polluted words.*

We just learned that to hear polluted words could cause you to lose your jing. This phrase directly teaches everyone not to hear polluted things. Then you will not lose jing.

Kou Bu Wang Yan. "Kou" means *mouth.* "Bu" means *not.* "Wang yan" means *speak polluted words.* "Kou bu wang yan" (pronounced *koe boo wahng yahn*) means *do not speak polluted words.*

We just learned that to speak polluted words could cause you to lose your qi. This is the correction for that mistake. Do not speak polluted words.

Wai San Bao Bu Lou. "Wai" means *external.* "San" means *three.* "Bao" means *treasures.* "Bu" means *not.* "Lou" means *leak.* "Wai san bao bu lou" (pronounced *wye sahn bao boo loe*) means *close your external treasures; do not leak your jing qi shen.*

Bu Shi An Shen Yu Xin. "Bu shi" means *do not see.* "An shen yu xin" means *your shen is peaceful in your heart.* "Bu shi an shen yu xin" (pronounced *boo shr ahn shun yü sheen*) means *do not see polluted things to make your shen reside peacefully in your heart.*

This is to teach every Tao practitioner not to see polluted things in order to benefit your shen.

Bu Ting Xu Jing Yu Shen. "Bu ting" means *do not hear.* "Xu jing yu shen" means *jing is stored in the kidneys.* "Bu ting xu jing yu shen" (pronounced *boo ting shü jing yü shun*) means *do not hear polluted words to store and increase the jing in your kidneys.*

This is to teach every Tao practitioner not to hear polluted words in order to benefit your jing.

Bu Yan Yun Qi Dan Tian. "Bu yan" means *do not speak.* "Yun qi dan tian" means *qi increases in the Dan Tian.* "Bu yan yun qi dan tian" (pronounced *boo yahn yün chee dahn tyen*) means *do not speak polluted things to increase the qi in the Dan Tian.*

This is to teach every Tao practitioner not to speak polluted words in order to benefit your qi.

Nei San Bao Zi He. "Nei" means *internal.* "San" means *three.* "Bao" means *treasures.* "Zi he" means *join together.* "Nei san bao zi he" (pronounced *nay sahn bao dz huh*) means *three internal treasures join together.*

The three internal treasures, shen qi jing, join together to form the Jin Dan. To form the Jin Dan is ming xin jian xing. To form a complete Jin Dan takes a long time. After ming xin jian xing, Yuan Shen will guide Shi Shen. Shi Shen will meld with Yuan Shen. To completely meld Shi Shen with Yuan Shen takes a long time also. But this is the process and these are the steps to meld with Tao.

Wai Bu Lou. "Wai" means *external*. "Bu lou" means *no leak*. "Wai bu lou" (pronounced *wye boo loe*) means *three external treasures do not leak*.

This is to teach you to close your three external treasures (eyes, ears, mouth) to avoid leaking your jing qi shen.

Nei Zi He. "Nei" means *internal*. "Zi he" means *join as one*. "Nei zi he" (pronounced *nay dz huh*) means *three internal treasures join as one*.

To join jing qi shen as one is to form the Jin Dan. To join jing qi shen together is to reach ming xin jian xing. This is an extremely significant accomplishment and step in the Tao journey.

Tong Tian Da Di. "Tong" means *connects*. "Tian" means *Heaven*. "Da" means *reach*. "Di" means *Earth*. "Tong tian da di" (pronounced *tawng tyen dah dee*) means *connect Heaven and Mother Earth*.

When you reach nei san bao zi he (three internal treasures join together), which means jing qi shen he yi, you will see your Yuan Shen. Yuan Shen is Tao. Tao creates Heaven and Mother Earth. Therefore, you will then connect with Heaven and Mother Earth automatically. Your Yuan Shen will guide you to connect with Heaven and Mother Earth further and further. Your Yuan Shen will meld with Shi Shen gradually. If your Yuan Shen and Shi Shen can meld completely together, then you will meld with Tao.

When you reach nei san bao zi he, your jing qi shen join as one, which means your Jin Dan has formed. You still need continuous and persistent practice to increase the Jin Dan. If you can form a complete Jin Dan, you will have gathered jing qi shen from countless planets, stars, galaxies, and universes in order to form Tao Dan. Then you will meld with Tao.

Xiao Yao Dao Zhong. "Xiao yao" means *true freedom and joy.* "Dao zhong" means *meld with Tao.* "Xiao yao Dao zhong" (pronounced *shee-yow yow dow jawng*) means *meld with Tao to have true freedom and joy.*

To reach jing qi shen he yi, to form Jin Dan, and to see one's Yuan Shen are the same. They are all the same stage of moving in the direction of melding with Tao.

After one melds with Tao, this one will become Tao. This one will have true freedom and joy. This one will go into the Tao fa zi ran (*follow nature's way*) condition. This one will be able to:

- Offer Tao love.

  Tao love is the highest and purest love. Tao love melts all blockages and purifies soul, heart, mind, and body for humanity, Mother Earth, countless planets, stars, and galaxies, and all universes.
- Offer Tao forgiveness.

  Tao forgiveness is the highest unconditional forgiveness. Tao forgiveness brings inner joy and inner peace for humanity, Mother Earth, countless planets, stars, and galaxies, and all universes.
- Offer Tao compassion.

  Tao compassion is the deepest compassion. Tao compassion boosts energy, stamina, vitality, and im-

munity for humanity, Mother Earth, countless planets, stars, and galaxies, and all universes.

- Offer Tao light.

    Tao light is the most powerful and purest light.
Tao light heals, prevents sickness, purifies, rejuvenates
soul, heart, mind, and body, transforms relationships
and finances, and enlightens soul, heart, mind, and
body for humanity, Mother Earth, countless planets,
stars, and galaxies, and all universes.

- Gain Tao intelligence.

    Tao intelligence is the highest intelligence.

- Have Tao kindness.

    Tao kindness is the highest kindness. Tao is kind
to everyone and everything. Tao treats everyone and
everything equally.

- Enjoy Tao happiness.

    Tao happiness is the truest happiness.

- Enjoy Tao freedom.

    Tao freedom is the most complete freedom.

Now I am ready to offer Tao Golden Light Ball and Golden
Liquid Spring of Tao Soul Mind Body Transplants as permanent
gifts to you and every reader.

Prepare.

Sit up straight. Put the tip of your tongue as close as you can
to the roof of your mouth without touching. Put both of your
palms on your lower abdomen. Totally relax. Open your heart
and soul to receive this great honor and these priceless treasures.
The Tao treasures will come to your lower abdomen.

Tao Order: Tao Golden Light Ball and Golden Liquid Spring of Tao Love Soul Transplant

Transmission!

Tao Order: Tao Golden Light Ball and Golden Liquid Spring of Tao Love Mind Transplant

Transmission!

Tao Order: Tao Golden Light Ball and Golden Liquid Spring of Tao Love Body Transplant

Transmission!

Tao Order: Tao Golden Light Ball and Golden Liquid Spring of Tao Forgiveness Soul Transplant

Transmission!

Tao Order: Tao Golden Light Ball and Golden Liquid Spring of Tao Forgiveness Mind Transplant

Transmission!

Tao Order: Tao Golden Light Ball and Golden Liquid Spring of Tao Forgiveness Body Transplant

Transmission!

Tao Order: Tao Golden Light Ball and Golden Liquid Spring of Tao Compassion Soul Transplant

Transmission!

Tao Order: Tao Golden Light Ball and Golden Liquid Spring of Tao Compassion Mind Transplant

Transmission!

Tao Order: Tao Golden Light Ball and Golden Liquid Spring of Tao Compassion Body Transplant

Transmission!

Tao Order: Tao Golden Light Ball and Golden Liquid Spring of Tao Light Soul Transplant

Transmission!

Tao Order: Tao Golden Light Ball and Golden Liquid Spring of Tao Light Mind Transplant

Transmission!

Tao Order: Tao Golden Light Ball and Golden Liquid Spring of Tao Light Body Transplant

Transmission!

Tao Order: Tao Golden Light Ball and Golden Liquid Spring of Tao Kindness Soul Transplant

Transmission!

Tao Order: Tao Golden Light Ball and Golden Liquid Spring of Tao Kindness Mind Transplant

Transmission!

Tao Order: Tao Golden Light Ball and Golden Liquid Spring of Tao Kindness Body Transplant

Transmission!

Tao Order: Tao Golden Light Ball and Golden Liquid Spring of Tao Happiness Soul Transplant

Transmission!

Tao Order: Tao Golden Light Ball and Golden Liquid Spring of Tao Happiness Mind Transplant

Transmission!

Tao Order: Tao Golden Light Ball and Golden Liquid Spring of Tao Happiness Body Transplant

Transmission!

Tao Order: Tao Golden Light Ball and Golden Liquid Spring of Tao Freedom Soul Transplant

Transmission!

Tao Order: Tao Golden Light Ball and Golden Liquid Spring of Tao Freedom Mind Transplant

Transmission!

Tao Order: Tao Golden Light Ball and Golden Liquid Spring of Tao Freedom Body Transplant

Transmission!

Tao Order: Join the twenty-one permanent Tao treasures as one.

Ya Hei Ya Hei Ya Hei Ya Hei You!

Here is a translation of this last Tao Order:

This is the Tao Order to join the twenty-one Tao Soul Mind Body Transplants that you have just received as one. These Tao treasures carry Tao power for healing, preventing sickness, purifying, rejuvenating, transforming, and enlightening your soul, heart, mind, and body, and transforming your relationships and finances that is beyond words, comprehension, and imagination.

You are extremely blessed. We cannot honor Tao enough. Let us chant or sing *Tao Gives Tao's Heart to Me* to express our greatest gratitude:

> *Tao gives Tao's heart to me*
> *Tao gives Tao's love to me*
> *My heart melds with Tao's heart*
> *My love melds with Tao's love*

Apply these Tao treasures a lot, anytime, anywhere. You can receive unlimited blessing.

Here is how to practice with divine and Tao treasures for healing. Apply the Four Power Techniques:

Body Power. Sit up straight. Put the tip of your tongue as close as you can to the roof of your mouth without touching. Contract your anus for a few seconds and then release. Place both palms on your lower abdomen.

Soul Power. Say *hello:*

> *Dear all of my Tao and divine permanent treasures,*
> *I love you, honor you, and appreciate you.*
> *You have the power to heal my sicknesses.*
> *Please heal* _____ (make your requests for healing
>   of your spiritual, mental, emotional, and physical
>   bodies).
> *I am extremely grateful.*
> *Thank you.*

Mind Power. Visualize your Jin Dan rotating in your abdomen. Visualize also that you are healed.

Sound Power. Chant repeatedly, silently or aloud, for several minutes:

> *Divine and Tao treasures heal me. Thank you, Divine and Tao.*
>
> *Divine and Tao treasures heal me. Thank you, Divine and Tao.*
>
> *Divine and Tao treasures heal me. Thank you, Divine and Tao.*
>
> *Divine and Tao treasures heal me. Thank you, Divine and Tao.*
>
> *Divine and Tao treasures heal me. Thank you, Divine and Tao.*
>
> *Divine and Tao treasures heal me. Thank you, Divine and Tao.*
>
> *Divine and Tao treasures heal me. Thank you, Divine and Tao . . .*

Close. After chanting and visualizing for several minutes, close this and every practice by saying:

> *Hao! Hao! Hao!*
> *Thank you. Thank you. Thank you.*

"Hao" means *good* or *perfect*. The first *thank you* is to the Divine and Tao. The second *thank you* is to your spiritual fathers and mothers and all the souls who came to assist you. The third *thank you* is to your own soul, heart, mind, and body.

As with Jin Dan Da Tao Xiu Lian, there is no time limit for this or any practice in this book. When you practice, you are receiving divine and Tao frequency and vibration, with divine and

Tao love, forgiveness, compassion, and light. The longer and the more often you practice, the better.

Next we will practice with divine and Tao treasures to rejuvenate. Apply the Four Power Techniques:

Body Power. Sit up straight. Put the tip of your tongue as close as you can to the roof of your mouth without touching. Contract your anus for a few seconds and then release. Place both palms on your lower abdomen.

Soul Power. Say *hello:*

> *Dear all of my Tao and divine permanent treasures,*
> *I love you, honor you, and appreciate you.*
> *You have the power to form my Jin Dan and rejuvenate my*
>   *soul, heart, mind, and body.*
> *I am extremely grateful.*
> *I cannot honor you enough.*
> *Thank you.*

Mind Power. Visualize your Jin Dan rotating in your abdomen. Visualize also that your soul, heart, mind, and body are rejuvenated.

Sound Power. Chant repeatedly, silently or aloud, for several minutes:

> *Divine and Tao treasures form my Jin Dan and rejuvenate*
>   *my soul, heart, mind, and body. Thank you, Divine*
>   *and Tao.*

Divine and Tao treasures form my Jin Dan and rejuvenate my soul, heart, mind, and body. Thank you, Divine and Tao.

Divine and Tao treasures form my Jin Dan and rejuvenate my soul, heart, mind, and body. Thank you, Divine and Tao.

Divine and Tao treasures form my Jin Dan and rejuvenate my soul, heart, mind, and body. Thank you, Divine and Tao.

Divine and Tao treasures form my Jin Dan and rejuvenate my soul, heart, mind, and body. Thank you, Divine and Tao.

Divine and Tao treasures form my Jin Dan and rejuvenate my soul, heart, mind, and body. Thank you, Divine and Tao.

Divine and Tao treasures form my Jin Dan and rejuvenate my soul, heart, mind, and body. Thank you, Divine and Tao . . .

Close. Close in the usual way.

Next, practice with divine and Tao treasures to prolong your life. Apply the Four Power Techniques:

Body Power. Sit up straight. Put the tip of your tongue as close as you can to the roof of your mouth without touching. Contract your anus for a few seconds and then release. Place both palms on your lower abdomen.

Soul Power. Say *hello:*

Dear all of my Tao and divine permanent treasures,
I love you, honor you, and appreciate you.

You have the power to form my Jin Dan and prolong my life.
I am extremely grateful.
I cannot honor you enough.
Thank you.

Mind Power. Visualize your Jin Dan expanding and that your life is prolonged.

Sound Power. Chant repeatedly, silently or aloud, for several minutes:

Divine and Tao treasures form my Jin Dan and have the
   power to prolong my life. Thank you, Divine and Tao.
Divine and Tao treasures form my Jin Dan and have the
   power to prolong my life. Thank you, Divine and Tao.
Divine and Tao treasures form my Jin Dan and have the
   power to prolong my life. Thank you, Divine and Tao.
Divine and Tao treasures form my Jin Dan and have the
   power to prolong my life. Thank you, Divine and Tao.
Divine and Tao treasures form my Jin Dan and have the
   power to prolong my life. Thank you, Divine and Tao.
Divine and Tao treasures form my Jin Dan and have the
   power to prolong my life. Thank you, Divine and Tao.
Divine and Tao treasures form my Jin Dan and have the
   power to prolong my life. Thank you, Divine and Tao . . .

Close. Close in the usual way.

⁂

I have explained the three external treasures and the three internal treasures. The three external treasures must be closed. Do not leak your jing qi shen, which are the three internal treasures. Finally, you want to have jing qi shen join as one.

After the teaching of the three internal treasures and three external treasures, you should understand the importance of jing qi shen further. At the same time, you should understand the power of Jin Dan Da Tao Xiu Lian further. Jin Dan Da Tao Xiu Lian gathers *jing qi shen xu dao* of Heaven, Mother Earth, humanity, and wan wu, including countless planets, stars, galaxies, and universes. To practice Jin Dan Da Tao Xiu Lian is to form the Tao Dan. To form the Tao Dan is to meld with Tao.

This is the perfect time to do Jin Dan Da Tao Xiu Lian with me one more time.

Sit up straight. Put both palms on your lower abdomen. Focus your mind on your lower abdomen. Then chant to form your Jin Dan. If you have a Divine or Tao Jin Dan Download, chant to increase the power of your Jin Dan:

> *Tian Zhi Jing*
> *Di Zhi Jing*
> *Ren Zhi Jing*
> *Tian Di Ren Zhi Jing*
> *Wan Wu Zhi Jing*
> *Quan Yu Zhou Zhi Jing*
> *Jie Shi Dao Zhi Jing*
>
> *Tian Zhi Qi*
> *Di Zhi Qi*
> *Ren Zhi Qi*
> *Tian Di Ren Zhi Qi*
> *Wan Wu Zhi Qi*
> *Quan Yu Zhou Zhi Qi*
> *Jie Shi Dao Zhi Qi*

Tian Zhi Shen
Di Zhi Shen
Ren Zhi Shen
Tian Di Ren Zhi Shen
Wan Wu Zhi Shen
Quan Yu Zhou Zhi Shen
Jie Shi Dao Zhi Shen

Tian Zhi Xu
Di Zhi Xu
Ren Zhi Xu
Tian Di Ren Zhi Xu
Wan Wu Zhi Xu
Quan Yu Zhou Zhi Xu
Jie Shi Dao Zhi Xu

Tian Zhi Dao
Di Zhi Dao
Ren Zhi Dao
Tian Di Ren Zhi Dao
Wan Wu Zhi Dao
Quan Yu Zhou Zhi Dao
Jie Shi Da Dao

Tian Jing Qi Shen Xu Dao He Yi
Di Jing Qi Shen Xu Dao He Yi
Ren Jing Qi Shen Xu Dao He Yi
Tian Di Ren Jing Qi Shen Xu Dao He Yi
Wan Wu Jing Qi Shen Xu Dao He Yi
Quan Yu Zhou Jing Qi Shen Xu Dao He Yi
Jie Shi Yu Dao He Yi

Tian Jin Dan
Di Jin Dan
Ren Jin Dan
Tian Di Ren Jin Dan
Wan Wu Jin Dan
Quan Yu Zhou Jin Dan
Jie Shi Dao Jin Dan

Tian Yu Dao He Zhen
Di Yu Dao He Zhen
Ren Yu Dao He Zhen
Tian Di Ren Yu Dao He Zhen
Wan Wu Yu Dao He Zhen
Quan Yu Zhou Yu Dao He Zhen
Jie Shi Yu Dao He Zhen

As I have stated previously, Jin Dan Da Tao Xiu Lian is the practice for your entire life. There is no time limit for this practice. You can never think that you have practiced Jin Dan Da Tao Xiu Lian enough.

Jin Dan Da Tao Xiu Lian is the fastest way to meld with Tao. To meld with Tao is the final destiny for one's spiritual journey and physical journey.

77

道生一

Dao Sheng Yi

Tao creates One

78

天一真水

Tian Yi Zhen Shui

Heaven's Oneness sacred liquid

79

金津玉液

Jin Jin Yu Ye

Gold liquid, jade liquid

80

咽入丹田

Yan Ru Dan Tian

Swallow into the Lower Dan Tian

81

神气精合一

Shen Qi Jing He Yi

Join soul energy matter as one

82

天地人合一

Tian Di Ren He Yi

**Join Heaven, Mother Earth,
human being as one**

83
金丹炼成

Jin Dan Lian Cheng

Jin Dan is formed

84
抱元守一

Bao Yuan Shou Yi

Hold both hands in a circle below the navel and concentrate on the Jin Dan

85
人命如灯油

Ren Ming Ru Deng You

A human's life is like the oil in a lamp

86
耗尽命归西

Hao Jin Ming Gui Xi

When the oil is exhausted, life ends

87
欲健康长寿

Yu Jian Kang Chang Shou

Wish to have good health and longevity

88
必添灯油
Bi Tian Deng You

Must add oil to the lamp

89
天一真水
Tian Yi Zhen Shui

Heaven's Oneness sacred liquid

90
金津玉液
Jin Jin Yu Ye

Gold liquid, jade liquid

91
犹如添油
You Ru Tian You

Is just like adding oil to the lamp

92
油灯常明
You Deng Chang Ming

The oil is always burning

Dao Sheng Yi. Tao or Dao is The Way. "Sheng" means *create.*
"Yi" means *one.* "Dao sheng yi" (pronounced *dow shung yee*)
means *Tao creates One.*

Dao sheng yi, tian yi zhen shui, jin jin yu ye, yan ru dan tian
are explained in detail and depth on pp. 92–95 of *Tao I: The Way
of All Life.* Here, I will just give the essence of these few sacred
phrases.

Tao is the source of all things. Tao is the creator of all things.
Tao is the Way. Tao is emptiness and nothingness. Dao sheng yi
means *Tao creates One.* One is unity. There are countless planets,
stars, galaxies, and universes, but they are one. One is Tao Oneness. In fact, Tao is One and One is Tao.

Remember this Tao Oneness. In Tao Xiu Lian practice, always remember Oneness. I will explain this Oneness much more
in the following sacred phrases. Put this Oneness in your heart
and consciousness first. I am preparing your Shi Shen.

Tian Yi Zhen Shui. "Tian" means *Heaven.* "Yi" means *one.*
"Zhen" means *sacred or true.* "Shui" means *water or liquid.* "Tian
yi zhen shui" (pronounced *tyen yee jun shway*) means *Heaven's
unique sacred liquid*, which is *Heaven's Oneness sacred liquid.*

Tian yi zhen shui is Heaven's unique sacred liquid. In fact,
tian yi zhen shui is Tao's sacred liquid. We can call it tian yi zhen
shui or Dao yi zhen shui, Heaven's or Tao's Oneness sacred liquid,
respectively. When you chant *tian yi zhen shui*, Heaven and Tao
will deliver their sacred liquid through the Bai Hui (pronounced
bye hway) acupuncture point at the top of your head[10] into your

---

10. Draw a line from the top of one ear over the head to the top of the other ear. Draw another
line from the tip of the nose up and over the top of the head to the nape of the neck. The Bai
Hui acupuncture point is located where these two lines cross at the top of the head.

brain. This sacred liquid then flows down through the palate into your mouth. You can literally feel the liquid in your mouth.

Jin Jin Yu Ye. "Jin" means *gold.* The second "jin" means *liquid.* "Yu" means *jade.* "Ye" means *liquid.* "Jin jin yu ye" (pronounced *jeen jeen yü yuh*) means *gold liquid, jade liquid.*

Jin jin yu ye is sacred liquid from Mother Earth. It is produced by *di qi,* Mother Earth's qi or energy. ("Di" means Mother Earth. "Qi" means energy.) "Di qi" (pronounced *dee chee*) flows up from Mother Earth through your Yong Chuan (Kidney 1) acupuncture points.[11] It then goes up through both legs to your Hui Yin acupuncture point in your perineum. From there, it goes up through the center of your body into your mouth. There are two acupuncture points under the tongue that are named Jin Jin and Yu Ye. Di qi comes out from these two acupuncture points and transforms to liquid. These two acupuncture points are like the entrance of spring. These are ancient secrets of the body. This liquid produced by the spring is Mother Earth's sacred liquid.

Yan Ru Dan Tian. "Yan" means *swallow.* "Ru" means *go into.* "Dan tian" means *Lower Dan Tian.* "Yan ru dan tian" (pronounced *yahn roo dahn tyen*) means *swallow tian yi zhen shui and jin jin yu ye into the Lower Dan Tian.*

When tian yi zhen shui and jin jin yu ye join as one inside your mouth, you must swallow this precious sacred liquid. This sacred liquid carries the essence of jing qi shen from Heaven and Mother Earth. It is the raw material to form your Jin Dan.

---

11. The Yong Chuan acupuncture points are located on the soles of the feet, just behind the balls of the feet. The essence of Mother Earth enters through the two Yong Chuan points, then goes up through the legs and body to the Jin Jin and Yu Ye acupuncture points under the tongue.

Jin Dan is formed by jing qi shen. Remember the *Tao I* teaching? A human being's jing qi shen are not enough to build the Jin Dan. Jin Dan is the sacred code of Tao. Jin Dan *is* Tao. But when you are just forming the Jin Dan, you have not melded with Tao. To form a complete Jin Dan takes time. After you form a complete Jin Dan, you are formally melded with Tao.

Jin Dan Da Tao Xiu Lian is to form your complete Jin Dan in the fastest way. I cannot honor Tao and the Divine enough for giving me the Jin Dan Da Tao Xiu Lian practice.

Shen Qi Jing He Yi. "Shen" means *soul*. "Qi" means *vital energy and life force*. "Jing" means *matter*. "He" means *join*. "Yi" means *one*. "Shen qi jing he yi" (pronounced *shun chee jing huh yee*) means *join soul energy matter as one*.

Shen qi jing he yi happens inside your lower abdomen. Shen qi jing he yi is to form the Jin Dan. The souls, energy, and matter of all of your systems, organs, and cells join as one in your lower abdomen to form the Jin Dan. At the same time, tian yi zhen shui and jin jin yu ye gather the essence of Heaven and Mother Earth to form your Jin Dan.

Tian Di Ren He Yi. "Tian" means *Heaven*. "Di" means *Mother Earth*. "Ren" means *human being*. "He yi" means *join as one*. "Tian di ren he yi" (pronounced *tyen dee wren huh yee*) means *join Heaven, Mother Earth, human being as one*.

Heaven has Heaven's jing qi shen. Mother Earth has Mother Earth's jing qi shen. Humanity has humanity's jing qi shen. Tian di ren he yi is to gather the jing qi shen of Heaven, Mother Earth, and humanity as one to form your Jin Dan.

Jin Dan Lian Cheng. "Jin dan" means *golden light ball*. "Lian" means *cook*. "Cheng" means *done*. In ancient times, Tao masters cooked Wai Dan, the external Dan, in an urn. ("Wai" means *external*. "Dan" means *ball*.) It is not necessary to give further teachings on this here. "Jin dan lian cheng" (pronounced *jeen dahn lyen chung*) means *form the (internal) Jin Dan*. The Jin Dan is not related to the external Dan, but Tao still uses the word "lian" (cook) to describe forming the Jin Dan.

Tian yi zhen shui and jin jin yu ye gather the sacred liquids from Heaven and Mother Earth to form your Jin Dan.

Shen qi jing he yi joins your jing qi shen as one to form your Jin Dan.

Tian di ren he yi joins the jing qi shen of Heaven, Mother Earth, and humanity as one to form your Jin Dan.

Bao Yuan Shou Yi. "Bao Yuan" is the name of a special Body Power hand position. "Bao" means *hold with both hands*. "Yuan" means *circle* or *ball*. "Shou" means *concentrate* or *focus*. "Yi" means *one*. "Bao yuan shou yi" (pronounced *bao ywen sho yee*) means *hold both hands as a circle, place them below the navel, and concentrate on your Jin Dan*.

Tao is a circle. Tao is a ball. It is a Tao Xiu Lian secret to use *yuan* as a symbol to represent Tao. A circle and a ball have no beginning and no ending. Tao is emptiness and nothingness, but Tao is also expressed as a ball. Tao is not two-dimensional or three-dimensional. Tao is multi-dimensional.

In this sacred phrase and practice, "yi" is not a straight line. This "yi" is one line to make a circle. The circle in two dimensions also represents a ball or sphere in three dimensions. The circle "yi" is one. This "yi" is the Jin Dan. Jin Dan is Tao. Therefore, Bao Yuan Shou Yi is Bao Yuan Shou Tao. Bao Yuan Shou Yi is to hold your Jin Dan and concentrate on your Jin Dan, which is to hold Tao and concentrate on Tao. In one sentence:

**Bao Yuan Shou Yi is the number one Tao sacred method
to do Tao Xiu Lian to form your complete Jin Dan.**

Because Bao Yuan Shou Yi is the number one sacred Tao
method to do Tao Xiu Lian, you will hear this special secret
phrase again and again. How do you practice with this method?
Here is the way to do it. Apply the Four Power Techniques:

Body Power. Sit up straight. Put the tip of your tongue as close
as you can to the roof of your mouth without touching. Gently
contract your anus, and then forget about it. It will naturally relax
later.

What is the Bao Yuan Shou Yi Hand Position? In fact, you
have already learned it and applied it several times. The Bao Yuan
Shou Yi Hand Position is the same as the Jin Dan Da Tao Xiu
Lian Hand Position. (See figure 4 below. It is the same as figure 1
on page 42.) Tao is One. The Body Power for Tao Xiu Lian is one.

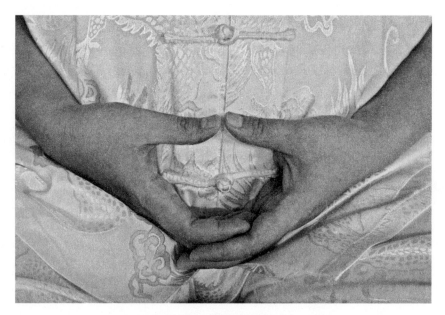

Figure 4. Bao Yuan Shou Yi Hand Position

Soul Power. Say *hello:*

> *Dear Tao,*
> *Dear Divine,*
> *Dear soul mind body of all spiritual fathers and mothers in*
>   *all layers of Heaven and on Mother Earth,*
> *Dear Heaven,*
> *Dear Mother Earth,*
> *Dear humanity,*
> *Dear countless planets, stars, galaxies, and universes,*
> *I love you, honor you, and appreciate you.*
> *Please form my Jin Dan.*
> *Thank you.*

Mind Power. Visualize a line from your navel going straight back to your back. Just below the center of this line, there is a fist-sized golden light ball. This golden light ball is your Jin Dan. Focus on your Jin Dan. If your Third Eye is open and you have already formed your Jin Dan, you can see the actual size of your Jin Dan. It could be smaller than your fist. It could be much bigger than your fist. It does not matter how big your Jin Dan is. Everyone needs to develop his or her Jin Dan further to form a complete Jin Dan. Focusing on the Jin Dan area in every Tao practice is the key.

Sound Power. Sing or chant repeatedly, silently or aloud:

> *Tao Sheng Yi*
> *Tian Yi Zhen Shui*
> *Jin Jin Yu Ye*
> *Yan Ru Dan Tian*
> *Shen Qi Jing He Yi*

Tian Di Ren He Yi
Jin Dan Lian Cheng

Tao Sheng Yi
Tian Yi Zhen Shui
Jin Jin Yu Ye
Yan Ru Dan Tian
Shen Qi Jing He Yi
Tian Di Ren He Yi
Jin Dan Lian Cheng

Tao Sheng Yi
Tian Yi Zhen Shui
Jin Jin Yu Ye
Yan Ru Dan Tian
Shen Qi Jing He Yi
Tian Di Ren He Yi
Jin Dan Lian Cheng

Tao Sheng Yi
Tian Yi Zhen Shui
Jin Jin Yu Ye
Yan Ru Dan Tian
Shen Qi Jing He Yi
Tian Di Ren He Yi
Jin Dan Lian Cheng . . .

Sing or chant as much as you can. You can learn the melody from the CD or audio download included with *Tao I*, the sixth book in my Soul Power Series. There is no time limit for this practice. The more you chant, the faster you will build your Jin Dan.

The more you chant, the closer you will come to forming a complete Jin Dan. To form a complete Jin Dan is to meld with Tao.

Bless your Tao Xiu Lian journey.

Bless your Jin Dan formation.

Bless your yu Dao he zhen.

Ren Ming Ru Deng You. "Ren" means *human being*. "Ming" means *life*. "Ru" means *like*. "Deng" means *lamp*. "You" means *oil*. "Ren ming ru deng you" (pronounced *wren ming roo dung yoe*) means *a human's life is like the oil in a lamp*.

A human being's life is just like the oil in a lamp. When a baby is born, the lamp is full of oil. When the baby grows and matures to be a child, a teenager, an adult, a senior, and then becomes sick, the oil is burning away.

Remember my earlier teaching about the three external treasures? One must see no evil, hear no evil, and speak no evil because any kind of pollution exhausts the oil in your lamp.

Hao Jin Ming Gui Xi. "Hao jin" means *oil is exhausted*. "Ming" means *life*. "Gui xi" means *die*. "Hao jin ming gui xi" (pronounced *how jeen ming gway shee*) means *when the oil is exhausted, life ends*.

Yu Jian Kang Chang Shou. "Yu" means *wish*. "Jian kang" means *good health*. "Chang shou" means *longevity*. "Yu jian kang chang shou" (pronounced *yü jyen kahng chahng sho*) means *wish to have good health and longevity*.

If you understand that a human being's life is just like the oil in a lamp, then it is easy to understand that if you exhaust the oil, life will end. If you wish to have good health and longevity, what should you do? See the next sacred phrase:

Bi Tian Deng You. "Bi" means *must*. "Tian" means *add*. "Deng you" means *lamp oil*. "Bi tian deng you" (pronounced *bee tyen dung yoe*) means *must add oil to the lamp*.

What is the oil for your good health and longevity? See the next sacred phrase:

Tian Yi Zhen Shui. As I have explained, "tian yi zhen shui" (pronounced *tyen yee jun shway*) means *Heaven's unique sacred liquid*, which is *Heaven's and Tao's Oneness liquid*.

Now you should understand much better the importance of tian yi zhen shui and jin jin yu ye. They are sacred liquids from Heaven and Mother Earth, respectively. They are sacred material for good health and longevity.

In Chinese, the verb "to live" or "to be alive" is huo, which is written:

活

The left half of this Chinese character for "alive" is the character for *liquid* (in pinyin: ye). The right half of this character is the character for *tongue* (in pinyin: she). The Chinese character for "to live" clearly explains that in order to be alive, the tongue must have liquid.

Jin Jin Yu Ye. As previously explained, jin jin yu ye is the sacred liquid from Mother Earth.

How do Heaven and Mother Earth balance? The sun shines on Mother Earth's oceans and rivers. The water turns to vapor and ascends. The vapor is Mother Earth's qi. In the yin yang world, Mother Earth's qi rises. In Chinese, *di qi shang sheng*. "Di" means *Mother Earth*. "Qi" means *energy*. "Shang sheng" means *ascend*. In the form of water vapor, Mother Earth's qi ascends to Heaven where it accumulates to form clouds. It then turns to rain or snow, which fall to Mother Earth. This is Heaven's qi descending. In Chinese, *tian qi xia jiang*. "Tian" means *Heaven*. "Qi" means *energy*. "Xia jiang" means *descend*. Di qi shang sheng (pronounced *dee chee shahng shung*) and tian qi xia jiang (pronounced *tyen chee shya jyahng*) is to balance Heaven and Mother Earth, yin and yang.

Think about Mother Earth now. It is 2010. There are so many natural disasters in Mother Earth. Too much rain is causing floods. Not enough rain is causing droughts. This is an imbalance between Heaven and Mother Earth. This imbalance is causing huge problems for Mother Earth. Many lives are being lost worldwide because of this imbalance. To balance Heaven and Mother Earth is vital.

Tian ren he yi, to join Heaven and human being as one, is an ancient spiritual teaching. Tian or Heaven is the big universe. Ren or human being is a small universe. "He yi" means *join as one*. What happens in the big universe is what happens in a small universe. What exists in a small universe is what exists in the big universe.

In a human being's body, everything above the diaphragm belongs to Heaven and everything below the diaphragm belongs to Mother Earth. Mother Earth's qi must ascend. Heaven's qi must descend. Tian yi zhen shui and jin jin yu ye are Heaven's and Mother Earth's sacred liquids. Tian yi zhen shui and jin jin yu ye are vital for a human being's life. They can bring balance. If they descend, then Mother Earth's qi ascends. If they descend, the whole body is balanced.

Therefore, when you do Jin Dan Da Tao Xiu Lian, you create

tian yi zhen shui and jin jin yu ye. Tian yi zhen shui and jin jin yu ye are swallowed into your Jin Dan. These sacred liquids form your Jin Dan and nourish your whole body, because Jin Dan is the source of energy, stamina, vitality, immunity, rejuvenation, longevity, and immortality.

Tian yi zhen shui and jin jin yu ye are the materials to form the Jin Dan. Jin Dan is the unity of jing qi shen. Jing qi shen is the oil. Tian yi zhen shui and jin jin yu ye will increase your jing qi shen. This means they will add oil to your life lamp. First, they will fulfill the oil that you have lost through your *lou ti*. Then, they will continue to increase your oil, which is jing qi shen. Your oil will be fulfilled more and more, until one day you will have a lamp full of oil. Then you will reach fan lao huan tong, because a healthy baby has a lamp full of oil.

Contine to practice Jin Dan Da Tao to keep your lamp full of oil continuously. Then you will have longevity.

Continue to practice to keep your lamp full of oil permanently. This is immortality.

I was honored to have been chosen as a lineage holder of Lao Zi's teacher, Peng Zu, the renowned "long life star" in China. Peng Zu lived to be 880 years old. He spent two hours every morning just swallowing tian yi zhen shui and jin jin yu ye.

To swallow tian yi zhen shui and jin jin yu ye is to form the Jin Dan. To form a complete Jin Dan is to meld with Tao. This is the absolute truth. This is the Tao secret of longevity and immortality.

Millions of people are searching for the secrets of longevity. There is only one secret. It can be summarized in one sentence:

Jin Dan Da Tao Xiu Lian is the highest secret and absolute truth of longevity and immortality.

You Ru Tian You. "You ru" means *just like*. "Tian you" means *add oil*. "You ru tian you" (pronounced *yoe roo tyen yoe*) means *it is just like adding oil to the lamp.*

Tian yi zhen shui and jin jin yu ye are the oil for prolonging life. One must add this oil to one's lamp. This means that one must practice Jin Dan Da Tao Xiu Lian. One must swallow tian yi zhen shui and jin jin yu ye all of the time.

When you do the Jin Dan Da Tao practice regularly, one day you will start to produce a lot of tian yi zhen shui and jin jin yu ye. Remember to swallow them. If you continue to practice, you will be surprised. Even without practicing Jin Dan Da Tao Xiu Lian, your body will still produce tian yi zhen shui and jin jin yu ye. When you speak, you will produce tian yi zhen shui and jin jin yu ye. Even when you are not speaking, you will still produce tian yi zhen shui and jin jin yu ye. That is the secret.

In traditional Tao teaching, there are two conditions in which you can practice: *you wei* (pronounced *yoe way*) and *wu wei* (pronounced *woo way*).

You wei means you know what you are doing. For example, we do meditations in this book together. We are chanting Jin Dan Da Tao Xiu Lian. Your mind understands what you are doing. This is you wei practice. In the you wei condition, you are guided by your Shi Shen or your mind to practice.

One day you will reach the wu wei condition. In the wu wei condition, you are guided by your Yuan Shen to practice. You do not use your Shi Shen or mind to practice. Wu wei means that your mind does not know what you are doing. When you meditate and chant Jin Dan Da Tao, you may suddenly forget where you are. You forget who you are. You forget yourself. You may stay in this emptiness condition for a few seconds, a few minutes, or much longer. This emptiness condition is wu wei.

In *wu wei* practice, your practice is automatic. Your Jin Dan rotates by itself. Your tian yi zhen shui and jin jin yu ye are created by themselves. Your you wei practice turns to wu wei practice gradually. Your wu wei practice increases little by little. It starts after ming xin jian xing. This means your wu wei practice starts after the Jin Dan is formed. Yuan Shen guides your Shi Shen little by little. Yuan Shen transforms your Shi Shen little by little. Shi Shen melds with Yuan Shen little by little.

When you do Xiu Tao practice, what will happen when you meld with Tao? You will not need to chant. You will not need to meditate. You are Tao. Tao is you. Tao is creating and manifesting. You are creating and manifesting. Your body has transformed to a Tao body. Every cell and every DNA and RNA of your body carries Tao frequency and Tao light. You have total purity in your soul, heart, mind, and body. No bacteria, viruses, or all kinds of other factors in Mother Earth will affect your body because these issues are in the yin yang world. The yin yang world is the *you* world. You have melded with Tao. You are in the *wu* world. The *wu* world creates the *you* world. The frequency of the *you* world cannot affect the frequency of the *wu* world. This is the condition of melding with Tao. This is the *wu wei* condition.

When you completely meld with Tao and form a complete Jin Dan, you will have gone completely into wu wei practice. This will take you into the true tao fa zi ran condition, which is to "follow nature's way." You have melded with Tao. You are Tao and Tao is you.

You Deng Chang Ming. "You deng" means *oil lamp*. "Chang" means *always*. "Ming" means *burning*. "You deng chang ming" (pronounced *yoe dung chahng ming*) means *the oil in the lamp is always burning*.

If you continually practice Jin Dan Da Tao, if you continue to create tian yi zhen shui and jin jin yu ye, then the oil in your lamp will become full and could always stay full. Even more, the quality of the oil is transforming.

If the oil is always full, you have returned to the baby condition. A healthy baby has a lamp full of oil. When your lamp is always full of oil, you have reached fan lao huan tong. As you continue to practice, the quality of the oil is transformed further and further.

Remember, the oil for your lamp is jing qi shen. To transform the quality of oil is to transform the quality of jing qi shen. Your Jin Dan gets bigger and bigger. One day your Jin Dan will grow to the size of your entire body. Every system, every organ, and every cell will transform to the quality of your Jin Dan. Your whole body becomes Jin Dan. You are Jin Dan. Jin Dan is you. At that moment, your Tao body is produced. When you have a Tao body, immortality is with you. Your body becomes Tao. Your body cannot die anymore.

This is not easy to do.

It *is* possible.

The absolute truth is present in front of you.

The highest secret is released.

Grabbing it is not enough.

Seriously practice it.

In ancient times, serious Tao practitioners did Jin Dan Da Tao Xiu Lian for ten years without doing anything else. Today, most Tao practitioners have work and families. There is no way you can dedicate ten years just to do Tao practice from morning to night. How can you do it? If you do not have ten years full time for Tao practice, grab the top secret I will release now. This top secret can be summarized in one sentence:

守一咽津液
Shou Yi Yan Jin Ye
is a twenty-four hour Xiu Tao practice

"Shou yi" (pronounced *sho yee*) means *concentrate on your Jin Dan in your abdomen.* "Yan jin ye" (pronounced *yahn jeen yuh*) means *swallow tian yi zhen shui and jin jin yu ye into your lower abdomen.*

This tells you to always put your mind on your Jin Dan. In ancient spiritual teaching, *yi dao qi dao.* "Yi" means *thinking.* "Dao" means *arrive.* "Qi" means *vital energy and life force.* "Yi dao qi dao" (pronounced *yee dow chee dow*) means *where you put your mind is where qi goes.* In fact, not only will qi accumulate in your area of concentration, jing will also gather there. In this case, if you "shou yi" (put your mind on the lower abdomen), the Jin Dan will form.

Put your mind on the Jin Dan. Tian yi zhen shui and jin jin yu ye will continue to form.

Put your mind on the Jin Dan. Remember to swallow tian yi zhen shui and jin jin yu ye.

Put your mind on your Jin Dan all of the time. The Jin Dan will form faster.

Continue to put your mind on the Jin Dan. The Jin Dan will expand.

Put your mind on the Jin Dan. Healing will happen automatically.

Put your mind on the Jin Dan. You will become younger.

Put your mind on the Jin Dan. Fan lao huan tong is coming.

Put your mind on the Jin Dan. Longevity is coming.

Put your mind on the Jin Dan. Melding with Tao is on the way.

Therefore, Shou Yi Yan Jin Ye is the key for Jin Dan Da Tao

Xiu Lian. When you do Jin Dan Da Tao Xiu Lian, put your mind on the Jin Dan. Swallow tian yi zhen shui and jin jin yu ye.

However, the top secret I have just offered is not only for Jin Dan Da Tao Xiu Lian. The teaching is to put your mind on your Jin Dan and swallow tian yi zhen shui and jin jin yu ye anytime, anywhere, twenty-four hours a day. Before sleep, do Shou Yi Yan Jin Ye. When you wake up, do Shou Yi Yan Jin Ye. When you are walking, working, cooking, or driving, do Shou Yi Yan Jin Ye. ***Always* put your mind on the Jin Dan.** This is called *xing zou zuo wo bu li zhe ge*. "Xing zou" means *walk*. "Zuo" means *sit*. "Wo" means *lie down*. "Bu li" means *do not leave*. "Zhe ge" means *this one* and refers to the Jin Dan. "Xing zou zuo wo bu li zhe ge" (pronounced *shing dzoe dzwaw waw boo lee juh guh*) means *anytime, anywhere in your whole life, always put your mind on your Jin Dan*. To put your mind on the Jin Dan is to connect with Tao.

93
修仙之道
Xiu Xian Zhi Dao

The way to become a saint

94
性命双修
Xing Ming Shuang Xiu

Do Xiu Lian to develop intelligence and body together

95
明心见性
Ming Xin Jian Xing

Enlighten your heart to see your Yuan Shen

96
超凡入圣
Chao Fan Ru Sheng

Go beyond an ordinary being and become a saint

97
静定慧明
Jing Ding Hui Ming

Quiet, still, intelligent, enlightened

98
静中生定
Jing Zhong Sheng Ding

Stillness comes from quietness

99
定中生慧
Ding Zhong Sheng Hui

Intelligence comes from stillness

100
慧中生明
Hui Zhong Sheng Ming

Enlightenment comes from intelligence

101
跳出欲海
Tiao Chu Yu Hai

Jump out from the sea of desire

102
服务万灵
Fu Wu Wan Ling

Serve all souls

103
抱元守一
Bao Yuan Shou Yi

Hold both hands in a circle below the navel and concentrate on the Jin Dan

104
通体透明
Tong Ti Tou Ming

Whole body is transparent

Xiu Xian Zhi Dao. "Xiu" means *Xiu Lian*. "Xian" means *saint*. Dao or Tao is The Way. "Xiu xian zhi Dao" (pronounced *sheo shyen jr dow*) means *the way to become a saint*.

To become a saint is to move toward Tao. As I explained earlier in this chapter, there are layers of saints: Human Being saints, Mother Earth saints, Heaven saints, and Tao saints.

Xing Ming Shuang Xiu. "Xing" means *Xing Gong, intelligence practice*. "Ming" means *Ming Gong, body practice*. "Shuang" means *both*. "Xiu" means *Xiu Lian*. "Xing ming shuang xiu" (pronounced *shing ming shwahng sheo*) means *do Xiu Lian to develop intelligence and body together*.

Earlier in this chapter, I shared the four stages of yu Dao he zhen:

- Bai Ri Zhu Ji – Practice for one hundred days to build a foundation for your body.
- Ju Zu Xing – Your body is fulfilled with sufficient jing qi shen to reach the baby state.
- Ming Xin Jian Xing – Enlighten your heart to see your Yuan Shen.
- Yu Dao He Zhen – Meld with Tao.

In the Tao journey, the final destiny is to meld with Tao. The first stage is to build a foundation for your body.

I would like to emphasize again that when you are sick, your body is *lou ti* (pronounced *loe tee*). "Lou" means *leak*. "Ti" means *body*. Lou ti, a "leaky body," means *your body lacks jing qi shen because your jing qi shen leaked out*.

Remember the teaching of the oil lamp. Jing qi shen is the oil. If you are sick, your oil is insufficient. Your body is lou ti. You need to spend one hundred days doing Jin Dan Da Tao Xiu Lian in order to fulfill your jing qi shen and add oil back to your lamp. If your jing qi shen becomes sufficient, your body foundation is built and your sicknesses will be healed.

The second stage is to reach fan lao huan tong. Stages one and two are the "must" stages for Tao Xiu Lian. They are the must stages for Ming Gong, which is body practice. You have to have a strong body.

I would like to share with you and every reader why millions of spiritual people in history have reached enlightenment but do not live a long life. Many great spiritual fathers and mothers on Mother Earth are still sick. The reason is very simple. They do not do enough Ming Gong practice. Some of them may not do Ming Gong practice at all.

The third stage is to enlighten your heart to see your Yuan Shen. This is Xing Gong, intelligence practice. To see your Yuan Shen is to gain the highest wisdom. Yuan Shen is Tao. When you reach Ming Xin Jian Xing, your Yuan Shen becomes the true boss. Your Yuan Shen will guide your Shi Shen. This is a big step on the journey to meld with Tao, which is the fourth and final stage.

I emphasize these four stages of yu Dao he zhen again to tell you clearly that to become a saint or to meld with Tao, you must do both Ming Gong and Xing Gong practice. You cannot meld with Tao just by practicing one or the other. You have to practice to develop your intelligence *and* your body. This is the vital wisdom and practice that you must follow. Millions of spiritual practitioners have learned huge lessons that when they only practice one, they cannot meld with Tao.

Jin Dan Da Tao Xiu Lian is beyond words. Jin Dan Da Tao Xiu Lian is to practice Ming Gong and Xing Gong together.

When you practice Jin Dan Da Tao Xiu Lian, you put your mind on your lower abdomen. The lower abdomen is the foundation center for energy, stamina, vitality, immunity, rejuvenation, and longevity. Therefore, when you practice Jin Dan Da Tao Xiu Lian, you are practicing Ming Gong.

Jin Dan is jing qi shen he yi. Jing qi shen he yi is ming xin jian xing. Ming xin jian xing is Xing Gong practice. Therefore, Jin Dan Da Tao Xiu Lian develops intelligence and body. Jin Dan Da Tao joins Ming Gong and Xing Gong together. This is how powerful Jin Dan Da Tao practice is.

Just focus your mind on your Jin Dan. You are doing Ming Gong and Xing Gong together.

Ming Xin Jian Xing. "Ming xin jian xing" means *enlighten your heart to see your Yuan Shen*. I have explained the wisdom of ming xin jian xing earlier in this chapter (sacred phrase 55). Please re-read those explanations if necessary.

Chao Fan Ru Sheng. "Chao" means *go beyond*. "Fan" means *ordinary being*. "Ru" means *go into*. "Sheng" means *saint*. "Chao fan ru sheng" (pronounced *chow fahn roo shung*) means *go beyond an ordinary being and become a saint*.

Do Xing Gong, intelligence practice, and Ming Gong, body practice, together in order to enlighten your heart and see your Yuan Shen. When you see your Yuan Shen, you reach ming xin jian xing. When you reach ming xin jian xing, you become a saint.

Saints have layers. After you reach ming xin jian xing, your Yuan Shen must continue to guide your Shi Shen. Yuan Shen will test Shi Shen. Shi Shen will listen to Yuan Shen more and more to gradually meld with Yuan Shen, but it takes time for Yuan Shen and Shi Shen to join as one.

To reach Ming Xin Jian Xing, the following four sacred phrases are the process one must follow:

Jing Ding Hui Ming
Jing Zhong Sheng Ding
Ding Zhong Sheng Hui
Hui Zhong Sheng Ming

Jing Ding Hui Ming. "Jing" means *quiet.* "Ding" means *stillness.* "Hui" means *intelligence.* "Ming" means *enlightenment.* "Jing ding hui ming" (pronounced *jing ding hway ming*) means *quiet, still, intelligent, enlightened.*

These are the four steps to reach enlightenment.

The first step is quietness. The best way to achieve quietness is to meditate and chant Jin Dan Da Tao Xiu Lian. Put your mind on your Jin Dan. To chant Jin Dan Da Tao Xiu Lian is to invoke *jing qi shen xu dao* of Heaven, Mother Earth, humanity, and wan wu, including countless planets, stars, and galaxies, and all universes. Jin Dan Da Tao Xiu Lian will help you go into quietness very quickly to start forming your Jin Dan.

To chant Jin Dan Da Tao Xiu Lian is to use one thought to replace all other thoughts. Beginners sometimes say that they cannot concentrate or meditate. The root cause for most of these blockages is bad karma. Dark souls come to these people and block them from meditating. If you are in this situation, use your mind to chant Jin Dan Da Tao as much as possbile. The more you chant, the more quietness will come to you. Remember to focus only on the Jin Dan. The golden light ball is forming in your lower abdomen.

If any thought comes, do not be upset. Continue to chant. The thoughts will decrease more and more. When you do this, yang qi will ascend in your body and yin qi will descend in your body. Yin yang balance will happen by itself.

The second step to reach enlightenment is given in the next phrase:

Jing Zhong Sheng Ding. "Jing zhong" means *inside quietness.* "Sheng" means *create.* "Ding" means *stillness.* "Jing zhong sheng ding" (pronounced *jing jawng shung ding*) means *stillness comes from quietness.*

Stillness is going into the emptiness condition. For example, when you practice Jin Dan Da Tao Xiu Lian, you suddenly do not know where you are. Your consciousness is empty. You do not have a single thought anymore. At that moment, you have gone into stillness. That is a very important step. The more you practice, the more time you will spend in stillness. That is a vital sign of progress for your Tao Xiu Lian practice.

The third step to reach enlightenment is described by the next phrase:

Ding Zhong Sheng Hui. "Ding zhong" means *inside stillness.* "Sheng" means *creates.* "Hui" means *intelligence.* "Ding zhong sheng hui" (pronounced *ding jawng shung hway*) means *intelligence comes from stillness.*

When you go into the stillness or emptiness condition, your Shi Shen is no longer guiding you. Your Yuan Shen is on duty. Your Yuan Shen is Tao. Therefore, in that stillness condition, your Yuan Shen is teaching your Shi Shen. You will gain Tao wisdom, which is the highest wisdom. This is how *intelligence comes from stillness.*

The fourth step to reach enlightenment is:

Hui Zhong Sheng Ming. "Hui zhong" means *inside intelligence.* "Sheng" means *create.* "Ming" means *enlightenment.* "Hui zhong sheng ming" (pronounced *hway jawng shung ming*) means *enlightenment comes from intelligence.*

As I just explained, when you reach stillness, your Yuan Shen starts to guide you and to deliver Tao wisdom. You have received wisdom from your Shi Shen, but now your Shi Shen realizes it does not know enough, and that it has to obey Yuan Shen. Yuan Shen is your spiritual father.

This will happen as you continue the Jin Dan Da Tao practice. One day your Shi Shen will receive an "aha!" moment. Your Shi Shen will realize and recognize the wisdom and the power of Yuan Shen. Then your Shi Shen will decide that it has to learn from Yuan Shen. Your Shi Shen will want Yuan Shen to guide its life.

At that moment, you will have reached ming xin jian xing. To reach ming xin jian xing means that your Yuan Shen is formally on duty to be the boss of your soul, heart, mind, and body. At that moment, you could experience complete emptiness inside and outside of your body. The inside and outside of your body join as one. This emptiness could create light. You could suddenly feel or, for those whose Third Eye is open, see light shining both inside and outside of your body.

Tiao Chu Yu Hai. "Tiao chu" means *jump out.* "Yu hai" means *sea of desire.* "Tiao chu yu hai" (pronounced *tee-yow choo yü hye*) means *jump out from the sea of desire,* which means all of the pollution.

Mother Earth is red dust. Mother Earth is the bitter sea. Mother Earth has all kinds of pollution such as killing, harming, taking advantage of others, stealing, cheating, anger, greed, lack of wisdom to distinguish between right and wrong, and more.

When you reach enlightenment, you have to jump out from

all of the pollution. When you jump out from all of the pollution, you are self-clearing bad karma and you are avoiding creating new bad karma.

This is the essence of all Xiu Lian practice. When you do Xiu Lian, you are self-clearing bad karma. At the same time, you avoid and prevent creating new bad karma in this life, as well as in future lifetimes.

Fu Wu Wan Ling. "Fu wu" means *serve*. "Wan ling" means *all souls*. "Fu wu wan ling" (pronounced *foo woo wahn ling*) means *serve all souls*.

To serve wan ling is Tao service because Tao created wan ling. Serve wan ling and you will gain virtue beyond imagination.

Jin Dan Da Tao Xiu Lian is the best way to serve wan ling. You are invoking *jing qi shen xu dao* of wan ling to come to your abdomen to form the Jin Dan. It is good for you. It is especially good for wan ling.

You are forming your Jin Dan to reach Tao or meld with Tao. To meld with Tao is to serve wan ling better. Therefore, to form the Jin Dan is to offer Tao service. This Tao service will self-clear your bad karma. The benefits cannot be underestimated. At the same time, invoke wan ling to chant with you. This will help wan ling to form their Jin Dan. Finally, wan ling will form Tao Dan together.

This is a long process, but it is the best way to serve wan ling.

Bao Yuan Shou Yi. As explained previously, "bao yuan" means *both hands held as a circle, the Bao Yuan Shou Yi Hand Position* (see figure 4 on p. 258). "Shou yi" means *focus on Jin Dan*. "Bao yuan shou yi" (pronounced *bao ywen sho yee*) means *both hands hold and your mind focuses on your Jin Dan*.

The essence of bao yuan shou yi is to focus your mind on your

Jin Dan. I shared the top secret earlier: put your mind on the Jin Dan day and night.

Tong Ti Tou Ming. "Tong ti" means *whole body*. "Tou ming" means *transparent*. "Tong ti tou ming" (pronounced *tawng tee toe ming*) means *whole body becomes transparent*.

Jin Dan Da Tao Xiu Lian is Bao Yuan Shou Yi practice. Jin Dan Da Tao Xiu Lian is to form your Jin Dan. Every soul is forming their Jin Dan. Finally, every soul is moving in the direction of forming Tao Dan.

When you practice Jin Dan Da Tao Xiu Lian, your *jing qi shen* is fulfilled quickly.

When you practice Jin Dan Da Tao Xiu Lian, all of your sicknesses can be healed quickly.

When you practice Jin Dan Da Tao Xiu Lian, you can prevent sickness very well.

When you practice Jin Dan Da Tao Xiu Lian, you can rejuvenate your soul, heart, mind, and body quickly.

When you practice Jin Dan Da Tao Xiu Lian, your *jing qi shen* can be transformed to Heaven's and Mother Earth's *jing qi shen*, and then transform further to Tao *jing qi shen*. When the quality of *jing qi shen* is transformed, your body will shine light. What is light? Light is the essence and highest form of energy.

When you practice Jin Dan Da Tao Xiu Lian, your body will transform to a light body. Your whole body could turn transparent.

105
人之初
Ren Zhi Chu

Origin of a human being

106
精卵化人
Jing Luan Hua Ren

Sperm and egg create a human being

107
内肾先生
Nei Shen Xian Sheng

Kidneys are produced first

108
渐长两目
Jian Zhang Liang Mu

Gradually grow both eyes

109
后生外肾
Hou Sheng Wai Shen

Grow the urinary system, including sexual organs

110
五脏六腑
Wu Zang Liu Fu

Five yin and six yang organs grow

111
四肢百骸
Si Zhi Bai Hai

Four extremities and skeleton

112
逐次而生
Zhu Ci Er Sheng

Gradually grow one by one

Ren Zhi Chu. "Ren zhi chu" (pronounced *wren jr choo*) means *beginning or origin of a human being*.

Jing Luan Hua Ren. "Jing" means *sperm*. "Luan" means *egg*. "Hua" means *produce*. "Ren" means *human being*. "Jing luan hua ren" (pronounced *jing lwahn hwah wren*) means *sperm and egg join as one to create a human being*.

A sperm and an egg joining together is yin yang jiao gan (pronounced *yeen yahng jee-yow gahn*), which means *yin yang connect and respond*. After the sperm and the egg have yin yang jiao gan, the physical and biochemical process will happen.

The sperm and the egg are the cause. The result is the embryo, which will grow to become a human being. Thus, the formation of a human being is itself a cause and effect relationship.

Nei Shen Xian Sheng. "Nei shen" means *kidneys*. "Xian sheng" means *produced first*. "Nei shen xian sheng" (pronounced *nay shun shyen shung*) means *kidneys are produced first in the embryo*.

Nei shen is in charge of water metabolism. Nei shen is the key organ for the urinary system.

Both kidneys carry genes and the Yuan Shen comes to the kidneys first. Later the Yuan Shen will move to the heart. Yuan Shen carries the Tao message code because Yuan Shen is Tao.

In traditional Chinese medicine, the kidneys are the root pre-natal organ.

Jian Zhang Liang Mu. "Jian" means *gradually*. "Zhang" means *grow*. "Liang mu" means *both eyes*. "Jian zhang liang mu" (pro-nounced *jyen jahng lyahng moo*) means *gradually grow both eyes*.

Hou Sheng Wai Shen. "Hou sheng" means *grows later* (after nei shen, the kidneys). "Wai shen" means *hypothalamic-pituitary-gonadal axis, externalia, and sexual organs*. "Hou sheng wai shen" (pronounced *hoe shung wye shun*) means *wai shen grows after nei shen*.

Wai shen is in charge of jing.

Human beings are in the yin yang world. Yin yang organs are the yin yang signal. Therefore, they grow earliest in the embryo. The kidneys and urinary bladder are followed by the other yin-yang organ pairs:

Wu Zang Liu Fu. "Wu zang" (pronounced *woo dzahng*) are the five *zang* or yin organs (liver, heart, spleen, lungs, kidneys). "Liu fu" (pronounced *leo foo*) are the six *fu* or yang organs (gallblad-der, small intestine, stomach, large intestine, urinary bladder, San Jiao—"three areas" of the body).

The Upper Jiao is everything above the diaphragm. The Middle Jiao is everything between the diaphragm and the level of the navel. The Lower Jiao is everything below the level of the navel down through the genitals.

Si Zhi Bai Hai. "Si zhi" means *four extremities.* "Bai hai" means *all bones of the body, which is the skeleton.* "Si zhi bai hai" (pronounced *sz jr bye hye*) means *four extremities and the skeleton.*

Zhu Ci Er Sheng. "Zhu ci er sheng" (pronounced *joo tszz ur shung*) means *all the above organs, the four extremities, and all bones gradually grow one by one according to their proper order.*

113
入静忘我
Ru Jing Wang Wo

Meditate deeply to go into stillness and forget yourself

114
刹那悟空
Cha Na Wu Kong

Go suddenly into emptiness and nothingness

115
恍兮惚兮
Huang Xi Hu Xi

Spiritual images appear and disappear

116
真气从之
Zhen Qi Cong Zhi

Zhen qi, the qi of Yuan Shen, is produced

117
真气升泥丸
Zhen Qi Sheng Ni Wan

Zhen qi rises to the Zu Qiao

118
化玉液
Hua Yu Ye

Transforms to jade liquid

119
入中元
Ru Zhong Yuan

Swallow into the abdomen

120
滋润丹田
Zi Run Dan Tian

Nourish the Lower Dan Tian

Ru Jing Wang Wo. "Ru jing" means *meditate to become quiet.* "Wang wo" means *forget yourself.* "Ru jing wang wo" (pronounced *roo jing wahng waw*) means *meditate deeply to go into stillness and forget yourself.*

Cha Na Wu Kong. "Cha na" means *suddenly.* "Wu kong" means *emptiness and nothingness.* "Cha na wu kong" (pronounced *chah nah woo kawng*) means *go suddenly into the emptiness and nothingness condition.*

When you practice Jin Dan Da Tao Xiu Lian or any spiritual meditation, you could suddenly go into the emptiness and nothingness condition. You do not know where you are. You forget yourself. That is the moment you have reached emptiness. In that emptiness moment, Yuan Shen appears and is in charge.

Huang Xi Hu Xi. "Huang xi hu xi" (pronounced *hwahng shee hoo shee*) means *spiritual images appear and disappear* (in the emptiness and nothingness condition).

Zhen Qi Cong Zhi. "Zhen qi" means *real* or *true qi.* It is also named yuan qi (*original qi*), which is produced by Yuan Shen. Yuan Shen is Tao. Therefore, zhen qi, the qi of Yuan Shen, is also the qi of Tao. "Cong zhi" means *produce.* "Zhen qi cong zhi" (pronounced *jun chee tsawng jr*) means *the qi of Yuan Shen and Tao is produced.*

Let me summarize the process described in the last four sacred phrases. When you practice Jin Dan Da Tao Xiu Lian for example, you chant, chant, chant. You focus your mind on the Jin Dan. Go into deep meditation. You become quiet. You have fewer and fewer thoughts.

Continue to practice. Suddenly you go into the emptiness or nothingness condition. You have forgotten yourself. In that condition, your Third Eye may see some images or perhaps you suddenly cannot see any images. A little later, some images will appear and then they will disappear again.

In that condition, zhen qi is produced. Zhen qi is the real or true qi. Zhen qi is the qi of Yuan Shen and Tao.

Zhen Qi Sheng Ni Wan. "Sheng" means *rises*. "Ni wan" means *Zu Qiao*. The Zu Qiao (pronounced *dzoo chee-yow*) is a cherry-sized energy center located in the bone cavity behind the Yin Tang acupuncture point between the eyebrows. It is a very important center for mind power. "Zhen qi sheng ni wan" (pronounced *jun chee shung nee wahn*) means *the qi of Yuan Shen or Tao rises to the Zu Qiao*. This is the movement of zhen qi.

Zhen qi is Tao qi. It belongs to yang. It moves up. This follows the rules of Tao inside the body.

Hua Yu Ye. "Hua" means *transform to*. "Yu ye" means *jade liquid*. "Hua yu ye" (pronounced *hwah yü yuh*) means *zhen qi transforms to jade liquid*. I have explained *yu ye* earlier in this chapter. It is part of Mother Earth's sacred liquid.

Ru Zhong Yuan. "Ru" means *go into*. "Zhong yuan" means *abdomen*. "Ru zhong yuan" (pronounced *roo jawng ywen*) means *swallow the jade liquid into the abdomen*.

Zi Run Dan Tian. "Zi run" means *nourish*. "Dan tian" means *Lower Dan Tian*. "Zi run dan tian" (pronounced *dz rwun dahn tyen*) means *jade liquid nourishes the Lower Dan Tian*.

I have explained many times already that this jade liquid is material to form the Jin Dan. This jade liquid is oil in the lamp for longevity and immortality.

121
何谓坤宫
He Wei Kun Gong

What is the Kun Temple?

122
肾上心下肝左脾右
Shen Shang Xin Xia Gan Zuo Pi You

Above the kidneys, below the heart, at the left of the liver, at the right of the spleen

123
两肾之前脐轮之后
Liang Shen Zhi Qian Qi Lun Zhi Hou

In front of both kidneys, behind the navel

124
中虚之窍真气产地
Zhong Xu Zhi Qiao Zhen Qi Chan Di

The space in Kun Temple is the land to produce zhen qi

125
母气坤宫
Mu Qi Kun Gong

Kun Temple carries Mother Earth's qi

126
阴阳交媾
Yin Yang Jiao Gou

Yin yang connect in Kun Temple

127
坤宫意守
Kun Gong Yi Shou

Concentrate on Kun Temple

128
真火自来
Zhen Huo Zi Lai

True fire from Yuan Shen comes by itself

129
产药之源
Chan Yao Zhi Yuan

Kun Temple is the source to create yao
(the material of Jin Dan)

130
真气自归
Zhen Qi Zi Gui

Zhen qi comes back to Kun Temple

He Wei Kun Gong. "He wei" means *what*. "Kun" is the name of one of the *gua* or hexagrams from *I Ching*. Kun gua represents Mother Earth. "Gong" means *temple*. "He wei kun gong" (pronounced *huh way kwun gawng*) means *what is the Kun Temple?*

The Kun Gong is vital for the Tao Xiu Lian journey. You will learn more in the following phrases.

Shen Shang Xin Xia Gan Zuo Pi You. "Shen" means *kidneys*. "Shang" means *above*. "Xin" means *heart*. "Xia" means *below*. "Gan" means *liver*. "Zuo" means *left*. "Pi" means *spleen*. "You" means *right*. "Shen shang xin xia gan zuo pi you" (pronounced *shun shahng sheen shya gahn dzwaw pee yoe*) means *the Kun Temple is located above the kidneys, below the heart, left of the liver, right of the spleen.*

Liang Shen Zhi Qian Qi Lun Zhi Hou. "Liang shen" means *both kidneys*. "Zhi qian" means *in front*. "Qi lun" means *the energy chakra located at the navel*. "Zhi hou" means *behind*.

"Liang shen zhi qian qi lun zhi hou" (pronounced *lyahng shun jr chyen chee lwun jr hoe*) means *the Kun Temple is also located in front of both kidneys and behind the navel.*

Zhong Xu Zhi Qiao Zhen Qi Chan Di. "Zhong xu zhi qiao" means *the space of the Kun Temple, which is an empty area.* "Zhen qi" means *the qi of Yuan Shen or Tao*. "Chan" means *produce*. "Di" means *land*.

"Zhong xu zhi qiao zhen qi chan di" (pronounced *jawng shü jr chee-yow jun chee chahn dee*) means *the Kun Temple is the space that is the land to produce zhen qi.*

Mu Qi Kun Gong. "Mu qi" means *the qi of Mother Earth.* "Kun gong" is the *Kun Temple.* "Mu qi kun gong" (pronounced *moo chee kwun gawng*) means *the Kun Temple carries Mother Earth's qi.*

Yin Yang Jiao Gou. "Yin yang" means *yin yang.* "Jiao gou" means *connect and join together.* "Yin yang jiao gou" (pronounced *yeen yahng jee-yow goe*) means *yin yang connect and join together* in the Kun Temple.

In the Kun Temple, zhen qi is zhen yang, the real yang that is the yang of Yuan Shen or Tao. Zhen yin or real yin is yu ye, the jade liquid. Zhen yang (zhen qi) and zhen yin (jade liquid) interact in the Kun Temple. They join together to form the Jin Dan. Zhen yang and zhen yin are two. When they join as one, yin yang return to one. This is the reverse creation of Tao. Yin yang, which are two, return to one. One is Tao. Therefore, Jin Dan is Tao practice.

Kun Gong Yi Shou. "Kun gong" means *Kun Temple.* "Yi shou" means *concentrate on.* "Kun gong yi shou" (pronounced *kwun gawng yee sho*) means *concentrate on the Kun Temple.*

During Jin Dan Da Tao Xiu Lian, focus on the Jin Dan day and night. Jin Dan is located in the Kun Temple. To focus on the Jin Dan is to focus on the Kun Temple, which is located in the lower abdomen just below the navel.

Zhen Huo Zi Lai. "Zhen huo" means *true fire,* which is produced by Yuan Shen or Tao. "Zi lai" means *comes by itself.* "Zhen huo zi lai" (pronounced *jun hwaw dz lye*) means *the true fire from Yuan Shen or Tao comes by itself.*

The Kun Temple is where zhen yang and zhen yin join. If you

focus on the Kun Temple when you do Xiu Lian, zhen huo or true fire will develop.

Chan Yao Zhi Yuan. "Chan" means *produce*. "Yao" is the material to form the Jin Dan. "Zhi yuan" means *source*. "Chan yao zhi yuan" (pronounced *chahn yow jr ywen*) means *the Kun Temple is the source to create yao (the material for the Jin Dan)*.

Jin Dan is formed in the Kun Temple. Jing qi shen he yi happens in the Kun Temple. Zhen yang and zhen yin join as one in the Kun Temple. The Kun Temple is the source to produce yao. Yao is the material for the Jin Dan. Yao is jing qi shen. Yao is the Jin Dan.

Zhen Qi Zi Gui. "Zhen qi" means *the qi of Yuan Shen or Tao*. "Zi gui" means *returns by itself*. "Zhen qi zi gui" (pronounced *jun chee dz gway*) means *zhen qi returns to the Kun Temple*.

The Kun Temple is the land to form Jin Dan. The Kun Temple is the source of zhen qi.

131
天地未判
Tian Di Wei Pan

Before Heaven and Mother Earth existed

132
清浊未定
Qing Zhuo Wei Ding

Clean qi and disturbed qi have not been created

133
混沌一气
Hun Dun Yi Qi

There is only one qi, which is Tao

134
时至气化
Shi Zhi Qi Hua

When the time comes for Tao to create

135
清升为天
Qing Sheng Wei Tian

Clean qi rises to form Heaven

136
浊降为地
Zhuo Jiang Wei Di

Disturbed qi falls to form Mother Earth

137
天地开化
Tian Di Kai Hua

Heaven and Mother Earth start

138
地气上升
Di Qi Shang Sheng

Mother Earth's qi rises

139
天气下降
Tian Qi Xia Jiang

Heaven's qi falls

140
万物孕生
Wan Wu Yun Sheng

Countless things are produced

Tian Di Wei Pan. "Tian" means *Heaven*. "Di" means *Mother Earth*. "Wei pan" means *not started*. "Tian di wei pan" (pronounced *tyen dee way pahn*) means *before Heaven and Mother Earth existed*.

The following phrases will explain how Tao produces One, One produces Two, Two produces Three, and Three produces everything.

Qing Zhuo Wei Ding. "Qing" means *clean qi*. "Zhuo" means *disturbed qi*. "Wei ding" means *not created*. "Qing zhuo wei ding" (pronounced *ching jwaw way ding*) means *clean qi and disturbed qi have not been created*.

Hun Dun Yi Qi. "Hun dun" means *formless mass before creation*. "Yi qi" means *one qi*. "Hun dun yi qi" (pronounced *hwun dwun* *yee chee*) means *before creation, Tao is one qi that appears as a formless mass.* This is the Tao sheng yi (Tao creates One) state. Tao is the source and creator of everything. Tao creates One. One is this formless mass before creation.

Shi Zhi Qi Hua. "Shi zhi" means *when the time comes.* "Qi hua" means *qi is transformed.* "Shi zhi qi hua" (pronounced *shr jr chee hwah*) means *when the time has come to transform hun dun yi qi to yin yang.* This is yi sheng er (One creates Two). Tao, One, is ready to create.

Qing Sheng Wei Tian. "Qing" means *clean qi,* which is yang qi. "Sheng" means *rise.* "Wei tian" means *form Heaven.* "Qing sheng wei tian" (pronounced *ching shung way tyen*) means *clean qi or yang qi rises to form Heaven.*

Zhuo Jiang Wei Di. "Zhuo" means *disturbed qi.* Zhuo qi is yin qi. "Jiang" means *fall.* "Wei" means *become.* "Di" means *Mother Earth.* "Zhuo jiang wei di" (pronounced *jwaw jyahng way dee*) means *disturbed qi or yin qi falls to form Mother Earth.*

The last two sacred phrases explain how hun dun yi qi divides into two qi: qing qi and zhuo qi. Qing qi rises to form Heaven. Zhuo qi falls to form Mother Earth. This is to explain yi sheng er, One creates Two.

Tian Di Kai Hua. "Tian" means *Heaven.* "Di" means *Mother Earth.* "Kai hua" means *start.* "Tian di kai hua" (pronounced *tyen dee kye hwah*) means *Heaven and Mother Earth are formed and start to function.*

Di Qi Shang Sheng. "Di" means *Mother Earth.* "Qi" means *vital energy and life force.* "Shang sheng" means *rise.* "Di qi shang sheng" (pronounced *dee chee shahng shung*) means *Mother Earth's qi rises*.

Tian Qi Xia Jiang. "Tian" means *Heaven*. "Qi" means *vital energy and life force*. "Xia jiang" means *fall*. "Tian qi xia jiang" (pronounced *tyen chee shya jyahng*) means *Heaven's qi falls*.

The last two phrases, di qi shang sheng and tian qi xia jiang, describe how Tao regulates Heaven and Mother Earth. They are Tao movement. They are how Heaven and Mother Earth are balanced.

Di qi rises to Heaven to become clouds. Rain or snow is Heaven's qi falling. This is the balancing of Heaven and Mother Earth. If this balance is broken, many problems will occur.

Wan Wu Yun Sheng. "Wan wu" means *countless things*. "Yun sheng" means *created or produced*. "Wan wu yun sheng" (pronounced *wahn woo yün shung*) means *countless things are produced*.

Tao creates One. One creates Two. Two is Heaven and Mother Earth, yang and yin. Tao plus Heaven and Mother Earth are three. Three creates all things.

141
抱元守一
Bao Yuan Shou Yi

Hold and concentrate on Jin Dan

142
真精自固
Zhen Jing Zi Gu

Real matter is produced nonstop

143
真气自在
Zhen Qi Zi Zai

Real qi continues to be produced

144
真神自现
Zhen Shen Zi Xian

Yuan Shen appears and is in charge

145
抱元守一
Bao Yuan Shou Yi

Hold and concentrate on Jin Dan

146
三宝合一
San Bao He Yi

Three treasures, jing qi shen, join as one

147
真气自行
Zhen Qi Zi Xing

Real qi moves by itself

148
真火自运
Zhen Huo Zi Yun

Real fire moves by itself

Bao Yuan Shou Yi. This is a key phrase that I explained earlier in this chapter (sacred phrase 84). "Bao" means *hold*. "Yuan" means *circle or ball*. "Shou" means *concentrate*. "Yi" means *one*. This *One* is Jin Dan. "Bao yuan shou yi" (pronounced *bao ywen sho yee*) means *hold and concentrate on the Jin Dan*.

Bao Yuan Shou Yi is a key for Jin Dan Da Tao Xiu Lian. Bao Yuan Shou Yi is the secret of the secret.

Zhen Jing Zi Gu. "Zhen" means *real*. "Jing" means *matter*. "Zi gu" means *produce itself and become solid*. "Zhen jing zi gu" (pronounced *jun jing dz goo*) means *the real matter is produced nonstop and becomes solid*.

Jin Dan Da Tao Xiu Lian applies Bao Yuan Shou Yi. This is the Tao secret. This practice creates yuan jing and yuan qi from Yuan Shen or Tao. Remember the oil in the lamp. When you are born, you are given a full bottle of oil in your lamp. You exhaust this oil due to age, poor health, and all kinds of pollution.

To do Jin Dan Da Tao Xiu Lian and use Bao Yuan Shou Yi is to create more jing.

To create more jing is to fulfill the oil in your lamp.

It is to restore your lou ti (leaky body).

It is to join jing qi shen as one.

It is to form the Jin Dan.

It is to heal.

It is to prevent sickness.

It is to rejuvenate.

It is to reach fan lao huan tong.

It is to have a long, long life.

Finally, it is to meld with Tao.

To meld with Tao is to reach immortality.

Zhen Qi Zi Zai. "Zhen" means *real*. "Qi" means *vital energy and life force*. "Zi zai" means *self-produce and exist*. "Zhen qi zi zai" (pronounced *jun chee dz zye*) means *real qi continues to be produced and exist*.

To do Jin Dan Da Tao Xiu Lian and Bao Yuan Shou Yi is to continuously produce your zhen qi. Then, just as in the previous phrase, zhen qi is increased constantly. Automatically, you will jing qi shen he yi, form Jin Dan, heal, prevent sickness, rejuvenate, fan lao huan tong, prolong life, and meld with Tao to reach immortality.

Zhen Shen Zi Xian. "Zhen shen" means *real and true shen, which is Yuan Shen*. "Zi xian" means *appear by itself*. "Zhen shen zi xian" (pronounced *jun shun dz shyen*) means *Yuan Shen appears by itself and is in charge*.

To do Jin Dan Da Tao Xiu Lian and Bao Yuan Shou Yi is to have your Yuan Shen appear by itself. Your Yuan Shen will be in charge. Your Shi Shen will listen to Yuan Shen. Your Shi Shen will meld with Yuan Shen. Then you will reach ming xin jian xing and your Jin Dan will be formed. Fan lao huan tong and immortality are on the way.

Bao Yuan Shou Yi. As before, "bao yuan shou yi" means *hold and concentrate on the Jin Dan*.

Bao Yuan Shou Yi (pronounced *bao ywen sho yee*) is absolutely the top secret for Jin Dan Da Tao Xiu Lian. Therefore, I emphasize it repeatedly.

San Bao He Yi. "San" means *three*. "Bao" means *treasures*. "He yi" means *join as one*. "San bao he yi" (pronounced *sahn bao huh yee*) means *three internal treasures, jing qi shen, join as one*.

To do Jin Dan Da Tao Xiu Lian and Bao Yuan Shou Yi is to join jing qi shen as one. To join jing qi shen as one is to form the Jin Dan. To form the Jin Dan is to reach fan lao huan tong, longevity, and immortality.

Zhen Qi Zi Xing. "Zhen qi" means *real qi*. "Zi xing" means *move by itself*. "Zhen qi zi xing" (pronounced *jun chee dz shing*) means *the real qi moves by itself*.

To do Jin Dan Da Tao Xiu Lian and Bao Yuan Shou Yi is not to need to worry about how and where qi moves inside your body. When you do Bao Yuan Shou Yi, the real qi will move by itself.

According to traditional Chinese medicine, every sickness is due to blockages of qi. If you do Jin Dan Da Tao Xiu Lian and Bao Yuan Shou Yi, your zhen qi will move by itself. Wherever the qi blockages may be in the body, they will be removed little by little. Therefore, Bao Yuan Shou Yi causing zhen qi to move by itself is to heal all sickness. You are producing more and more zhen qi. The oil in your lamp is fulfilled more and more. All kinds of benefits will follow.

Zhen Huo Zi Yun. "Zhen" means *real*. "Huo" means *fire*. "Zi yun" means *move by itself*. "Zhen huo zi yun" (pronounced *jun hwaw dz yün*) means *the real fire of the body moves by itself*.

Zhen huo is the driving force of a human's life. It is just like an engine in a car. One must have zhen huo to survive. One must have zhen huo to rejuvenate. One must have zhen huo to prolong life.

149

百日筑基

Bai Ri Zhu Ji

**Practice one hundred days to build
a foundation for your body**

150

补足漏体

Bu Zu Lou Ti

Completely fulfill your leaky body

151

抱元守一

Bao Yuan Shou Yi

Hold and concentrate on Jin Dan

152

行走坐卧不离这个

Xing Zou Zuo Wo Bu Li Zhe Ge

Walking, sitting, or lying down, always focus on Jin Dan

Bai Ri Zhu Ji. As explained in depth earlier in this chapter, "bai
ri zhu ji" (pronounced *bye rr joo jee*) means *practice one hundred
days to build a foundation for your body*. Bai ri zhu ji is the first
stage to yu Dao he zhen.

Everyone has some imbalances in the spiritual, mental, emotional, and physical bodies. Sickness is an imbalance of jing qi

shen. To do one hundred days of practice is to fulfill your jing qi shen.

The purpose of these one hundred days is to build a foundation for your body in order to form your Jin Dan. To form the Jin Dan is to move in the direction of melding with Tao.

Bu Zu Lou Ti. "Bu zu" means *fulfill completely.* "Lou ti" means *leaky body.* "Bu zu lou ti" (pronounced *boo dzoo loe tee*) means *completely fulfill your leaky body.*

I have explained before that in Tao teaching, all sickness is due to a lack or imbalance of jing qi shen. The lack or imbalance of jing qi shen is named lou ti. To practice Jin Dan Da Tao Xiu Lian and Bao Yuan Shou Yi for one hundred days is to fulfill your jing qi shen. To fulfill jing qi shen is to fulfill the lou ti completely. Everything else to move you in the direction of melding with Tao will follow.

Bao Yuan Shou Yi. As previously explained, "bao yuan" means *hold a circle or ball.* To hold a circle or ball is to hold Tao, because Tao is the circle or ball. "Shou" means *concentrate.* "Yi" means *one,* which is Jin Dan. "Bao yuan shou yi" (pronounced *bao ywen sho yee)* means *hold and concentrate on your Jin Dan.*

Xing Zou Zuo Wo Bu Li Zhe Ge. "Xing zou" means *walk.* "Zuo" means *sit.* "Wo" means *lie down.* "Bu li" means *do not leave.* "Zhe ge" means *this one,* which is Bao Yuan Shou Yi. "Xing zou zuo wo bu li zhe ge" (pronounced *shing dzoe dzwaw waw boo lee juh guh)* means *always remember Bao Yuan Shou Yi whenever and wherever you are walking, sitting, or lying down.*

This is the most important Xiu Lian method to meld with

Tao. This is also the most difficult thing for the Tao practitioner to do. If you can always follow this principle, which means you always put your mind on your Jin Dan, then your Tao Xiu Lian journey will move much faster.

The moment you wake up, your mind is on the Jin Dan.
While you brush your teeth, your mind is on the Jin Dan.
While you eat breakfast, your mind is on the Jin Dan.
While you drive to work, your mind is on the Jin Dan.
Before work, your mind is on the Jin Dan.
While you work, your mind is on the Jin Dan.
During work breaks, your mind is on the Jin Dan.
Before you go to sleep, your mind is on the Jin Dan.

Put your mind on the Jin Dan not only when you are formally meditating; put your mind on the Jin Dan all the time.

This is the absolute secret that everybody must remember and put into practice.

Grab this absolute secret.

Do it.

You will receive benefits beyond, beyond imagination.

153
千日文武火
Qian Ri Wen Wu Huo

Practice gentle fire and strong fire for one thousand days

154
守一咽津液
Shou Yi Yan Jin Ye

Bao Yuan Shou Yi and swallow jade liquid

155
性命双修
Xing Ming Shuang Xiu

Do Xiu Lian to develop intelligence and body together

156
明心见性
Ming Xin Jian Xing

Enlighten your heart to see your Yuan Shen

157
穿岁月无形
Chuan Sui Yue Wu Xing

Time passes without notice

158
贯金墙无碍
Guan Jin Qiang Wu Ai

Go through the golden wall without blockage

Qian Ri Wen Wu Huo. "Qian ri" means *one thousand days*. "Wen huo" means *gentle fire*. "Wu huo" means *strong fire*. "Qian ri wen wu huo" (pronounced *chyen rr wun woo hwaw*) means *practice gentle fire and strong fire for one thousand days*.

In traditional Tao, there are many practices for wen huo and wu huo. The purpose of practicing wen huo, gentle fire, is to nourish the Jin Dan. The purpose of practicing wu huo, strong fire, is to practice the Jin Dan. For example, breathing practices can apply wen huo and wu huo. But I do not want to introduce too many ways to practice wen huo and wu huo. I want you to learn only one way, because Da Tao zhi jian—The Big Way is extremely simple.

The one way to practice wen huo and wu huo is the next phrase:

Shou Yi Yan Jin Ye. "Shou yi" means *Bao Yuan Shou Yi*. "Yan" means *swallow*. "Jin ye" means *jade liquid*. "Shou yi yan jin ye" (pronounced *sho yee yahn jeen yuh*) means *Bao Yuan Shou Yi and swallow jade liquid*.

If you practice shou yi yan jin ye consciously, you are practicing wu huo, strong fire.

If you practice shou yi yan jin ye in a natural condition, which is to naturally focus on your Jin Dan and swallow your jade liquid *without* conscious effort or intent, then you are practicing wen huo, gentle fire.

You cannot reach this natural condition right away. That is always the process. You must start by consciously practicing shou yi yan jin ye as wu huo. Then you will go into the emptiness condition, forgetting time and space. You are in the wen huo condition.

Wu huo and wen huo will alternate constantly. At the final stage, you will reach the completely natural state, which is the Tao fa zi ran state. Tao fa zi ran is to follow nature's way.

Bao Yuan Shou Yi is to form the Jin Dan.

To form the Jin Dan is to heal all sickness.

To form the Jin Dan is to prevent all sickness.

To form the Jin Dan is to reach fan lao huan tong.

To form the Jin Dan is to prolong life.

To form the Jin Dan is to meld with Tao.

To meld with Tao is to reach immortality.

Yan jin ye is wu huo. The purpose of yan jin ye is to form the Jin Dan. After the Jin Dan is formed, continue yan jin ye in order to form a complete Jin Dan.

To form a complete Jin Dan is to meld with Tao. To meld with Tao is to reach immortality.

Bao Yuan Shou Yi and yan jin ye are the two major secrets I reveal to you in this book.

Wen huo and wu huo are traditional Tao practice. Shou yi is the new wen huo practice. Yan jin ye is the new wu huo practice. These treasures are being released for the first time to humanity.

Grab the treasures.

Practice.

Benefit.

Xing Ming Shuang Xiu. "Xing" means *Xing Gong*, intelligence practice. "Ming" means *Ming Gong*, body practice. "Shuang xiu" means *practice together*. "Xing ming shuang xiu" (pronounced *shing ming shwahng sheo*) means *practice Xing Gong to develop intelligence and Ming Gong to develop body together.*

I emphasize again Jin Dan Da Tao Xiu Lian is xing ming shuang xiu. The purpose of Xing Gong is to reach ming xin jian xing. To reach ming xin jian xing is to enlighten your heart to see your Yuan Shen.

The purpose of Ming Gong is to have ju zu xing. Recall that ju zu xing means your body is fulfilled with complete jing qi shen to reach the baby state, which is fan lao huan tong.

To meld with Tao, you must xing ming shuang xiu—practice Ming Gong and Xing Gong together. Without both, you cannot meld with Tao.

If you do not practice Xing Gong, you can never reach ming xin jian xing. Your Yuan Shen will never be shown.

If you do not practice Ming Gong, you cannot have a perfect body. Before you can meld with Tao, your physical body may transition. When your body transitions, your Yuan Shen will leave. Later, your original soul will reincarnate again. You will have to do Tao Xiu Lian again in your next lifetime because you could not accomplish melding with Tao in this lifetime.

To practice Jin Dan Da Tao and do xing ming shuang xiu is a must to meld with Tao.

Let us do Jin Dan Da Tao Xiu Lian together one more time:

Sit up straight. Put both palms on your lower abdomen, below the navel. Keep your back straight. Put your mind on your Jin Dan. Chant Jin Dan Da Tao to develop your Xing Gong and Ming Gong together:

> *Tian Zhi Jing*
> *Di Zhi Jing*
> *Ren Zhi Jing*
> *Tian Di Ren Zhi Jing*
> *Wan Wu Zhi Jing*
> *Quan Yu Zhou Zhi Jing*
> *Jie Shi Dao Zhi Jing*
>
> *Tian Zhi Qi*
> *Di Zhi Qi*
> *Ren Zhi Qi*
> *Tian Di Ren Zhi Qi*
> *Wan Wu Zhi Qi*
> *Quan Yu Zhou Zhi Qi*
> *Jie Shi Dao Zhi Qi*

Tian Zhi Shen
Di Zhi Shen
Ren Zhi Shen
Tian Di Ren Zhi Shen
Wan Wu Zhi Shen
Quan Yu Zhou Zhi Shen
Jie Shi Dao Zhi Shen

Tian Zhi Xu
Di Zhi Xu
Ren Zhi Xu
Tian Di Ren Zhi Xu
Wan Wu Zhi Xu
Quan Yu Zhou Zhi Xu
Jie Shi Dao Zhi Xu

Tian Zhi Dao
Di Zhi Dao
Ren Zhi Dao
Tian Di Ren Zhi Dao
Wan Wu Zhi Dao
Quan Yu Zhou Zhi Dao
Jie Shi Da Dao

Tian Jing Qi Shen Xu Dao He Yi
Di Jing Qi Shen Xu Dao He Yi
Ren Jing Qi Shen Xu Dao He Yi
Tian Di Ren Jing Qi Shen Xu Dao He Yi
Wan Wu Jing Qi Shen Xu Dao He Yi
Quan Yu Zhou Jing Qi Shen Xu Dao He Yi
Jie Shi Yu Dao He Yi

Tian Jin Dan
Di Jin Dan
Ren Jin Dan
Tian Di Ren Jin Dan
Wan Wu Jin Dan
Quan Yu Zhou Jin Dan
Jie Shi Dao Jin Dan

Tian Yu Dao He Zhen
Di Yu Dao He Zhen
Ren Yu Dao He Zhen
Tian Di Ren Yu Dao He Zhen
Wan Wu Yu Dao He Zhen
Quan Yu Zhou Yu Dao He Zhen
Jie Shi Yu Dao He Zhen

Chant again. Chant more. There is no time limit. The more you chant, the more benefits you will receive.

Jin Dan Da Tao Xiu Lian can develop your Xing Gong and Ming Gong beyond any thought. Practice more and more.

Ming Xin Jian Xing. "Ming xin jian xing" (pronounced *ming shing jyen shing*) means *enlighten your heart to see your Yuan Shen.*

I do not need to explain ming xin jian xing further. See my previous explanations in this chapter.

Chuan Sui Yue Wu Xing. "Chuan" means *go through.* "Sui yue" means *time.* "Wu xing" means *no shape.* "Chuan sui yue wu xing" (pronounced *chwahn sway yoo-eh woo shing*) means *time passes without notice.*

When you reach ming xin jian xing, your Jin Dan is formed.

Then, your rejuvenation starts. You become younger and younger. Time could pass quickly without your even realizing it. One day you could suddenly think, "Wow, twenty years have passed." But you are becoming younger. That is the key. When people think about twenty years passing, they may feel old or tired. But when you do Jin Dan Da Tao Xiu Lian, you become younger. This is a completely different feeling and condition.

Guan Jin Qiang Wu Ai. "Guan" means *go through.* "Jin qiang" means *golden wall.* "Wu ai" means *no resistance.* "Guan jin qiang wu ai" (pronounced *gwahn jeen chyahng woo eye*) means *go through the golden wall without blockage.*

This is a Tao ability. An ordinary human being cannot do this at all. Tao creates all things. Tao is bigger than biggest and smaller than smallest. Tao has no shape, no image, no time, no space.

When you reach Tao, you will reach a condition described five thousand years ago in *The Yellow Emperor's Internal Classic*, the authority book of traditional Chinese medicine:

Ju zhe cheng xing, san zhe cheng feng

"Ju" means *accumulation.* "Zhe" means *the person* or *the thing.* "Cheng" means *become.* "Xing" means *shape.* "San" means *dissipation.* "Feng" means *wind.* "Ju zhe cheng xing, san zhe cheng feng" (pronounced *jü juh chung shing, sahn juh chung fung*) means *energy accumulates to form a shape; energy dissipates just like wind flowing away.*

When you meld with Tao, you are Tao. You can do much more than going through walls. This is just one sacred phrase to explain Tao abilities. When you reach Tao, you will know much more. My ten-year Tao training program includes training for special Tao abilities.

When you are ready, I welcome you to this special training. To gain Tao abilities is to be a better servant. To have Tao abilities is nothing to be proud of. In fact, when you gain these Tao abilities, do not show off. Be a humble servant.

159
三千日抱元守一
San Qian Ri Bao Yuan Shou Yi

Practice Bao Yuan Shou Yi for three thousand days

160
修得与道合真
Xiu De Yu Dao He Zhen

Xiu Lian to meld with Tao

San Qian Ri Bao Yuan Shou Yi. "San qian ri" means *three thousand days*. "Bao yuan shou yi" means *hold and focus on the Jin Dan*. "San qian ri bao yuan shou yi" (pronounced *sahn chyen rr bao ywen sho yee*) means *practice Bao Yuan Shou Yi for three thousand days*.

In Xiu Tao practice, there are three major periods to achieve great progress.

The first period is bai ri zhu ji (pronounced *bye rr joo jee*), *practice one hundred days to build a foundation for the body*. The purpose of this is to fulfill your lou ti (leaky body) in order to heal all of your sicknesses.

The second period is qian ri xiao cheng. "Qian ri" means *one thousand days*. "Xiao cheng" means *small achievement*. "Qian ri xiao cheng" (pronounced *chyen rr shee-yow chung*) means *do one thousand days of Xiu Lian for a small achievement.*

This achievement includes ming xin jian xing, forming the Jin Dan, fan lao huan tong, and more.

The third stage is three thousand days, san qian ri da cheng. "San qian ri" means *three thousand days.* "Da cheng" means *big achievement. Do three thousand days of Xiu Lian for a big achievement.*

"San qian ri bao yuan shou yi" (pronounced *sahn chyen rr bao ywen sho yee*) is to reach yu Dao he zhen. See the next sacred phrase:

Xiu De Yu Dao He Zhen. "Xiu de" means *Xiu Lian to achieve.* "Yu Dao he zhen" means *meld with Tao.* "Xiu de yu Dao he zhen" (pronounced *sheo duh yü dow huh jun*) means *Xiu Lian to meld with Tao.*

If you follow the teachings in this book seriously and practice seriously, you and humanity will know that you can meld with Tao in ten years. This could be very hard to believe for many people.

The three stages of Xiu Lian achievement are vital. The first stage is the most important. If you can, spend one hundred days to completely discipline yourself. Practice. Seriously purify your soul, heart, mind, and body. What you do, what you say, and what you hear must be completely disciplined. As explained earlier, close your three external treasures:

Do not see pollution in order to reach ming xin jian xing.

Do not hear pollution in order to fulfill your jing.

Do not speak pollution in order to boost your qi.

Most important in the first hundred days is to purify your heart in order to remove all kinds of pollution.

To remove all kinds of pollution is to self-clear bad karma.

To self-clear bad karma is the first step in Xiu Lian.

To Bao Yuan Shou Yi and yan jin ye is to add oil to your lamp.

Continue Bao Yuan Shou Yi and yan jin ye to fulfill your jing qi shen and join jing qi shen as one.

To join jing qi shen as one is to form the Jin Dan and to reach ming xin jian xing.

To reach ming xin jian xing is to bring your Yuan Shen to be in charge.

Fan lao huan tong follows.

Longevity follows.

Finally, meld with Tao.

Immortality is waiting for you.

161
天地淡定
Tian Di Dan Ding

Heaven and Mother Earth have no emotion, no desire, no attachment

162
阳升阴降
Yang Sheng Yin Jiang

Yang qi ascends, yin qi descends

163
日往月来
Ri Wang Yue Lai

Sun goes, moon comes

164
万物昌盛
Wan Wu Chang Sheng

All things flourish

Tian Di Dan Ding. "Tian" means *Heaven*. "Di" means *Mother Earth*. "Dan ding" means *no emotion, no desire, no attachment*. "Tian di dan ding" (pronounced *tyen dee dahn ding*) means *Heaven and Mother Earth have no emotion, no desire, and no attachment*.

Why do Heaven and Mother Earth have long, long lives? Nobody can figure out exactly how long Heaven and Mother Earth have lived. Their lives are very long because Heaven and Mother Earth have no emotions, desires, or attachments. They follow Tao movement, principles, and rules.

Why is a human being's life limited? Because a human being has emotions, desires, and attachments. Emotions, desires, attachments, sickness, age, all types of pollution, and more exhaust the oil in a human being's lamp. Therefore, a human being's life is limited.

To do Xiu Tao practice is to remove emotions, desires, attachments, and all kinds of pollution. To do Xiu Tao practice is to heal all sickness. To do Xiu Tao practice is to reach ming xin jian xing and more. These are the important purposes of Xiu Tao practice. A human being must also follow Tao movement, principles, and laws.

Yang Sheng Yin Jiang. "Yang" means *yang qi*. "Sheng" means *ascends*. "Yin" means *yin qi*. "Jiang" means *descends*. "Yang sheng yin jiang" (pronounced *yahng shung yeen jyahng*) means *yang qi ascends and yin qi descends*.

Yang sheng yin jiang is the rule of Tao. Therefore, a human

being's body has to follow this rule. If the body does not follow this rule, sickness occurs. If yang qi ascends and yin qi descends within the body, then a human being has health, rejuvenation, and longevity.

Ri Wang Yue Lai. "Ri" means *sun*. "Wang" means *go*. "Yue" means *moon*. "Lai" means *come*. "Ri wang yue lai" (pronounced *rr wahng yoo-eh lye*) means *sun goes, moon comes.*

Think about each day. In the morning, the sun comes and the moon goes. At night, the moon comes and the sun goes. This is yin yang exchange, which is Tao movement.

Wan Wu Chang Sheng. "Wan wu" means *all things.* "Chang sheng" means *flourish.* "Wan wu chang sheng" (pronounced *wahn woo chahng shung*) means *all things flourish.*

Let me summarize the last four sacred phrases. Because Heaven and Mother Earth have no emotions, desires, and attachments, yang qi ascends and yin qi descends. Heaven and Mother Earth are balanced. These are the natural rules of Tao.

The sun comes and the moon goes. The moon comes and the sun goes. This is the natural rule of Tao also.

Because Heaven and Mother Earth follow Tao's natural rules, all things flourish.

165
静中至寂
Jing Zhong Zhi Ji

Meditate to extreme quietness where you forget yourself

166
神气相抱
Shen Qi Xiang Bao

Yuan Shen and yuan qi hold together

167
气结精凝
Qi Jie Jing Ning

Yuan qi and yuan jing accumulate and concentrate

168
结成金丹
Jie Cheng Jin Dan

Jing Qi Shen He Yi to form Jin Dan

169
丹田温暖
Dan Tian Wen Nuan

Dan Tian area is warm

170
三关升降
San Guan Sheng Jiang

Energy ascends and descends in three gates

171
上下冲合
Shang Xia Chong He

Di qi ascends, tian qi descends; yang qi and yin qi collide and join in order to balance

172
醍醐灌顶
Ti Hu Guan Ding

Suddenly achieve enlightenment

173
甘露洒心
Gan Lu Sa Xin

Dew sprays to the heart

174
玄天妙音
Xuan Tian Miao Yin

Hear Heaven's profound sounds

175
耳中常闻
Er Zhong Chang Wen

Often hear Heaven's music and voices

176
至宝玄珠
Zhi Bao Xuan Zhu

Jing Qi Shen He Yi forms the initial Jin Dan, just like a pearl

177
真真景象
Zhen Zhen Jing Xiang

See the real images

178
永存道中
Yong Cun Dao Zhong

These images always exist within Tao

179
犹如灯光
You Ru Deng Guang

Just like the lamp light

180
长明不熄
Chang Ming Bu Xi

The light always shines continuously

Jing Zhong Zhi Ji. "Jing zhong" means *quiet*. "Zhi ji" means *extremely quiet*. "Jing zhong zhi ji" (pronounced *jing jawng jr jee*) means *meditate to extreme quietness where you forget yourself.*

When you do Xiu Tao practice, Jin Dan Da Tao Xiu Lian is the key. When you do Jin Dan Da Tao Xiu Lian, you are meditating, chanting, and doing Bao Yuan Shou Yi. You become calm and more quiet. Suddenly you do not know where you are. You have forgotten yourself. In that moment, you have gone into the stillness condition.

I will continue to explain this process in the next phrase:

Shen Qi Xiang Bao. "Shen" means *Yuan Shen*. "Qi" means *yuan chi*. "Xiang bao" means *hold together*. "Shen qi xiang bao" (pronounced *shun chee shyahng bao*) means *Yuan Shen and yuan qi hold together.*

When you do Jin Dan Da Tao Xiu Lian, you go into the emptiness and nothingness condition. In Tao practice, this is named "ding," which means *stillness*. When you reach stillness, you go into the condition of "wang wo zhuang tai" (pronounced *wahng waw jwahng tye*), which means *forget yourself.*

When you forget yourself, you are in the emptiness and nothingness condition. Your Yuan Shen appears. Yuan Shen is Tao. Your Yuan Shen created your yuan qi and yuan jing. When you are in the stillness condition, yuan qi and yuan jing "hold" or join together. This is Xing Gong practice.

Recall that the purpose of Xing Gong is to develop your big intelligence. Big intelligence comes from your Yuan Shen.

Qi creates jing. When Yuan Shen and yuan qi join as one, jing is created.

The next phrase explains the process further:

Qi Jie Jing Ning. "Qi" means *vital energy and life force.* "Jie" means *accumulation.* "Jing" means *matter.* "Ning" means *concentration.* "Qi jie jing ning" (pronounced *chee jyeh jing ning*) means *yuan qi and yuan jing accumulate and concentrate.*

When Yuan Shen and yuan qi hold or join together, yuan qi accumulates and yuan jing concentrates. This will create your Jin Dan.

The process continues in the next phrase:

Jie Cheng Jin Dan. "Jie cheng" means *concentrate to form.* "Jin" means *golden.* "Dan" means *light ball.* "Jie cheng jin dan" (pronounced *jyeh chung jeen dahn*) means *jing qi shen he yi to form Jin Dan.*

When Yuan Shen, yuan qi, and yuan jing join as one, the Jin Dan is formed. Jing qi shen he yi (matter energy soul joining as one) is yuan jing, yuan qi, and Yuan Shen joining as one. Yuan Shen is Tao. Yuan Shen is given at the moment the father's sperm and the mother's egg join as one.

Yuan Shen creates yuan qi and yuan jing. Tao gives jing qi shen to every human being. As a newborn baby, everyone is given a full bottle of oil in the lamp. This full bottle of oil is the jing qi shen from Tao.

As I have explained, in one's life this orignal jing qi shen is constantly exhausted due to all kinds of reasons. To do Jin Dan Da Tao Xiu Lian is to fulfill jing qi shen. To fulfill jing qi shen is to form the Jin Dan.

When jing qi shen he yi, the Jin Dan is formed.

I will continue to explain in the next sacred phrase:

Dan Tian Wen Nuan. "Dan tian" means *Lower Dan Tian.* "Wen nuan" means *warm.* "Dan tian wen nuan" (pronounced *dahn tyen wun nwahn*) means *Dan Tian area is warm.*

When the Jin Dan is formed, your jing qi shen join as one. Your lower abdomen will feel warm. This warmth is the energy created by jing qi shen.

The next step in this process is:

San Guan Sheng Jiang. "San" means *three*. "Guan" means *gate*. "Sheng" means *ascend*. "Jiang" means *descend*. "San guan sheng jiang" (pronounced *sahn gwahn shung jyahng*) means *energy ascends and descends in three gates*.

There are three energy gates on the back of the body. Wei Lu Guan (pronounced *way lü gwahn*) is the first gate. Wei Lu is in the tailbone area, in the area of the Chang Jiang acupuncture point. The Chang Jiang point is Du (Governing Vessel) meridian 1. It is located midway between the tip of the coccyx and the anus. The second gate is Jia Ji Guan (pronounced *jyah jee gwahn*), which is the area of the Shen Tao acupuncture point, which is Du (Governing Vessel) meridian 11. It is located on the midline of the back below the level of the fifth thoracic vertebrae. The third gate is Yu Zhen Guan (pronounced *yü jun gwahn*), which is in the area of the Feng Fu acupuncture point. The Feng Fu point is Du (Governing Vessel) meridian 16. It is located one *cun* above the midpoint of the posterior hairline, directly below the occipital protuberance on the back of the head.

For a normal human being, these three energy gates are not fully open. When you do Jin Dan Da Tao practice, your Jin Dan is formed. When your Jin Dan is formed, energy will move to these three gates to fully open them.

After energy flows freely through these three areas, it then flows down the front side of the body. The entire flow of energy becomes a circle.

In traditional Tao practice, one special practice is named *xiao zhou tian*, the "microcosmic orbit." This is an energy circle that starts in the genital area, goes up through the back of the body to the top of the head, and then comes back down through the front of the body.

Many people in history used mind power to practice this circle of qi flow. Some people did not practice correctly; they used too strong mind power to create energy flow, which caused major problems. They focused so much and so strongly that it caused irritation, headaches, and, in the worse cases, mental disorders. Therefore, it does not matter what kind of meditation you are doing. Always remember the very important principle: focus very gently. Focus for a little while, and then relax for a little while. Then focus again for a little while, and then relax again. That is the secret. Follow this principle and you will not create any side effects.

There is an ancient statement: *yi zhong qi huo.* "Yi" means *thinking* or *concentrating.* "Zhong" means *heavy.* "Qi" means *produce.* "Huo" means *fire.* "Yi zhong qi huo" (pronounced *yee jawhng chee hwaw*) means *concentrating too much produces fire.* That is why you have to do gentle meditation like I said in the previous paragraph.

For the Xiao Zhou Tian or any energy circle, remember this point and do not focus your mind on the energy circle. In fact, in my teaching, you do not need to think about the energy circle at all. Just focus on your Jin Dan! When your Jin Dan is formed and when your jing qi shen is full in your Jin Dan, this energy circle will flow by itself. *All energy circles will flow by themselves.* This is a major secret! You do not need to think at all. Therefore, you cannot create any side effects by practicing in the wrong way.

Shang Xia Chong He. "Shang" means *ascend.* "Xia" means *descend.* "Chong he" means *collide and join.* "Shang xia chong he" (pronounced *shahng shya chawhng huh*) means *di qi* (Mother Earth's qi) *ascends, tian qi* (Heaven's qi) *descends; yang qi and yin qi collide and join in order to balance.*

Ti Hu Guan Ding. "Ti hu" means *awakening.* "Guan ding" means *jade liquid pours into the head* (through the crown chakra). "Ti hu guan ding" (pronounced *tee hoo gwahn ding*) means *jade liquid pours into your head and goes into your heart; you suddenly awaken and realize the Tao wisdom.* This is another expression of ming xin jian xing. "Ti hu guan ding" can be translated as *suddenly achieve enlightenment.*

In the Xiu Tao journey, you will have a sudden awakening. In fact, this is to reach ming xin jian xing. You see the happiness and the light in the bitter sea.

Gan Lu Sa Xin. "Gan lu" means *dew.* "Sa xin" means *spray the heart.* "Gan lu sa xin" (pronounced *gahn loo sah sheen*) means *dew sprays to the heart.*

When you reach ming xin jian xing and are suddenly awakened and enlightened, it is like the purest and most refreshing dew spraying on your heart. You feel so clear and fresh.

Xuan Tian Miao Yin. "Xuan tian" means *Heaven.* "Miao yin" means *profound sound.* "Xuan tian miao yin" (pronounced *shwen tyen mee-yow yeen*) means *hear Heaven's profound sounds.*

When you are enlightened, your spiritual channels may open. You may hear profound sounds from Heaven.

Er Zhong Chang Wen. "Er zhong" means *inside the ear*. "Chang" means *often*. "Wen" means *hear*. "Er zhong chang wen" (pronounced *ur jawhng chahng wun*) means *often hear Heaven's music and voices*.

After enlightenment, your spiritual channels may open. You may often hear Heaven's music and voices.

Zhi Bao Xuan Zhu. "Zhi bao" means *the most precious treasure*. "Xuan zhu" means *Heaven's pearl*. "Zhi bao xuan zhu" (pronounced *jr bao shwen joo*) means *jing qi shen he yi forms the initial Jin Dan, just like a pearl*. At its initial stages of formation, the Jin Dan is the size of a small grain of rice, but it grows bigger and bigger as you do Xiu Tao practice. Zhi bao xuan zhu tells us that the Jin Dan grows like a pearl. The normal size of the Jin Dan would be between the size of a pigeon egg and a chicken egg. The Jin Dan could grow bigger and bigger.

Zhen Zhen Jing Xiang. "Zhen zhen" means *real*. "Jing xiang" means *images*. "Zhen zhen jing xiang" (pronounced *jun jun jing shyahng*) means *see the real images*.

After you begin to form your Jin Dan, if your Third Eye is open, you could clearly see your intital Jin Dan as a pearl.

Of course, you have to open your spiritual channels to see Heaven's pearl and hear Heaven's profound sounds. Some people reach enlightenment and still see nothing. Never expect to see anything. You may see something else. The important principle is always no expectation.

Yong Cun Dao Zhong. "Yong" means *always*. "Cun" means *exist*. "Dao zhong" means *within Tao*. "Yong cun Dao zhong" (pronounced *yawng tsoon dow jawng*) means *these images always exist within Tao.*

Tao creates all things. If you reach ming xin jian xing, you could see Yuan Shen. Yuan Shen is Tao. You could see Heaven's images and hear Heaven's profound music and voices. However, you can see and hear only when you go into the Tao condition. Remember the teaching. Do not expect to see Heaven's images or hear Heaven's voices. If you see special images or hear special sounds from Heaven, great. If you cannot see or hear them, have no attachment. This is to follow nature's way (Dao fa zi ran).

You Ru Deng Guang. "You ru" means *just like.* "Deng guang" means *lamp light.* "You ru deng guang" (pronounced *yoe roo dung gwahng*) means *just like the lamp light.*

When you reach ming xin jian xing and form the initial Jin Dan, it is just like the lamp light is on.

Chang Ming Bu Xi. "Chang ming" means *light is always on.* "Bu xi" means *continuously.* "Chang ming bu xi" (pronounced *chahng ming boo shee*) means *the light always shines continuously.* In order for your lamp's light to shine continuously, you have to fulfill the jing qi shen in the lamp all of the time. To fulfill jing qi shen is to fulfill the oil in your life lamp. If the oil is always fulfilled, you have reached fan lao huan tong. If you continuously keep your life lamp full of oil, then you have longevity. If you can keep your lamp full of oil permanently, then you have achieved immortality.

181
先天真阳
Xian Tian Zhen Yang

Innate real yang is Yuan Shen

182
后天真阴
Hou Tian Zhen Yin

After birth, real yin is Shi Shen plus the body

183
两气氤氲
Liang Qi Yin Yun

Yin yang unification

184
结成仙胎
Jie Cheng Xian Tai

Form a saint baby

185
仙胎道胎
Xian Tai Dao Tai

Saint baby and Tao Baby

186
道乳哺养
Dao Ru Pu Yang

Tao milk feeds the saint baby and Tao Baby

187
成长壮大
Cheng Zhang Zhuang Da

Baby grows bigger and stronger

188
提高等级
Ti Gao Deng Ji

Your joined Yuan Shen and Shi Shen are uplifted

189
十月功成
Shi Yue Gong Cheng

**Saint baby or Tao Baby
takes ten months to grow**

190
脱胎飞升
Tuo Tai Fei Sheng

Soul baby travels

191

超乎阴阳

Chao Hu Yin Yang

Go beyond yin yang laws

192

无形无拘

Wu Xing Wu Ju

No shape, no control, no restraint from anything

193

通身浊阴

Tong Shen Zhuo Yin

Whole body is disturbed yin after birth

194

尽化纯阳

Jin Hua Chun Yang

**Whole body transforms to pure yang,
which is your Yuan Shen**

195

跳出樊笼

Tiao Chu Fan Long

Jump out from the control of yin, yang, and San Jie

196
逍遥无穷
Xiao Yao Wu Qiong

Freedom and joy are endless within Tao

Xian Tian Zhen Yang. "Xian tian" means *innate*. "Zhen yang" means *real yang*. "Xian tian zhen yang" (pronounced *shyen tyen jun yahng*) means *innate real yang is Yuan Shen*.

Yuan Shen is given to every human being. The Xiu Tao journey is to see your Yuan Shen first. Then everything else will follow. Xian tian zhen yang is your Yuan Shen.

Hou Tian Zhen Yin. "Hou tian" means *postnatal*. "Zhen yin" means *Shi Shen*. "Hou tian zhen yin" (pronounced *hoe tyen jun yeen*) means *after birth, real yin is Shi Shen plus the body*.

After birth, your whole body is controlled by Shi Shen. Shi Shen is the body soul who reincarnates. Shi Shen carries karma. Shi Shen plus the whole body are zhen yin.

Liang Qi Yin Yun. "Liang qi" means *yin yang*. "Yin yun" means *unification*. "Liang qi yin yun" (pronounced *lyahng chee yeen yün*) means *yin yang unification*.

Yuan Shen is xian tian zhen yang, innate real yang. Shi Shen and the whole body are real yin, zhen yin, which is the real postnatal yin. When real yin and real yang join as one, it is yin yang unification. This is Shi Shen and Yuan Shen joining as one. This is ming xin jian xing. This is also Jin Dan formation. They are all the same thing, only explained in different ways.

Jie Cheng Xian Tai. "Jie cheng" means *form*. "Xian tai" means *saint baby*. "Jie cheng xian tai" (pronounced *jyeh chung shyen tye*) means *form a saint baby*.

A saint baby is not a baby created from a sperm and an egg. A saint baby is a soul baby. The purpose of this baby is to train you to become a saint and move further to meld with Tao. It does not matter if you are male or female; receiving a saint baby is a "must" process to meld with Tao. This is absolutely the top Tao secret.

This saint baby is created by the unification of your Yuan Shen and Shi Shen.

Xian Tai Dao Tai. "Xian tai" again means *saint baby*. "Dao tai" means *Tao Baby*. "Xian tai Dao tai" (pronounced *shyen tye dow tye*) means *saint baby and Tao Baby*.

A saint baby and a Tao Baby are different. There are many layers of saint baby. Finally, you can reach the level where you can receive a Tao Baby.

A saint baby is a soul baby from Heaven and Mother Earth, the yin yang world. A Tao Baby is a soul baby from the Tao realm, which is the wu world or emptiness-and-nothingness world. When you form a complete Jin Dan, the Tao Baby will be formed.

During the Xiu Lian process, the Jin Dan is continually developed after its initial formation. To form a complete Jin Dan takes many years. If you cannot accomplish this process, in the next life you will start all over again. If in your next life you still cannot meld with Tao, you will start the Xiu Tao journey yet again in your following life.

Dao Ru Pu Yang. Dao or Tao is The Way, emptiness and nothingness, the source of all universes, and the universal principles and laws. "Ru" means *milk*. "Pu yang" means *feed baby*. "Dao ru pu yang" (pronounced *dow roo poo yahng*) means *Tao milk feeds the saint baby and Tao Baby*.

When you have a saint baby or a Tao Baby, Heaven, Mother Earth, and Tao will feed the milk of Heaven, Mother Earth, and Tao to the baby. The milk of Heaven, Mother Earth, and Tao are the nutrients. They directly come from Heaven, Mother Earth, and Tao to feed your saint soul baby or Tao Soul Baby.

Cheng Zhang Zhuang Da. "Cheng zhang" means *grow*. "Zhuang da" means *bigger and stronger*. "Cheng zhang zhuang da" (pronounced *chung jahng jwahng dah*) means *baby grows bigger and stronger*.

When the saint baby or Tao Baby is formed, it will be nourished by the milk of Heaven, Mother Earth, and Tao. The baby will grow and grow.

Ti Gao Deng Ji. "Ti gao" means *uplift*. "Deng ji" means *layers of soul standing in Heaven*. "Ti gao deng ji" (pronounced *tee gao dung jee*) means *your joined Yuan Shen and Shi Shen are uplifted*.

When you reach ming xin jian xing, your Yuan Shen is in charge. Your Shi Shen is in the process of melding with your Yuan Shen, but they have not yet melded with Tao. This process is one of transforming quantity to quality. It takes time to accomplish the process.

When each successive level of your saint baby or Tao Baby is created, your soul standing will be uplifted in Heaven.

Shi Yue Gong Cheng. "Shi yue" means *ten months*. "Gong cheng" means *grow your saint baby or Tao Baby*. "Shi yue gong cheng" (pronounced *shr yoo-eh gawng chung*) means *saint baby or Tao Baby takes ten months to grow*.

Tuo Tai Fei Sheng. "Tuo tai" means *to be born*. "Fei sheng" means *flying*. "Tuo tai fei sheng" (pronounced *twaw tye fay shung*) means *soul baby travels*.

This is a very sacred step. When your soul baby is ready, it will soul travel to Heaven, Mother Earth, and universes to absorb the nutrients of Heaven, Mother Earth, and universes.

The Tao Baby will travel to Tao to receive Tao nutrients. This is a very important stage of melding with Tao.

Chao Hu Yin Yang. "Chao hu" means *go beyond*. "Yin yang" means *yin yang world*. "Chao hu yin yang" (pronounced *chow hoo yeen yahng*) means *go beyond yin yang laws*.

When you meld with Tao, you are Tao. When you are at the Tao level, you cannot be controlled by anything in the yin yang world anymore, because Tao creates yin yang. You will gain many extraordinary abilities that you have read about in fairy tales.

Wu Xing Wu Ju. "Wu" means *no*. "Xing" means *shape*. "Ju" means *control*. "Wu xing wu ju" (pronounced *woo shing woo jü*) means *no shape, no control, no restraint from anything*.

When you meld with Tao, you have true freedom. Nothing can control you anymore.

Tong Shen Zhuo Yin. "Tong shen" means *whole body*. "Zhuo yin" means *disturbed yin*. "Tong shen zhuo yin" (pronounced *tawng shun jwaw yeen*) means *whole body is disturbed yin after birth*.

After birth, the whole body and any part of it from head to toe, skin to bone, can be considered yin compared to the pure Yuan Shen, which is pure yang. Before you reach ming xin jian xing, your Shi Shen is in charge, so your Shi Shen is also yin. This is all "disturbed" yin because your true self, which is your Yuan Shen, is not in charge yet.

Jin Hua Chun Yang. "Jin hua" means *all transforms*. "Chun yang" means *pure yang*. "Jin hua chun yang" (pronounced *jeen hwah chwun yahng*) means *the whole body transforms to pure yang, which is to meld with Yuan Shen*.

Tao gives Yuan Shen when the sperm and egg join as one. Yuan Shen is pure yang. After birth, Shi Shen is in charge. Do Jin Dan Da Tao Xiu Lian and Bao Yuan Shou Yi to reach ming xin jian xing and to form your Jin Dan.

After forming your Jin Dan, your Yuan Shen is on duty. Yuan Shen starts to guide and lead Shi Shen. The body transforms gradually from yin to pure yang. Shi Shen gradually melds with Yuan Shen.

When you form a complete Jin Dan, your Jin Dan will be the size of your whole body. Every part of your body, from head to toe, skin to bone, will be transformed by the Jin Dan. Every part of the body's frequency will have completely changed. At that moment, your body is a pure yang body.

To have a pure yang body is to reach the baby stage. When you reach this stage, you have accomplished fan lao huan tong.

Tiao Chu Fan Long. "Tiao chu" means *jump out*. "Fan long" means *cage*. "Tiao chu fan long" (pronounced *tee-yow choo fahn long*) means *jump out from the control of yin, yang, and San Jie*. "San Jie" (pronounced *sahn jyeh*) means *Heaven, Mother Earth, and human being*.

A human being on Mother Earth is controlled in many ways. Birth and death is the first control. There are many others. There are all kinds of rules in the yin yang world.

A purpose of doing Jin Dan Da Tao Xiu Lian and Bao Yuan Shou Yi is to jump out from the control of yin yang. Yin yang control is just like a cage. To jump out from the cage is to go beyond the control of yin yang laws.

Xiao Yao Wu Qiong. "Xiao yao" means *freedom*. "Wu qiong" means *endless*. "Xiao yao wu qiong" (pronounced *shee-yow yow woo chyawng*) means *freedom and joy are endless within Tao*.

When you meld with Tao, you have reached true freedom. There is no more control from the yin yang world and from Heaven and Mother Earth. To be a human being is to be controlled by so many rules in Heaven, Mother Earth, and the yin yang world. To be a human being is to have to follow all kinds of principles and rules. To meld with Tao is to achieve true freedom.

197
炼己炼心
Lian Ji Lian Xin

Xiu Lian for your body and heart

198
炼心不动
Lian Xin Bu Dong

The Xiu Lian heart cannot be shaken

199
离宫修定
Li Gong Xiu Ding

Xiu Lian for the heart leads to stillness

200
定则神和
Ding Ze Shen He

**Stillness leads to harmonization of
Yuan Shen and Shi Shen**

201
和则气安
He Ze Qi An

**Harmonization of Yuan Shen and Shi Shen will balance
and increase qi and bring true peace in the heart**

202
安则精满
An Ze Jing Man

Sufficient qi and a peaceful heart will create full jing

203
满则丹结
Man Ze Dan Jie

Sufficient jing accumulates to form the Jin Dan

204
结则造化
Jie Ze Zao Hua

Jin Dan forms and follows nature's way

Lian Ji Lian Xin. "Lian" means *Xiu Lian*. "Ji" means *yourself*. "Xin" means *heart*. "Lian ji lian xin" (pronounced *lyen jee lyen sheen*) means *Xiu Lian for your body and heart*.

To practice Jin Dan Da Tao Xiu Lian is to do Xing Gong and Ming Gong practice. To do Xiu Lian for your heart is Xing Gong practice. To do Xing Gong practice is to reach ming xin jian xing.

To do Xiu Lian for your body is Ming Gong practice. To do Ming Gong practice is to reach ju zu xing. "Ju zu xing" (pronounced *jü dzoo shing*) means *full of jing qi shen joined as one*. This is to transform the body to the pure yang body, which is to reach fan lao huan tong.

Therefore, lian ji lian xin, to do Xiu Lian for your body and heart, is to do both Xing Gong and Ming Gong practice.

Lian Xin Bu Dong. "Lian" means *Xiu Lian*. "Xin" means *heart*. "Bu dong" means *not affected by pollution*. "Lian xin bu dong" (pronounced *lyen sheen boo dawng*) means *the Xiu Lian heart cannot be shaken*.

The key to Xiu Lian is purification. In fact, "xiu" means *purification*. Your Shi Shen or body soul carries bad karma. Mother Earth is the bitter sea and red dust. There are all kinds of pollution on Mother Earth.

To do Xiu Lian for your heart is to avoid all that pollutes your heart. None of the pollution around you can shake your heart at all.

Li Gong Xiu Ding. "Li gong" means *the Li Temple*. This is wisdom teaching of the *I Ching*. The Li Temple is the fire temple and the heart temple. "Xiu" means Xiu Lian. "Ding" means *stillness*. "Li gong xiu ding" (pronounced *lee gawng sheo ding*) means *Xiu Lian for the heart leads to stillness*.

This sacred phrase continues to emphasize the phrase immediately before (lian xin bu dong).

When you do Jin Dan Da Tao Xiu Lian, you cannot be affected by any kind of pollution. Your heart must go into the stillness condition. Then, nothing can attract you. Nothing can distract you. Nothing can affect you.

All kinds of emotions, greed, selfishness, and much more can affect your Xiu Lian. The key for Xiu Lian is to purify your heart. This most important thing is also the most difficult thing for a Xiu Lian practitioner. Give your greatest effort to not let anything affect your Xiu Lian practice.

If you can bring your heart to the stillness condition, that is a very special condition.

Ding Ze Shen He. "Ding" means *stillness*. "Ze" means *become*. "Shen" represents *Yuan Shen and Shi Shen*. "He" means *harmony*. "Ding ze shen he" (pronounced *ding dzuh shun huh*) means *harmonization of Yuan Shen and Shi Shen*.

If you can Xiu Lian to purify your heart and reach the stillness condition, you are no longer affected by any pollution. Your Yuan Shen and Shi Shen will connect when you are in the stillness condition. The more time you can spend in the stillness condition, the more your Yuan Shen and Shi Shen will be harmonized. Finally, Yuan Shen and Shi Shen will completely meld as one. If you reach that condition then you have reached Tao. You have melded with Tao.

He Ze Qi An. "He" means *harmony*. "Ze" means *become*. "Qi" means *vital energy and life force*. "An" means *balance and peace*.

"He ze qi an" (pronounced *huh dzuh chee ahn*) means *harmonization of Yuan Shen and Shi Shen will balance and increase qi and bring true peace in the heart.*

An Ze Jing Man. "An" means *true peace.* "Ze" means *become.* "Jing" means *matter.* "Man" means *full.* "An ze jing man" (pronounced *ahn dzuh jing mahn*) means *sufficient qi and a peaceful heart will create full jing.*

When your heart reaches true peace and is full of qi, qi will produce jing. Jing will then increase. This is an important Ming Gong practice.

Man Ze Dan Jie. "Man" means *full.* "Ze" means *become.* "Dan" means *Jin Dan.* "Jie" means *form.* "Man ze dan jie" (pronounced *mahn dzuh dahn jyeh*) means *sufficient jing accumulate to form the Jin Dan.*

When your heart reaches the stillness condition, your qi is fulfilled and your heart will have true peace. The qi will produce jing and your jing will be fulfilled also. Jing will concentrate to form a Jin Dan.

Jie Ze Zao Hua. "Jie" means *Dan.* "Ze" means *become.* "Zao hua" means *follow nature's way.* "Jie ze zao hua" (pronounced *jyeh dzuh dzow hwah*) means *Jin Dan forms and follows nature's way.*

After the Jin Dan is formed, you will follow Tao's way, which is nature's way. Continue to practice Jin Dan Da Tao Xiu Lian and Bao Yuan Shou Yi. Your Jin Dan will grow. Finally the Jin Dan will grow to the size of your whole body to transform every system, every organ, every cell, and every DNA and RNA of the body. Your whole body's frequency will change to Tao frequency. Finally, you are moving in the direction of melding with Tao. Your body turns to the Tao body. The quality of your whole body will turn to Tao quality. Finally, you are moving in the direction of melding with Tao. You become Tao. Tao is you. The normal creation and reverse creation of Tao will happen inside of your body.

205
玄珠成象
Xuan Zhu Cheng Xiang

Initial stage of Jin Dan formation like a pearl

206
太乙含真
Tai Yi Han Zhen

Everyone has the real yang of Tao, which is Yuan Shen

207
津液炼形
Jin Ye Lian Xing

Tian Yi Zhen Shui and Jin Jin Yu Ye transform your body

208
神形俱妙
Shen Xing Ju Miao

Xing Gong and Ming Gong Xiu Lian
have been accomplished

209
奋勇精进
Fen Yong Jing Jin

Try your greatest best to do Xiu Lian

210
舍生忘死
She Sheng Wang Si

Give your life to do Xiu Lian

211
心死神活
Xin Si Shen Huo

Shi Shen gives up the position, Yuan Shen is in charge

212
方可修成
Fang Ke Xiu Cheng

Xiu Lian can reach Tao

Xuan Zhu Cheng Xiang. "Xuan zhu" means *Heaven's pearl*, which is the Jin Dan. "Cheng xiang" means *shows images*. "Xuan zhu cheng xiang" (pronounced *shwen joo chung shyahng*) means *initial stage of Jin Dan formation like a pearl.*

In Jin Dan Da Tao Xiu Lian, to form the Jin Dan is to reach ming xin jian xing. It is vital to form the Jin Dan because after forming the Jin Dan, your Yuan Shen is in charge. Yuan Shen is

Tao. Yuan Shen will guide you to continue to do Tao Xiu Lian. Every step will follow to meld with Tao.

Tai Yi Han Zhen. "Tai yi" means *Tao*. "Han" means *hold*. "Zhen" means *Yuan Shen*. "Tai yi han zhen" (pronounced *tye yee hahn jun*) means *everyone has the real yang of Tao, which is Yuan Shen*.

A normal human being cannot see this real yang of Tao, which is Yuan Shen. Only through practicing Jin Dan Da Tao can you start to form your initial Jin Dan. It could be the size of a grain of rice at first. Then it could grow to the size of a pearl. Then it can become a formal Jin Dan. Then the Jin Dan can grow bigger and bigger.

Jin Ye Lian Xing. "Jin ye" means *tian yi zhen shui and jin jin yu ye*. "Lian" means *transform*. "Xing" means *body*. "Jin ye lian xing" (pronounced *jeen yuh lyen shing*) means *tian yi zhen shui and jin jin yu ye transform your body*.

This is to continue to emphasize that tian yi zhen shui and jin jin yu ye are the materials to form your Jin Dan. After the Jin Dan's formation, tian yi zhen shui and jin jin yu ye will continue to fulfill the Jin Dan. Then the oil in your lamp can be fulfilled further and further until it is full.

When you reach a full lamp, you have reached the fan lao huan tong condition. You are in the baby condition. If you can, always keep the lamp full. That means you are staying in the baby condition forever. That is how fan lao huan tong and immortality are possible and available.

Shen Xing Ju Miao. "Shen" means *Yuan Shen*, which represents Xing Gong practice. "Xing" means *body*, which represents Ming Gong practice. "Ju miao" means *profound and successful*. "Shen xing ju miao" (pronounced *shun shing jü mee-yow*) means *Xing Gong and Ming Gong Xiu Lian have been accomplished.*

Only when Yuan Shen completely melds with Shi Shen does your body completely transform. Tao teaching uses the phrase *tuo tai huan gu.* "Tuo tai" means *give birth,* which represents rebirth. "Huan gu" means *change the bones,* which represents changing every part of the body, from head to toe, skin to bone.

"Tuo tai huan gu" (pronounced *twaw tye hwahn goo*) means that after you form the Jin Dan, you continue to do Jin Dan Da Tao Xiu Lian and Bao Yuan Shou Yi. You continue to swallow tian yi zhen shui and jin jin yu ye. Then your Jin Dan will grow to the size of your body. It will transform every part of the body including all systems, all organs, all cells, all cell units, all DNA and RNA, all spaces between cells, and all tiny matter inside the cells.

This is tuo tai huan gu. This is rebirth. Every part of the body is transformed to the Tao body. This is to accomplish Xing Gong and Ming Gong.

Fen Yong Jing Jin. "Fen yong" means *extreme will power.* "Jing jin" means *forge ahead vigorously.* "Fen yong jing jin" (pronounced *fun yawng jing jeen*) means *try your greatest best to do Xiu Lian.*

This is to encourage every Tao practitioner, because if you want to meld with Tao, there will be blockages. The number one blockage is the soul blockage of your bad karma.

All kinds of karma can block your Xiu Tao journey.

Mind blockages, which include negative mind-sets, negative beliefs, negative attitudes, attachments, and ego, can block your Xiu Tao journey.

Emotional blockages can block your Xiu Tao journey.

Body blockages, which include energy and matter blockages, can block your Xiu Tao journey.

All kinds of pollution, including selfishness, greed, jealousy, anger, and much more, can block your Xiu Tao journey.

Therefore, fen yong, *extreme will power*, and jing jin, *forging ahead vigorously*, are very important for your Xiu Tao practice. To do Xiu Tao practice is to meld with Tao. To meld with Tao is to become a Tao servant or Tao saint to serve wan ling, all souls.

She Sheng Wang Si. "She sheng" means *give your life.* "Wang si" means *forget death.* "She sheng wang si" (pronounced *shuh shung wahng sz*) means *give your life to do Xiu Lian.*

In the Xiu Tao journey there are many blockages that I just shared in explaining the previous sacred phrase. There is a lot of spiritual testing. When your Yuan Shen is in charge, your Yuan Shen will test you. Your Yuan Shen will test your Shi Shen. When your Shi Shen passes the tests, your Shi Shen will completely meld with your Yuan Shen.

To pass spiritual testing, you must have the courage to commit your life to Xiu Tao practice. It does not matter how difficult it is. This is your commitment to accomplish your soul journey. The final destiny for the soul journey is to meld with Tao.

To meld with Tao is to have immortality.

This is not a small goal.

This is the highest goal for your spiritual journey and also for your physical journey.

Move forward.

Overcome all kinds of difficulties.

Remove all kinds of blockages.

Do not be afraid of anything.

Give your life for your Xiu Tao journey.

You will meld with Tao.

Xin Si Shen Huo. "Xin" literally means *heart*. Here it represents your Shi Shen. "Si" means *die*. "Shen" here means *Yuan Shen*. "Huo" means *alive*. "Xin si shen huo" (pronounced *sheen sz shun hwaw*) means *Shi Shen gives up the position and Yuan Shen is in charge*.

The Xiu Tao journey is the journey to meld with Tao. Jin Dan Da Tao Xiu Lian is the fastest way to meld with Tao.

I emphasize again that ming xin jian xing is the key for the Xiu Tao journey. If you do not reach ming xin jian xing, there is no way you can reach Tao.

To reach ming xin jian xing, your Shi Shen has to give up its leadership position. Your Yuan Shen must be in charge. For Shi Shen to give up its position, your view of the world must be transformed. All the knowledge you have learned in your whole life may not be right for your Xiu Tao journey because that knowledge comes from a yin-yang view of the yin yang world.

To transform your view of the world to the Tao view of the world, you have to go into the Tao condition. Use Tao to see the world.

Yuan Shen is Tao. When Yuan Shen is on duty, Yuan Shen will guide you to move your Xiu Tao journey.

Your Shi Shen must give up the leadership position completely. Your view of the world must be completely changed. Then your Yuan Shen will be fully in charge and your view of the world will be transformed to the Tao view of the world.

To have your Yuan Shen in an absolute leadership position and to have Shi Shen completely meld with Yuan Shen takes time. To transform your view of the world from a yin-yang view to the Tao view takes time also.

This is the key wisdom: Shi Shen must totally give up. Yuan

Shen must be totally in charge. This is another vital step to meld with Tao.

Fang Ke Xiu Cheng. "Fang ke" means *can*. "Xiu cheng " means *accomplish melding with Tao*. "Fang ke xiu cheng" (pronounced *fahng kuh sheo chung*) means *Xiu Lian can reach Tao*.

This sacred phrase summarizes and emphasizes the several phrases that preceed it. If your Shi Shen completely gives up its position in order to meld with Yuan Shen; if your Yuan Shen completely guides your life; and if your view of the world completely transforms to the view of Tao, then you can meld with Tao. This is the direction to follow. This is The Way for your spiritual journey.

213
灵脑身圆满
Ling Nao Shen Yuan Man

Soul mind body enlightenment

214
金丹道体生
Jin Dan Dao Ti Sheng

Jin Dan and Tao body are produced

215
海枯石烂
Hai Ku Shi Lan

The seas run dry and the rocks crumble

216
道体长存
Dao Ti Chang Cun

The Tao body lives forever

217
阴阳归道
Yin Yang Gui Dao

Yin yang returns to Tao

218
与道合真
Yu Dao He Zhen

Meld with Tao

219
道法自然
Dao Fa Zi Ran

Follows nature's way

220
神哉妙哉
Shen Zai Miao Zai

Miraculous and profound

Ling Nao Shen Yuan Man. "Ling" means *soul*. "Nao" means *consciousness*. "Shen" means *body*. "Yuan man" means enlightenment. "Ling nao shen yuan man" (pronounced *ling now shun ywen mahn*) means *soul mind body enlightenment*.

Since 2002, I have offered soul enlightenment to humanity. In the authoritative book of my Soul Power Series, *The Power of Soul: The Way to Heal, Rejuvenate, Transform, and Enlighten All Life*, I have a chapter that teaches soul enlightenment. I will give you a little essence here. Read more in my other books.

Soul enlightenment is ming xin jian xing.

Soul enlightenment is also to form the Jin Dan.

Soul enlightenment is jing qi shen he yi.

Soul enlightenment is to fulfill the oil in your lamp.

Soul enlightenment is to uplift your soul standing in Heaven.

Mind enlightenment is to enlighten your consciousness. To reach mind enlightenment is to remove your negative mind-sets, negative beliefs, negative attitudes, attachments, ego, and more.

Body enlightenment is tuo tai huan gu, to rebirth and completely change your body from head to toe, skin to bone, including every system, organ, cell, cell unit, DNA, RNA, space between the cells, and tiny matter inside the cells.

Body enlightenment is to reach immortality.

Reach soul enlightenment first.

Then, achieve mind enlightenment.

Finally, accomplish body enlightenment.

Jin Dan Dao Ti Sheng. "Jin Dan" means *golden light ball*. "Dao ti" means *Tao body*. "Sheng" means *produced*. "Jin Dan Dao ti sheng" (pronounced *jeen dahn dow tee shung*) means *Jin Dan and Tao body are produced*.

Jin Dan Da Tao Xiu Lian is to form the Jin Dan first.

To form the Jin Dan is to reach ming xin jian xing.

When you reach ming xin jian xing, your Yuan Shen assumes leadership from your Shi Shen.

Continue Bao Yuan Shou Yi (hold and concentrate on your Jin Dan) and yan jin ye (swallow tian yi zhen shui and jin jin yu ye).

This will form your complete Jin Dan. When your Jin Dan grows to the size of your body, it will do tuo tai huan gu for you. Tuo tai huan gu is to transform your body from head to toe, skin to bone, completely to the Tao body.

Then your Tao body is produced. When you have a Tao body, you have melded with Tao. You have reached immortality.

Hai Ku Shi Lan. "Hai ku" means *dry sea.* "Shi lan" means *rocks crumble.* "Hai ku shi lan" (pronounced *hye koo shr lahn*) means *the seas run dry and the rocks crumble.*

This sacred phrase is to explain the power of the Tao body. If the seas run dry and the rocks crumble, what will happen to the Tao body?

The next phrase gives the answer:

Dao Ti Chang Cun. "Dao ti" means *Tao body.* "Chang cun" means *live forever.* "Dao ti chang cun" (pronounced *dow tee chahng tsoon*) means *the Tao body lives forever.*

If the seas run dry and the rocks crumble, the Tao body still stays and lives forever. This is the immortal body. This is immortality.

Yin Yang Gui Dao. "Yin yang" means *yin yang world.* "Gui" means *return.* Dao or Tao is The Way, the source. "Yin yang gui Dao" (pronounced *yeen yahng gway dow*) means *yin yang returns to Tao.*

In *Tao I: The Way of All Life,* as well as earlier in this book, I shared Tao normal creation: Tao creates One. One creates Two. Two creates Three. Three creates countless things. I also shared Tao reverse creation: Countless things return to Three. Three returns to Two. Two returns to One. One returns to Tao.

We are in the yin yang world. In Xiu Tao practice, we have to return to Tao from the yin yang world.

Jin Dan Da Tao Xiu Lian is a yin yang returning to Tao practice.

Forming the Jin Dan is a yin yang returning to Tao practice.

Bao Yuan Shou Yi practice is a yin yang returning to Tao practice.

Ming xin jian xing is a ying yang returning to Tao practice.

Practice more and more.

I wish you will reach Tao earlier.

Yu Dao He Zhen. "Yu" means *with.* Dao or Tao is The Way, the source. "He zhen" means *meld with Tao.* "Yu Dao he zhen" (pronounced *yü dow huh jun*) means *meld with Tao.*

This book is the way of healing, rejuvenation, longevity, and immortality. Immortality is the final step for the Xiu Tao journey.

Jin Dan Da Tao Xiu Lian is the highest secret and fastest way to move on this Xiu Tao journey.

It is vital to emphasize the four major stages of yu Dao he zhen:

- **Bai Ri Zhu Ji.** Practice for one hundred days to build a foundation for your body. Heal your spiritual, mental, emotional, and physical bodies. Prevent all sickness in your spiritual, mental, emotional, and physical bodies.

- **Ju Zu Xing.** Rejuvenate your soul, heart, mind, and body to have a stronger body.
- **Ming Xin Jian Xing.** Enlighten your heart to see your Yuan Shen. Form your Jin Dan. Yuan Shen is in charge and Shi Shen melds with Yuan Shen. Your body is fulfilled with complete jing qi shen to reach the baby state, which is fan lao huan tong.
- **Yu Dao He Zhen.** Form your complete Jin Dan. Meld with Tao.

These four steps can be summarized in one sentence. I am honored to reveal this one-sentence secret now:

守一咽津液金丹大道修炼
Practice Shou Yi Yan Jin Ye within Jin Dan Da Tao Xiu Lian all of the time to meld with Tao as fast as you can.

Jin Dan Da Tao Xiu Lian is to chant as much as you can all of the time. "Shou yi" means *Bao Yuan Shou Yi.* Hold and concentrate on your Jin Dan all of the time. "Yan jin ye" (pronounced *yahn jeen yuh*) means *swallow tian yi zhen shui and jin jin yu ye all of the time.*

This one-sentence secret will serve your four stages of melding with Tao.

This one-sentence secret is the absolute truth.

This one-sentence secret will serve millions and billions of people for their healing, rejuvenation, and longevity.

This one-sentence secret will create more immortals.

This one-sentence secret is the summary of this entire book.

Grab it.

Seriously practice it.

I wish you will meld with Tao sooner.

Dao Fa Zi Ran. Dao or Tao is The Way, the source. "Fa" means *method*. "Zi ran" means *natural*. "Dao fa zi ran" (pronounced *dow fah dz rahn*) means *follows nature's way*. Dao fa zi ran is the condition of melding with Tao.

When you meld with Tao, you are Tao and Tao is you. You are breathing with Tao. You are enjoying Tao normal creation and Tao reverse creation. You are serving countless planets, stars, galaxies, and universes. You are a Tao servant.

Shen Zai Miao Zai. "Shen" means *miraculous*. "Zai" is a sound with no specific meaning. "Miao" means *profound*. "Shen zai miao zai" (pronounced *shun dzye mee-yow dzye*) means *miraculous and profound*.

Tao is The Way. Tao is the source for all things. Tao is the universal principles and laws.

Since creation, countless people have practiced to meld with Tao. Very few have accomplished it.

I wish this book can be a servant for you and humanity to move on your Tao journey in order to meld with Tao.

I have shared the absolute truth, The Way of Healing, Rejuvenation, Longevity, and Immortality.

The Divine, Tao, many top Taoist saints, buddhas, and other spiritual fathers and mothers have been above my head from the beginning to the end. I flowed out their teachings. I cannot honor and bow down to them enough that I am to be a servant to deliver these sacred teachings, secrets, wisdom, knowledge, and practical techniques.

Are they profound?

The answer is in your heart and soul.

I love my heart and soul
I love all humanity
Join hearts and souls together
Love, peace and harmony
Love, peace and harmony

God gives his heart to me
God gives his love to me
My heart melds with his heart
My love melds with his love

Tao gives Tao's heart to me
Tao gives Tao's love to me
My heart melds with Tao's heart
My love melds with Tao's love

Conclusion

I AM EXTREMELY HONORED to conclude this book.

A human being's life follows the normal creation of Tao: birth, childhood, adolescence, adulthood, senior citizenship, sickness, and then death.

Can you reverse your age? Yes, you can. That is exactly the teaching in this book.

To reverse your age, you must follow the reverse creation of Tao.

Can you heal your spiritual, mental, emotional and physical bodies? Yes, you can. To heal them is to fulfill your *lou ti*, your "leaky body." To have a leaky body is to have insufficient jing qi shen. This book teaches you exactly how to fulfill your jing qi shen and transform your leaky body to a healthy body.

Can you reach fan lao huan tong, transforming old age to the health and purity of the baby state? Yes, you can. This book shares with you the sacred teachings and practices to achieve fan lao huan tong.

Can you live a long life? Absolutely! This book shares with you the sacred teachings and practices to achieve a long, long life.

Can you reach immortality? Yes, but you have to gain this belief little by little. If you heal your spiritual, mental, emotional and physical bodies, you will start to believe the teachings and practices solidly.

If you reach fan lao huan tong, you will believe more.

If you live to be 100 years old, you will believe further.

If you live to be 150 years old or more, you will believe much more.

If you can keep your fan lao huan tong condition forever, immortality is possible.

To experience is to believe.

How can you achieve all of the above? The answer is a one-sentence secret plus a few stages to go through.

The one-sentence secret is:

Practice Shou Yi Yan Jin Ye within Jin Dan Da Tao Xiu Lian all of the time to meld with Tao as fast as you can.

"Shou yi" means *Bao Yuan Shou Yi*, which is the practice of "holding" and concentrating on your Jin Dan all of the time.

"Yan jin ye" is the practice of swallowing tian yi zhen shui (Heaven's unique sacred liquid) and jin jin yu ye (Mother Earth's sacred liquid) all of the time.

Jin Dan Da Tao Xiu Lian is to chant The Big Tao Golden Light Ball Xiu Lian text as much as you can all of the time.

I summarize and emphasize again the four stages to meld with Tao:

Stage 1. Bai Ri Zhu Ji

Practice for one hundred days to build a foundation for your body.

Stage 2. Ju Zu Xing

Fulfill your body with sufficient jing qi shen to be completely healthy.

Stage 3. Ming Xin Jian Xing and Fan Lao Huan Tong

Enlighten your heart to see your Yuan Shen and transform your age to the health and purity of the baby state.

Stage 4. Yu Dao He Zhen

Meld with Tao.

A human being's life is like an oil lamp. A newborn baby has a lamp full of oil. See figure 5.

Figure 5.

Let's use a woman aged fifty as an example. This person could be halfway through her life. Her lamp would therefore be about half full of oil. See figure 6.

Figure 6.

If this fifty-year-old woman has a chronic or serious health condition, the oil in her lamp could be significantly reduced. See figure 7. Such a person has *lou ti,* a leaky body as described above.

Figure 7.

The purpose of bai ri zhu ji, stage 1 of melding with Tao, is to fulfill the lou ti by replenishing jing qi shen. If the person does the most secret and powerful practice in this book, Shou Yi Yan Jin Ye with Jin Dan Da Tao Xiu Lian, this can restore her body to the normal fifty-year-old healthy condition, as depicted in figure 6.

If this person, as a Tao student and practitioner, continues to practice Shou Yi Yan Jin Ye with Jin Dan Da Tao Xiu Lian, she could reach stage 2, ju zu xing.

The purpose of ju zu xing is to make one's body healthier, stronger, and younger than a normal healthy body of a 50-year-old woman. Her jing qi shen will continue to increase. She will start to become younger. Her lamp could become 75 percent full. See figure 8.

Figure 8.

If she continues to practice Shou Yi Yan Jin Ye with Jin Dan Da Tao Xiu Lian seriously and persistently all of the time, she could reach stage 3, ming xin jian xing.

To achieve ming xin jian xing and fan lao huan tong is to enlighten the person's heart so that she can see her Yuan Shen and to transform her fifty-year-old age to the health and purity of a child. At this stage, her lamp could be 90 percent full or more. See figure 9.

Figure 9.

Extremely encouraged by the results, she could continue to practice Shou Yi Yan Jin Ye with Jin Dan Da Tao Xiu Lian even more seriously to reach fan lao huan tong. When she reaches fan lao huan tong, she has completely accomplished stage 3. Her lamp is completely full of oil, just like a newborn baby's. She has transformed her fifty-year-old age and returned to the baby state. See figure 10.

By now, she will definitely continue to practice Shou Yi Yan Jin Ye with Jin Dan Da Tao Xiu Lian to keep her lamp 100 percent full of oil constantly, which means forever. Her lamp will always look like the one in figure 10.

Figure 10.

If she can keep her lamp full all of the time, then longevity and immortality are possible.

Jin Dan Da Tao is the only way to receive immortality. As I said before, gain this belief little by little.

Millions of people in history have searched for the secrets of healing, rejuvenation, fan lao huan tong, longevity, and immortality. Serious spiritual seekers have spent hundreds, even thousands of lifetimes to find the secrets of longevity and immortality. It is very difficult to find this absolute truth.

People have spent billions of dollars trying to achieve healing, beauty, rejuvenation, and longevity. People use all kinds of ways to try to become younger. Remember the teaching. The teaching can be summarized in a few one-sentence secrets. The first one-sentence secret is:

Inner beauty comes first; then outer beauty will follow.

Another one-sentence secret:

Fan lao huan tong is possible by doing Jin Dan Da Tao Xiu Lian.

Another one-sentence secret:

Longevity is possible by following the Tao practice of Jin Dan Da Tao Xiu Lian.

Another one-sentence secret:

Immortality is on the way by following the teachings and practices of The Way of Healing, Rejuvenation, Longevity, and Immortality, as well as Jin Dan Da Tao Xiu Lian

The absolute truth for healing, rejuvenation, longevity, and immortality is released in this book. I wish for you to understand this and grab it. In history, the absolute truth has often been hard to believe in the beginning. For example, for a long time, people did not believe that Mother Earth rotates around the sun.

You may not realize the importance of this teaching right now. You could realize it more a few years later or even ten to twenty years later, when you experience an "aha!" or "wow!" moment.

I wish for you to realize this absolute truth earlier.

I wish for you to be awakened to this absolute truth earlier.

I wish for you to practice Jin Dan Da Tao Xiu Lian and The Way of Healing, Rejuvenation, Longevity, and Immortality right now.

I wish for you to heal yourself quickly.

I wish for you to become younger and happier quickly.

I wish for you to live to be one hundred or one hundred fifty years old, even hundreds of years old.

I wish for you to meld with Tao in order to live forever.

Practice. Practice. Practice.

Practice Jin Dan Da Tao Xiu Lian and the two hundred twenty sacred phrases of The Way of Healing, Rejuvenation, Longevity, and Immortality.

Each of these two hundred twenty sacred phrases and each phrase in Jin Dan Da Tao Xiu Lian text is Tao dew and Tao jade liquid dropping to your Jin Dan to form your complete Jin Dan in order to meld with Tao as soon as possible.

Each of these two hundred twenty sacred phrases and each phrase in Jin Dan Da Tao Xiu Lian text is a Tao pearl to transform your physical life and your soul journey completely.

Each of these two hundred twenty sacred phrases and every phrase in the Jin Dan Da Tao Xiu Lian are the Tao priceless sacred treasures to fulfill your dream of fan lao huan tong, longevity and immortality.

Each of these two hundred twenty sacred phrases and each phrase in Jin Dan Da Tao Xiu Lian text is a Tao blessing to bring wan ling rong he (all souls joining as one) and create love, peace, and harmony for humanity, Mother Earth, and all universes.

I am extremely honored to receive the Divine and Tao teachings in this book and share them right away with humanity and wan ling.

Thank you, Divine.

Thank you, Tao.

Thank you, all spiritual fathers and mothers in all layers of Heaven.

Thank you, countless planets, stars, galaxies, and all universes.

Thank you, all souls.

Thank you for reading this book and receiving the benefits from the teachings and practices. May these teachings serve your soul journey and physical journey forever.

I am your servant forever.

> *I love my heart and soul*
> *I love all humanity*
> *Join hearts and souls together*
> *Love, peace and harmony*
> *Love, peace and harmony*

Acknowledgments

$\mathcal{I}$ FLOWED THIS BOOK from the Divine and Tao, and from many major spiritual fathers and mothers in Heaven. They were above my head for my entire flow of this book. My "flow" means they talk; I receive and deliver. I could not write this book without their wisdom and knowledge. I deeply appreciate them.

Second, I appreciate an incredible Tao master who does not want to be recognized by the public. This one's guidance for the Tao of Healing, Rejuvenation (Fan Lao Huan Tong), Longevity, and Immortality has been vital. I deeply appreciate this one.

Third, I would like to thank Master and Dr. Zhi Chen Guo, the founder of Zhi Neng Medicine and Body Space Medicine, Professor and Dr. De Hua Liu, my Peng Zu lineage grantor, Professor and Dr. Da Jun Liu, one of the world authority scholars and practitioners of *I Ching* and feng shui, as well as another major Tao master who also does not want public acknowledgment. I also thank all of my spiritual fathers and mothers for their teaching since my childhood. I cannot thank them enough. I deeply appreciate all of them.

Next, my appreciation goes to Allan Chuck, who currently is one of my top Worldwide Representatives. He is going to the whole world to teach the Soul Power Series. He is the primary and final editor of this book and all of my last ten books. I deeply appreciate his total GOLD and great contribution of editing my books and for his unconditional service to the mission.

Next, my deep appreciation goes to Elaine Ward for her assistance to Allan for this book and other books from Heaven's Library. She has offered great support for producing many of these books. I deeply appreciate Shu Chin Hsu, Min Lei, and Shi Gao for their assistance in proofreading the Chinese and pinyin in this book. I deeply appreciate Rick Riecker and several other Divine Editors for their proofreading assistance. Rick also assisted greatly in creating the final audio tracks comprising the CD or audio downloads included with this book. I appreciate Chester Chin for his creation of several of the figures in this book.

Next, my deep appreciation goes to my assistant, Cynthia Deveraux. She typed this book and a few other books. Whenever I flow my books, she is totally moved and touched in the moment. Her great energy field is very important for flowing these books from the Divine and Tao.

Next, my appreciation goes to Peter Hudoba, another one of my top Worldwide Representatives. He is another Total GOLD servant for humanity. Peter was my first student who received soul enlightenment. Peter has studied Taoist arts and practices for more than forty years. For this book, he has contributed his deep understanding of my Tao teachings. I deeply appreciate him.

Next, my appreciation goes to my team at my co-publisher, Atria Books and Simon & Schuster, for their great support of my

Soul Power Series. The team includes Judith Curr, Chris Lloreda, Johanna Castillo, Amy Tannenbaum, Isolde Sauer, Lisa Keim, Christine Saunders, Michael Selleck, Tom Spain, Dan Vidra, others whom I may have inadvertently omitted, as well as many whose names I do not know.

Next, my appreciation goes to the Divine Composer Chun-Yen Chiang. He has produced incredible divine music for the Tao Jing ("Tao Classic") that is the core of *Tao I: The Way of All Life*. Thousands of people worldwide listen to a CD of my *Tao Jing* singing with Mr. Chiang's music for healing and blessing. He also just composed (August 2010) music for the Jin Dan Da Tao Xiu Lian and the two hundred twenty sacred phrases of The Way of Healing, Rejuvenation, Longevity, and Immortality that are the core of this book. In the last few years he has composed much heart-touching, moving, and powerful music for the mission. I deeply appreciate him.

My appreciation to my more than one thousand Divine Teachers and Healers worldwide, led by all of my Worldwide Representatives whom I deeply appreciate for their total commitment to serve humanity and all souls: Marilyn Smith, Francisco Quintero, Allan Chuck, Peter Hudoba, Petra Herz, David Lusch, Roger Givens, Patricia Smith, Peggy Werner, Lynne Nusyna, Shu Chin Hsu, Trevor Allen, Hannah Stevens, and Maria Sunukjian.

I deeply appreciate my wife and my children for their great support.

I deeply appreciate my mother, my brother, and my sisters for their great support. I flowed this book in two weeks in my mother's residence in China.

I deeply thank my mother and father for their teaching since my childhood. I cannot express my love and gratitude for the two of them enough.

I deeply appreciate all of my students worldwide for their great contributions to the mission.

I deeply appreciate the opportunity and honor to be a servant of you, humanity, and all souls.

> *I love my heart and soul*
> *I love all humanity*
> *Join hearts and souls together*
> *Love, peace and harmony*
> *Love, peace and harmony*

Thank you. Thank you. Thank you.

A Special Gift

THE ENCLOSED CD is an essential component of this book, *Tao II: The Way of Healing, Rejuvenation, Longevity, and Immortality*. It includes only two tracks, but these two tracks are the most sacred, most secret, most powerful, and most profound Tao texts that are the core of the book. As explained in the book itself, the practice of these Tao Songs is a practice for your whole life. The benefits for your Tao journey are immeasurable. Your Tao journey includes your healing journey, your rejuvenation journey, your longevity journey, and your entire spiritual journey.

Heal all your sicknesses.

Rejuvenate to the health and purity of a baby.

Attain a long, long life.

Move in the direction of immortality to be a better servant for humanity, Mother Earth, and all universes.

Reach Tao.

Meld with Tao.

You are blessed beyond words, thought, comprehension, and imagination.

Track 1   *Jin Dan Da Dao Xiu Lian—The Big Tao Golden Light Ball Xiu Lian*

Track 2   *Zhi Liao Fan Lao Huan Tong Chang Shou Yong Sheng Zhi Dao—Tao of Healing, Rejuvenation (Fan Lao Huan Tong), Longevity, and Immortality*

Index

Evolution of humanity, 3
Eyes/sight
  Bu Shi An Shen Yu Xin (do not see polluted
    things to make your shen reside peacefully in
    your heart), 228
  Er Mu Kou (ears eyes mouth), 227
  Jian Zhang Liang Mu (gradually grow both
    eyes), 280
  Ming Xin Jian Xing (enlighten your heart to
    see your true self, your Yuan Shen), 146–47,
    159–61, 222, 225–26, 270, 275–77, 303, 304,
    308
  Mu Bu Wang Shi (do not see polluted things),
    228, 234
  Wei He Bu Jian (why can't a human being see the
    Yuan Shen?), 221, 224
  Wood element practice and, 73
  Zhen Zhen Jing Xiang (see the real images),
    317, 323

F

Fan Fu Lun Hui (reincarnation continues),
    177–78, 182
Fan lao huan tong is possible by doing Jin Dan Da
    Tao Xiu Lian, 360
Fan lao huan tong (transform old age to health and
    purity of baby state)
  absolute truth and, 121
  achievability, 353
  Bu Er Fa Men (no second way for fan lao huan
    tong, longevity, and immortality), 134–38
  explanation of, lxxviii, lxxiv
  immortality and, 90–93
  Jin Dan and, lxxix, lxxxvi, xliii, 49, 161
  Jin Dan Da Tao Xiu Lian and, lxxviii–lxxix,
    lxxxvi, xciii, 179, 183
  practice Tao and, 86
  search for, 118
  sickness and, 195
  Tao I (Sha) and, 20
  Tao Jing and, 6
  Tao practice and, 90–93
  Xiu Lian practice and, 139
Fang Ke Xiu Cheng (Xiu Lian can reach Tao),
    339, 344
Fear, lxxxiii, 83
Fei Chang Tao (Is not the eternal Tao or true Tao),
    4, 25
Fen Yong Jing Jin (try your greatest best to do Xiu
    Lian), 339, 341–42
Feng Fu acupuncture point, 320
Feng shui, liv, lxxx
Finances
  absolute truth and, 121
  chanting and transformation of, 49
  Jin Dan and, 37, 123
  Jin Dan Da Tao practice and, 40
  Jin Dan Xiu Lian practice and, 68
  Tao and transformation of finances, 3
  Xiu Lian practice and, 139
Fire
  Fire element, 77–79, 297, 299

Qian Ri Wen Wu Huo (practice gentle fire and
    strong fire for one thousand days), 302–304
Yi zhong qi huo (concentrating too much
    produces fire), 321
Zhen Huo Zi Lai (true fire from Yuan Shen
    comes by itself), 288, 290–91
Zhen Huo Zi Yun (real fire moves by itself), 297,
    299
Five elements
  Earth element practice, 79–81
  Fire element practice, 77–79
  Metal element practice, 81–83
  Water element practice, 83–85
  Wood element practice, 73–79
  yang and, 71, 78
  yin and, 71
Follow Tao, flourish. Go against Tao, finish, 3, 25
Forgiveness, 51, 161, 180, 202, 203, 237
Forgiveness practice, 181
Four Power Techniques
  dark souls and, 197
  explanation of, 11–12, 41–42
Free will, xlviii–xlix
Fu Wu Di Qiu (serve Mother Earth), 6
Fu Wu Ren Lei (serve all humanity), 5
Fu Wu San Jie (serve Heaven, Earth, and Human
    Being), 9
Fu Wu Wan Ling (serve all souls), 5, 271, 278
Fu Wu Xiu Lian (Service Xiu Lian), 194, 210–11,
    212
Fu Wu Yu Zhou (serve all universes), 6

G

Gallbladder, 73, 282
Gan Lu Sa Xin (dew sprays to the heart), xxvii,
    111, 316, 322
God Gives His Heart to Me (Divine Soul Song),
    204, 351
GOLD (gratitude, obedience, loyalty, devotion),
    xlvi, xlvi(n4)
Golden Pill elixir of immortality, lxxiii–lxxiv
Gong De Yuan Man (serve unconditionally
    and gain complete virtue to reach
    enlightenment), 6
Good virtue, 90
Greed, 149, 193, 204–205, 224, 231, 277, 336, 342
Greed is the source of all evil, 204
Grief/sadness, 81
Guan Jin Qiang Wu Ai (go through the golden
    wall without blockage), 303
Guan Yin
  compassion, xxxvi
  identity, xxxvin1
  miracles and, xxxvi
Gums, 79
Guo, Zhi Chen, liv, lxiv, lxx, 363
Gurus, 119

H

Hai Ku Shi Lan (the seas run dry and the rocks
    crumble), 344, 347
Han Dynasty, lxiv

Other Books of the Soul Power Series

Soul Wisdom: Practical Soul Treasures to Transform Your Life (revised trade paperback edition). Heaven's Library/Atria Books, 2008. Also available as an audio book.

The first book of the Soul Power Series is an important foundation for the entire series. It teaches five of the most important practical soul treasures: Soul Language, Soul Song, Soul Tapping, Soul Movement, and Soul Dance.

Soul Language empowers you to communicate with the Soul World, including your own soul, all spiritual fathers and mothers, souls of nature, and more, to access direct guidance.

Soul Song empowers you to sing your own Soul Song, the song of your Soul Language. Soul Song carries soul frequency and vibration for soul healing, soul rejuvenation, soul prolongation of life, and soul transformation of every aspect of life.

Soul Tapping empowers you to do advanced soul healing for yourself and others effectively and quickly.

Soul Movement empowers you to learn ancient secret wisdom and practices to rejuvenate your soul, mind, and body and prolong life.

Soul Dance empowers you to balance your soul, mind, and body for healing, rejuvenation, and prolonging life.

This book offers two permanent Divine Soul Transplants as gifts to every reader. Includes bonus Soul Song for Healing and Rejuvenation of Brain and Spinal Column MP3 download.

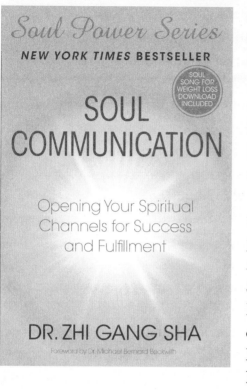

Soul Communication: Opening Your Spiritual Channels for Success and Fulfillment (revised trade paperback edition). Heaven's Library/Atria Books, 2008. Also available as an audio book.

The second book in the Soul Power Series empowers you to open four major spiritual channels: Soul Language Channel, Direct Soul Communication Channel, Third Eye Channel, and Direct Knowing Channel.

The Soul Language Channel empowers you to apply Soul Language to communicate with the Soul World, including your own soul, all kinds of spiritual fathers and mothers, nature, and the Divine. Then, receive teaching, healing, rejuvenation, and prolongation of life from the Soul World.

The Direct Soul Communication Channel empowers you to converse directly with the Divine and the entire Soul World. Receive guidance for every aspect of life directly from the Divine.

The Third Eye Channel empowers you to receive guidance and teaching through spiritual images. It teaches you how to develop the Third Eye and key principles for interpreting Third Eye images.

The Direct Knowing Channel empowers you to gain the highest spiritual abilities. If your heart melds with the Divine's heart or your soul melds with the Divine's soul completely, you do not need to ask for spiritual guidance. You know the truth because your heart and soul are in complete alignment with the Divine.

This book also offers two permanent Divine Soul Transplants as gifts to every reader. Includes bonus Soul Song for Weight Loss MP3 download.

The Power of Soul: The Way to Heal, Rejuvenate, Transform, and Enlighten All Life. Heaven's Library/Atria Books, 2009. Also available as an audio book and a trade paperback.

The third book of the Soul Power Series is the flagship of the entire series.

The Power of Soul empowers you to understand, develop, and apply the power of soul for healing, prevention of sickness, rejuvenation, transformation of every aspect of life (including relationships and finances), and soul enlightenment. It also empowers you to develop soul wisdom and soul intelligence, and to apply Soul Orders for healing and transformation of every aspect of life.

This book teaches Divine Soul Downloads (specifically, Divine Soul Transplants) for the first time in history. A Divine

Soul Transplant is the divine way to heal, rejuvenate, and transform every aspect of a human being's life and the life of all universes.

This book offers eleven permanent Divine Soul Transplants as a gift to every reader. Includes bonus Soul Song for Rejuvenation MP3 download.

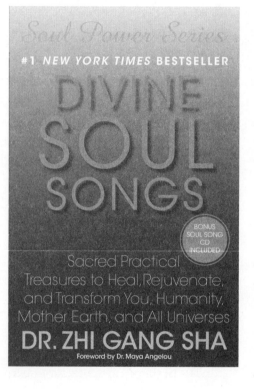

Divine Soul Songs: Sacred Practical Treasures to Heal, Rejuvenate, and Transform You, Humanity, Mother Earth, and All Universes. Heaven's Library/Atria Books, 2009. Also available as an audio book and a trade paperback.

The fourth book in the Soul Power Series empowers you to apply Divine Soul Songs for healing, rejuvenation, and transformation of every aspect of life, including relationships and finances.

Divine Soul Songs carry divine frequency and vibration, with divine love, forgiveness, compassion, and light, that can transform the frequency and vibration of all aspects of life.

This book offers nineteen Divine Soul Transplants as gifts to every reader. Includes bonus Soul Songs CD with seven samples of the Divine Soul Songs that are the main subjects of this book.

Divine Soul Mind Body Healing and Transmission System: The Divine Way to Heal You, Humanity, Mother Earth, and All Universes. Heaven's Library/Atria Books, 2009. Also available as an audio book.

The fifth book in the Soul Power Series empowers you to receive Divine Soul Mind Body Transplants and to apply Divine Soul Mind Body Transplants to heal and transform soul, mind, and body.

Divine Soul Mind Body Transplants carry divine love, forgiveness, compassion, and light. Divine love melts all blockages and transforms all life. Divine forgiveness brings inner peace and inner joy. Divine compassion boosts energy, stamina, vitality, and immunity. Divine light heals, rejuvenates, and transforms every aspect of life, including relationships and finances.

This book offers forty-six permanent divine treasures, including Divine Soul Transplants, Divine Mind Transplants, and Divine Body Transplants, as a gift to every reader. Includes bonus Soul Symphony of Yin Yang excerpt MP3 download.

Tao I: The Way of All Life. Heaven's Library/Atria Books, 2010. Also available as an audio book.

The sixth book of the Soul Power Series shares the essence of ancient Tao teaching and reveals the Tao Jing, a new "Tao Classic" for the twenty-first century. These new divine teachings reveal how Tao is in every aspect of life, from waking to sleeping to eating and more. This book shares advanced soul wisdom and practical approaches for *reaching* Tao. The new sacred teaching in this book is extremely simple, practical, and profound.

Studying and practicing Tao has great benefits, including the ability to heal yourself and others, as well as humanity, Mother Earth, and all universes; return from old age to the health and purity of a baby; prolong life; and more.

This book offers thirty permanent Divine Soul Mind Body Transplants as gifts to every reader and a fifteen-track CD with Master Sha singing the entire Tao Jing and many other major practice mantras.

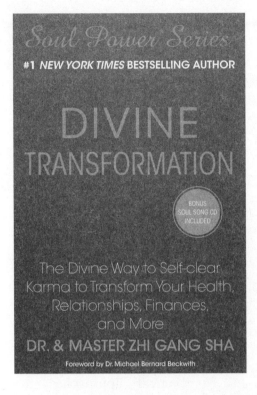

Divine Transformation: The Divine Way to Self-clear Karma to Transform Your Health, Relationships, Finances, and More. Heaven's Library/ Atria Books, 2010. Also available as an audio book.

The teachings and practical techniques of this seventh book of the Soul Power Series focus on karma and forgiveness. Bad karma is the root cause of any and every major blockage or challenge that you, humanity, and Mother Earth face. True healing is to clear your bad karma, which is to repay or be forgiven your spiritual debts to the souls you or your ancestors have hurt or harmed in all your lifetimes. Forgiveness is a golden key to true healing. Divine self-clearing of bad karma applies divine forgiveness to heal and transform every aspect of your life.

Clear your karma to transform your soul first; then transformation of every aspect of your life will follow.

This book offers thirty rainbow frequency Divine Soul Mind Body Transplants as gifts to every reader and includes four audio tracks of major Divine Soul Songs and practice chants.